Design Dialogues

Steven Heller and Elinor Pettit

ALLWORTH PRESS
NEW YORK

Design Dialogues

Steven Heller and Elinor Pettit

Allworth Press, New York
© 1998 Steven Heller

Published by Allworth Press
An imprint of Allworth Communications
10 East 23rd Street, New York, NY 10010

Cover and book design by James Victore, New York, NY

Page composition/typography by Sharp Des!gns, Inc., Lansing, MI

ISBN: 1-58115-007-5

Library of Congress Catalog Card Number: 98-72753

Printed in Canada

Contents

Massaging the Message

A Swell of Interactivity

This book is dedicated to Paul Rand for his immense influence on design.

ACKNOWLEDGMENTS

Thanks to Tad Crawford, publisher, and Ted Gachot, editor, at Allworth Press for their support, enthusiasm, and expertise in making this book a reality. Thanks also to James Victore for his splendid cover and interior design.

A number of these interviews were previously published and edited. Thanks go to Martin Fox, Julie Lasky, and Joyce Rutter Kaye at *Print* magazine, who edited the interviews with Nicholas Callaway, Johanna Drucker, Stuart Ewen, Jules Feiffer, Tibor Kalman, Ellen Lupton, Katherine McCoy, Philip Meggs, and Rick Poynor for my "Back Talk" column; and thanks to Rick Poynor and Max Bruinsma at *Eye* magazine, who edited the interviews with Michael Bierut, Milton Glaser, John Plunkett, and Richard Saul Wurman for the "Reputations" column.

Of course, this book would not be possible if not for the cooperation of the interviewees. We are grateful for their generosity, good humor, and attention to detail.

Introduction

Steven Heller on Design Dialogues

Let's begin with an easy question: Why did you and Elinor Pettit author *Design Dialogues*?

Well, for over fifteen years I have conducted interviews with artists of all kinds, sometimes simply as background for articles and essays that I've written and other times as Q&As for publication. While an interview is not always an appropriate way to profile an individual, I find that candid interviews are extremely informative and often quite entertaining. The best interviews are those where the interviewee has something important to say and is comfortable enough to be him- or herself, avoiding both formality and predictability.

About two years ago I decided to build an even larger inventory of interviews and proposed to Martin Fox, editor of *Print* magazine, that he publish a regular interview feature, called "Back Talk." Likewise, I did a few interviews for *Eye* magazine's "Reputations" column. Some of the interviews in this book are versions of these, but many are previously unpublished, and some were conducted by my collaborator Elinor Pettit. This book is a selection from the interview bank.

Despite the structure of the various thematic sections, the interviews are with very diverse individuals covering a wide range of ideas. What is the glue that binds *Design Dialogues* together?

This book is not focused on one particular theme as are my other books. One might call it a flaw, but I call it a virtue. There are interviews with a broad range of people because my interests are varied. However, there *is* a common thread: design in the broadest sense. While these interviews are rooted in graphic design, or at least disciplines that intersect with graphic design, I've included individuals who have something to say about the visual culture as a whole. For example, the interview with Stuart Ewen, a professor and communications critic, is about public relations and spin, yet it focuses on the power of the image to manipulate public opinion. The interview with Johanna Drucker, a professor and bookmaker, is about the pedagogy of theory in academe, but it addresses the role that theory has in graphic design too. The interview with Nicholas Callaway, a book editor and publisher, is about book packaging, but he advocates the marriage of content and design, and has had an influence on the current trends in illustrated books. The interview with Jules Feiffer is not about design per se, but he is a visual artist—also a veteran novelist, playwright, and screenwriter—who has, late in life, become a children's book author/illustrator. His change of priorities is a subject that all designers, indeed all artists, face at some time in their lives. While Feiffer's interview can be read for its insight into the process of writing and drawing for children, it can also be appreciated as a positive example of creative turmoil. Finally, the interview with Morris Wyszogrod, a former advertising artist and designer, addresses design in a very unusual way. He survived Nazi death camps in large part because he was a graphic designer. We often talk about design having an effect on society, but this is the story of a man who used his talent and skill to save his life under extreme circumstances. So each interview is a story of how visual culture plays a role in individual lives—and by extension, in all our lives.

I accept that you have eclectic tastes, and that this compilation reflects your interests. But eclecticism does not a book make. Please tell me why this book will benefit readers.

I'll answer that first by saying that the organizing scheme is simple. Each interviewee addresses a specific aspect of the individual's life in—or practice of—design. Stephen Doyle speaks about humor, Katherine McCoy discusses design education, Richard Saul Wurman extols the virtues of information architecture, and Philip Meggs explains the methodology behind writing his landmark book *A History of Graphic Design*. I have further grouped and categorized the interviews according to broader themes, which I admit are somewhat arbitrary as well as intersecting (I'm told that I have a habit of making arbitrary divisions, but I think they help the reader to focus). I have a section that covers issues of art and craft ("Whys and Wherefores"), in which Jonathan Hoefler talks about his life as a type designer and Michael Ian Kaye discusses his career as a book-jacket designer. These are very specific interrogatories on how and why they do what they do. In the section on past and present ("Where We Were, Where We're Going"), I include Rick Prelinger on using history as a commodity, exploring his work as a film documentarian; in addition, there is an interview with Ellen Lupton about being a curator of design at the Smithsonian and how decisions are made to document the legacy (or legacies) of graphic design. In the section on design as message ("Massaging the Message"), Sue Coe talks about art, politics, and propaganda; Michael Ray Charles explains the reasons for using black stereotypes in his artwork; and Tibor Kalman confronts his practice in relation to social responsibility. In the new media section ("A Swell of Interactivity"), John Plunkett reveals the motivations behind founding *Wired* magazine; David Vogler talks about what prompted his online invention D-Toys; and Rodney Alan Greenblat talks about the popular video game *Parappa the Rapper*.

With design as the armature holding *Design Dialogues* together, these are really more like short stories than interrogations. What the reader will get out of them? I believe insight into specific methods of working but, more important, an introduction to individuals with both passion and mission.

Do you have a method of interviewing that sets your work apart from others?

We interviewed two different ways: face-to-face and computer-to-computer. My usual method in the past was one-on-one with a subject, which was then transcribed, edited, sent to the subject for comment, and then reedited. It was a cumbersome process, which usually clarified thoughts that were confused in the conversation and transcription. Some of the interviews in this book were done that way, but the majority were e-mail interviews. Three or four back-and-forths usually covered the necessary ground. With e-mail, the interviewee has time to consider an answer and revise if needed. Of course, I edited the result to achieve a narrative flow.

Each interview has a very distinct voice. There is very little consistency, which is to be expected. But do you think this is a function of e-mail being a writer's rather than a speaker's medium?

Remember, some of these were done in the traditional way (Feiffer, Doyle, Wyszogrod, Lupton, Ewen, Wurman), and I defy you to tell the difference between the taped and e-mail interviews. But, I think that speech is indeed different from writing, and even the oral interviews have been rewritten. This means that language has been changed from voice to paper (or screen). I like these interviews because there is a literary quality. Some of the subjects are more articulate than others, but I'd say they are all fairly good reads. What really differentiates voice from e-mail is the serendipity that comes from personal interaction. But in the end, the interviewees are more or less candid in both forms.

Some critics have argued that making books out of interviews is somewhat lazy. Analysis is much harder. In this regard I have two questions: Was this easier than writing narrative profiles? And isn't the interview form more ephemeral?

Let me answer the last question first. Yes, an interview is more ephemeral in that the questions and answers often deal with issues of the moment. But the nature of the questioning and responses can be timely or timeless. Some of the interviews in *Design Dialogues* may be out-of-date in a year, others will not. We've tried to ask questions that elicit deeper answers.

Now I'll respond to the first question: Is an interview easier than an analytical profile? No. I'd say it is different. An interview relies on the interviewee to provide the meat of the story. We can ask questions, but we're not creating ideas from whole cloth. In that sense, I'm relieved because it may be easier (although I'm not sure I like that word) to ask rather than to answer. But the preparation and editing is not always easy. It takes time to work an interview into shape. When an interview is really tight, there is a chemistry between the two parties, but in the end, the better stories are the result of generous and articulate interviewees.

Are there any interviews that you would like to have but could not get?

There are a slew of people to whom I'd like to talk, yes. And a few of them were asked and declined. Maybe next time. Maybe never. I also conducted some interviews that did not work out, where the questions were not smart enough or where the answers were too superficial. That's the nature of the game.

Finally, what will we learn from *Design Dialogues* that we don't already know?

Come on, that's not a fair question. I suspect the reviewers will answer that one. But I think that the reader will gain insight into the personalities of the subjects. Some they will like, others they will not. I presume that there is enough new material that readers will also extract some history, useful facts, and interesting ideas. The interviews need not be read in the order in which they appear. The reader is encouraged to dip in where he or she is stimulated to do so. I hope that the reader will feel some kind of intellectual satisfaction after spending valuable time with this volume. Does that answer your question?

Whys and Wherefores

Massimo **Vignelli** on Rational Design

Massimo Vignelli studied architecture in Milan. He came to the United States in 1957 on a fellowship from Twole Silversmiths in Massachusetts and the Institute of Design, Illinois Institute of Technology. In 1960, with Lella Vignelli, he established the Vignelli Office of Design and Architecture in Milan. In 1965, he became cofounder and design director of Unimark International Corporation, and in 1971, he and Lella Vignelli opened Vignelli Associates in New York. His work includes corporate identity programs, architectural graphics, and exhibition, interior, and product design.

You began your career in Italy as an architect, yet your work today covers every aspect of design.

It goes back to my growing up in Milan where the saying was "One should be able to design anything from a spoon to a city," a statement attributed to the architect Adolf Loos. Indeed, it's not what we design but how we design that's important. I started in architecture because it was the basic training that was available at the time, but over the course of time, I switched to graphics, furniture, objects, glass, and other materials, and that became an attitude, a way of life.

So, you are not comfortable with specialization.

The versatility of our work is great because of the cross-pollination of one thing to another. I happen, as you can imagine, not to like specialization because it brings entropy; you keep doing one thing over and over because you have to do it and not because you are motivated. We specialize in graphic design and packaging, we specialize in product design, we specialize in interior design, we specialize in fashion design, and we do them with joy and flair and seriousness.

Are there situations where you do a number of different design projects for one specific client?

Yes, that's usually the case. A prospective client may come in because he thinks he needs a logo, but maybe a logo isn't the right thing for him. Once we talk about his needs and problems, we probably will end up doing a corporate identity program, then packaging or maybe his offices or a product itself. By the time he goes away, it's a miracle if he hasn't bought one of our suits.

Do you have specialists in all areas of design within Vignelli Associates?

We have specialists in all areas of design; however, about 60 percent of our work is in graphic design. Because of this, we do have specialists come in on some projects that are more complex, for instance, corporate identity programs and other projects that require advanced technology. Sometimes we have computer specialists come in to help us.

How do you get started with a new or prospective client? With so many different components, how do you get to the heart of the problem?

We know in advance as much about the client and his company as possible. We call in our associates to listen and talk about possible directions at the outset—discuss the nature of the problems. Usually by the time he leaves, we know the direction we will take. This is why we don't do a lot of research; nobody knows better the nature of the problem than the owner or president of the company. We don't like to work with managers because they have to interpret what we do and our ideas to their boss and very often they pass along the wrong information. When we work directly with the boss, we are able to suggest alternatives, a different approach, on-the-spot problem solving. Another person could not begin to second-guess what someone else would like.

Your motto at Vignelli Associates, then, must be "We start at the top."

Yes. If you want to stay at the top, start at the top. This is our suggestion to young people starting out in design—only work with people who are going to make final decisions. This is the only way. It's also important to go after the top jobs, not mediocre jobs.

Do you mean in terms of the kind of jobs or the kind of clients?

The kind of clients. It's very important to get the good clients and establish a good working relationship and put quality first. It is much better to do a good job than to do a job that pays a lot of money. If you can combine these two things, it's ideal. You should never work for money because if you work for money, that's not the stuff that makes good design. You should work to make great designs for whatever problems might come along—demonstrate a commitment to quality.

We say that design is a profession to solve problems; however, you would need to say there's not such a thing as solving a problem in absolute terms. It's always an interpretation of a problem; therefore, it shows right away there's no reality in this business—it's only the interpretation of reality that's real.

Over the years you have carried the torch of what Richard Saul Wurman has dubbed "information architecture." What is the difference between this and other forms of graphic design?

There are two kinds of graphic designers: One is rooted in history and semiotics and problem solving. The other is more rooted in the liberal arts—painting, figurative arts, advertising, trends, and fashion. These are really two different avenues. The first kind is more interested in looking to the nature of the problem and organizing information. That's our kind of graphic design. To me, graphic design is the organization of information. The other kind is interested in the look and wants to change things all the time. It wants to be up-to-date, beautiful, trendy. David Carson is a perfect example of the other kind. I have tremendous respect for guys like Carson. I don't think he's a graphic designer, but he's an articulator, he's clever, and he's a terrific self-promoter. His work is fascinating. There are really two channels, completely different from each other: one side is the structured side, the other is the emotional side.

Are you saying that your side, problem solving and organization of information, is the better avenue to take?

I think there's a place for both, and they could benefit from some integration. Because of my background in architecture, my work is rooted in structure: structure of information, structure in design, structure in language; in one way you could say we are structuralists. I don't have a problem with fashion or trends, but we would never follow a trend; it would be in conflict with what we do. We are interested in designing things that will last because we feel we have a responsibility, which is something often overlooked—this notion of responsibility. As designers, we have two kinds of responsibility, one to our clients and the other to society.

We have a responsibility to our client not to design something that will become obsolete quickly; his investment should be justified; he should have something that will last. If a designer feels the responsibility to give the client something that's up-to-the-moment, then when that's obsolete, the client will get something else. This goes back to the notion of obsolescence, fashion, and trends. From my point of view, all are equally detestable.

We have a responsibility to society to look for meaning in design, structure, and information, in such a way that will last a long time, not be something you have to throw away. For example, look at the Heller designs; they have been around for thirty years. And we are producing objects and furniture that were designed many years ago.

There used to be a time when people had to design things to last a long time. It wasn't a natural kind of commitment, however. Of course there were fashions and fabulous art deco and trendy stuff. Probably the best period of trendiness in this century was the art deco period, and maybe art nouveau, especially in the United States where it was the best.

You consider yourself a modernist. What is the most important tenet of the modern movement?

One of the greatest things about the modern movement was the sense of responsibility. It was the modern movement that created people like Charles Eames, and many, many others; not me, but many others. What we have in the last fifty years is an incredible collection of junk. Maybe you have some major personalities like Michael Graves. He has a very different style, but I like him. This doesn't mean that I agree with what he does all the time, but I do respect him. There are many contemporaries of his whom I do not respect, or contemporaries of mine, especially in the graphic design field. However, this is why I say it's important to clarify fields by saying there are two avenues, not just one.

Does this mean that it's alright by you that there's room in graphic design for the other kind?

I think it's perfectly alright. There is a need for that too. What you hope is that one side takes care of the sublime and the other side takes care of the ridiculous.

I see a tremendous amount of what I perceive as trash coming out as graphic design all over the world, particularly from England and the United States. I think it's perfectly alright to experiment with this kind of thing as a fine artist, but it's not perfectly alright at all if you are a graphic designer. If you perceive graphic design as the organization of information, all this kind of computer layering, these trends, are not enriching design one bit. It's just a way of making the form bigger, which has nothing to do with quality. It's totally irrelevant. I see irrelevance in other aspects of design, like in revivalism; all are desperate forms of intelligence for the unintelligent, if I can put it that way. They are lifesavers for the desperate. As you know, graphic design has been sinking like the *Titanic*.

Do you think this "sinking of graphic design" will continue, or is it just another trend?

Like in every profession, again, quantity versus quality. If you have few doctors, you are bound to have a lot of good doctors. If you have a lot of doctors, there are going to be a few good doctors and a lot of mediocre doctors. This is true in every profession. One has to go through phases of development; one is the ability to recognize trash. When you can recognize trash, then you can control trash. Otherwise you just live with trash, right?

Or it becomes kitsch.

Yes, or it becomes classic; that's even worse. Speaking of kitsch, there are so many chefs today. There used to be few chefs, and now look at how many there are. They go through incredible preparations, and they all have one direct thing in common—kitsch! There's so much kitsch in food preparation. It's unbelievable.

Not only in how it looks but in how it tastes, like nouvelle cuisine. Strawberries look pretty on fish, but the taste is rather strange.

Exactly. It's the exact same thing that you see in graphic design. Nouvelle cuisine is ultimate kitsch. It has no special tradition; it changes the value from taste to visual; it becomes only a visual thing. Cooking never had serious visual connotations, at least in our culture. Of course in the Japanese culture, food has always been very visual, and you get very little too. And the Chinese make everything look like something else.

There are more people graduating from design school now than ever before. Isn't it the responsibility of educators to teach design as organization of information?

If one can make this distinction very clear [structural design/emotional design] and give the proper education on both sides to the new generation coming along, then it will be up to the individual to choose one or the other. It's like architects and engineers. Architects always hated engineers, and engineers always hated architects. But you need both. In graphic design it's the same thing. On one side you have structural designers involved in structural information, and on the other side there is more involvement in the appearance of things. Maybe this is alright because you get something from it, and maybe that something has nothing to do with legibility, but it sets a mood, like in music. So I cannot anymore be ferociously against this side because there is indeed room for it too. Of course, I do resent that because of the lack of structure, we have more people falling in love with the other side. And because of the lack of training on the structural side, we have more people going to the other side. This is not the fault of the students but the fault of schools. You cannot have better design unless you have better schools. It's as simple as that.

In the last twenty years, we have seen teachers more interested in teaching an attitude of "why not?" and "what if?" That is the postmodern mentality. It is what's emerging from people who were rejected by the mainstream of thinking because they were incapable, and eventually there were so many, they became a culture. They are the generation of the why-nots who have a "let's-try, who-cares" attitude as opposed to those who have social responsibility and involvement, a commitment to making a better world. It's not up to graphic designers to change the world, but everything visual and everything that surrounds us can be better design if you don't offer the alternative of bad design.

How do you feel about new technology?

It's fantastic. It's never been as great as it is today; it's fabulous. Can you imagine being without it?

No, I can't. However, so many seasoned designers complain that it's just a tool, blah, blah, blah. Do you believe that out of it there will come a new discipline?

Never in the history of typography, for example, could a designer control as much as he can control today. We can do so many good things that we couldn't do before. We can also do bad things we never did before. But all the sloppiness of the past is gone. You can create beautiful things—even sizes of type that didn't exist in the past. Technology gives us the opportunity to do better what we do. It gives us the control between the tool and the mind.

Out of the industrial revolution came the Bauhaus. Do you think there is going to be a kind of Bauhaus emerging from computer technology?

Yes, definitely. The basic meaning of the Bauhaus was to provide quality in mass production whether it was printing, molding, casting, whatever. The same thing will happen here. Already the new tool is providing so much trash that I think there will be a demand for people who can organize a way of thinking so that the quality will come back.

People like Massimo?

Oh, I'm on my way out, but by someone who is on the way in. One has to be young enough to do these things. You need to be at a time in your life when you are at your full capacity.

H. L. Mencken

Paul Rand

made by
James T
Farrell
and with an
introduction
by him.

A Vintage Book
K58 $1.25

Prejudices:
A Selection

Paul Rand on the Play Instinct

Paul Rand was America's leading modern graphic designer in the disciplines of advertising, book, and corporate design. He studied at Parsons School of Design, Pratt Institute, and the Art Students League (where George Grosz was his teacher), all in New York City, but was primarily self-taught in the ways of modernism. In the early 1930s, he became a devoted follower of the European moderns and employed their economical and functional methods in his editorial design for *Esquire* and *Apparel Arts*. In 1941, he joined the William H. Weintraub Advertising Agency as its chief art director and proceeded to change the look and feel of American advertising, introducing a unique blend of wit, humor, and art-based aesthetics for mass-market clients. A master of many disciplines, he moved from editorial and advertising to corporate and packaging design, creating identities for IBM, Westinghouse, Cummins Engine, NeXT, Enron, and USSB. He is the author of three books, *Paul Rand: A Designer's Art* (Yale, 1985), *Design, Form, and Chaos* (Yale, 1993), and *From Lascaux to Brooklyn* (Yale, 1996). He passed away in 1996. This interview was conducted in 1990.

What is the play instinct?

It is the instinct for order, the need for rules that, if broken, spoil the game, create uncertainty and irresolution. "Play is tense," says Johan Huizinga. "It is the element of tension and solution that governs all solitary games of skill." Without play, there would be no Picasso. Without play, there is no experimentation. Experimentation is the quest for answers.

You design as though you were playing a game or piecing together a puzzle. Why don't you just settle on a formula and follow it through to its logical conclusion?

There are no formulas in creative work. I do many variations, which is a question of curiosity. I arrive at many different configurations—some just slight variations, others more radical—of an original idea. It is a game of evolution.

Then, the play instinct is endemic to all design?

There can be design without play, but that's design without ideas. You talk to me as if I were a psychologist. I can speak only for myself. Play requires time to make the rules. All rules are custom-made to suit a special kind of game. In an environment in which time is money, one has no time to play. One must grasp at every straw. One is inhibited, and there is little time to create the conditions of play.

Is there a difference between play and, say, work?

I use the term "play," but I mean coping with the problems of form and content, weighing relationships, establishing priorities. Every problem of form and content is different, which dictates that the rules of the game are different, too.

Is play humor? Or do the two have different meanings?

Not necessarily. It is one way of working. Its product may be very serious even if its spirit is humorous. I think of Picasso. His famous *Bull's Head,* made up of a bicycle seat and handlebars transformed into the head of a bull, is certainly play and humor. It's curious, a visual pun. Picasso is almost always humorous—but this does not rule out seriousness—when he creates images that are contrary to what one would expect. He might put a fish in a birdcage, or a flower with little bulls climbing up the stem. The notion of taking things out of context and giving them new meanings is inherently funny. My friend Shigeo Fukuda, the Japanese designer, is a good candidate for one whose sense of play is pertinent. Almost all of his work is the product of playfulness.

You've discussed play as experimentation. Would you also describe play as doing things unwittingly?

I don't think that play is done unwittingly. At any rate, one doesn't dwell over whether it's play or something more serious—one just does it. Why does one want to see something rendered in many different ways? Why does one prefer to see a solution in different color combinations or in different techniques? That is an aspect of the play instinct, although it may also be a kind of satisfaction in being prolific. Still, most of the time, many variations provide a good reason to be confused and indiscriminate. I often have to stand away from a project for a while and return in a few weeks.

As a painter one can do that, but as a designer do you have the time?

Sure, I do it. Sometimes I find what's wrong on that second look. But most of the time the work gets printed, *and then* I see my mistakes. Sometimes I'm able to catch it by having a job reprinted, paying for it myself, or, if the client is generous, getting him to do it. A good example of this is the UPS logo. I recently had an interview with a public relations person from UPS about the thirtieth anniversary of the logo. I said that I would like to correct the drawing because some things ought to be changed. I added that I was certain the company would not approve any changes. She tried; regrettably, I was right.

What's wrong with the logo? It's recognizable, aesthetically pleasing, and distinctively witty compared to the logos of the other package carriers.

Aesthetically pleasing is not aesthetically perfect. There are two problems: one is that the configuration of the bow is unharmonious with the letterform; the other is that the counter of the *p* is incompatible with the other two letters.

But the bow makes it a playful logo.

Of course it does. In fact, the idea of taking something that's traditionally seen as sacred, the shield, and sort of poking fun at it—which I'm doing by sticking a box on top of it—is a seemingly frivolous gesture. The client, however, never considered it that way, and as it turned out the logo is meaningful because of that lighthearted intent. But that's not the issue. The bow is drawn freely. Today I would use a compass.

Isn't the fact that it is freehand what gives it the needed light touch?

Whether a drawing is done with or without the benefit of a tool—the compass—is unimportant. The spirit and intent are what counts. It would be more consistent to construct it geometrically, as are the shield and letters. All elements would be consistent and no one would be the wiser.

For most corporations, their logo is sacrosanct and not meant to be an object of or for humor.

Most corporations think the logo is a kind of rabbit's foot or talisman—although sometimes it can be an albatross—and believe that if it is altered, something terrible will happen.

Along those lines, you've designed some of the most recognizable logos in America, specifically the one for IBM. Years later, after you showed how this logo could be applied, you designed a poster that showed the *I* as an eye, the *B* as a bee, and the *M* as itself. You said that the company didn't publish it until later. Was that because it poked fun at the company?

They thought that it might encourage people working for IBM to misuse or misinterpret the logo. Later, though, they changed their minds because it didn't become the license they anticipated. What I did turned out to be a humorous idea; in fact, virtually any rebus is a humorous vehicle. Look at the rebuses of Lewis Carroll. A rebus is a form of dramatization making an idea more memorable.

When you begin a project, regardless of medium, are you playing with forms?

I don't just play around with form or forms. That implies a paucity of ideas. I always start with an idea, otherwise I'm working with mere abstractions. It's like taking a trip without a destination. Form develops an idea. You see, form is the manipulation of ideas—or content, if you prefer. And that's exactly what designers are, manipulators of content.

Do you intentionally try to create humorous ideas?

No. There are designers with a sense of humor and there are those without. Given the same content, the success is in the delivery. Groucho Marx can make anything funny, while others with similar material might just be tiresome. Still, something can be funny without being humorous—with irony. It helps, of course, if the material is amusing, but someone with a sense of humor can make almost anything funny. *How* something is done or delivered is often more important than *what*.

One of your jackets, for a book called *Leave Cancelled,* comes to mind in this regard. It shows a classical figure flying on a pink background with a number of die-cut bullet holes through the paper.

I wouldn't call that funny. The image is Eros, the god of love. That's not inherently funny. The bullet holes have to do with the plot; the protagonist has to return to his regiment before his date is over. Rather than funny, the cover was a literal translation of the plot. For me, a much funnier idea is the H. L. Mencken cover *Prejudices*. But the solution was built into the material—I had a lousy photograph of Mencken. What could one do with a bad portrait of the guy? I cut up the photo into a silhouette of someone making a speech, which bore no relation to the shape of the photo. That was funny, in part because of the ironic cropping and because Mencken was such a curmudgeon. But not everything I do is intended to be funny, particularly when the subject matter doesn't warrant it. Conversely, though I try to do things with a certain wit, I don't always succeed.

Can you be funny without a drawn line? Can type be an element of humor?

Of course. One can make letters correspond to an action, like letting them lie down if a text is about resting or dying. Apollinaire did that kind of thing with his concrete poetry. And it was done long before Apollinaire. In Hebrew typography there's a lot of humor. The way Hebrew was written in the Bible involves all sorts of grammatical tricks. And even when one prays, the prayers are written so that prefixes or suffixes are repeated. These were used as mnemonic devices. Indeed, humor is very Jewish.

Jumping from ancient Israel back to logos, the NeXT logo is a very humorous approach.

Humor was not intended. It's playful and friendly. One critic described it as a child's building block. While that wasn't the idea, it does suggest the association. One can't make people perceive ideas as intended.

Actually, I assumed that Steve Jobs, the founder of NeXT and the man behind the Apple computer, liked cute things, like the Apple logo in rainbow colors with a bite taken out of it. I was told that the reason it was called Apple was that Jobs challenged his staff to come up with an idea—and nobody did—so he decided upon the apple, for no other reason than he liked them. This is a classic example of how arbitrary symbols and logos are—or even should be.

Calling the computer an Apple also humanized it.

Yes, I think by accident. But it's evidence that a logo does not have to illustrate one's business. If it does, great. Look at the symbol of a bat for Bacardi rum or the alligator for Lacoste sports clothes. Other than the originator, who really wants a bat or an alligator for a corporate symbol? But these are so ingrained in the consumer's mind that it doesn't really matter. The fact is, if one recognizes a bat or an alligator in association with these products, its purpose has been served. The function of a signature, which is what a logo really is, is to be authoritative and not necessarily original or humorous.

Right, but we were discussing your reason for selecting the NeXT cube.

I have a tendency to veer off. The reason was, Jobs liked cutesy things. I believed that I should try to find some kind of object, like a cube. It seemed reasonable because Jobs indicated that his computer was going to be housed in a cube. He did not say, however, that I should use a cube—he just shot off a bunch of adjectives describing the machine. I thought, what's comparable to a cute little apple? A little cube—something to play with. And it was positioned askew on the envelope, like a Christmas seal.

Someone at the presentation meeting told me the thing that sold him on this logo was just that—the skewed logos—which is amusing because I originally did two versions. The first showed the logo parallel to the picture plane. The only one that was askew was the one on the back of the envelope. While the presentation was being printed, someone asked, "Why don't you do them all like they appear on the envelope?" I agreed. That made it more playful and more lively.

It's like timing in the delivery of a joke.

Yes.

Have you ever done parody?

I've done a poster for Yale that I would call parody in which I use the step motif—so common today among the trendy. But this old ziggurat motif goes back to ancient times. It is also a common motif in Dutch architecture. It's a common motif that has been dragged out by the postmodernists. Because of all this charged meaning, I decided to do a parody of it, just for fun.

It's a recruiting poster in the form of an accordion folder. The cover shows the title and a dramatized rendition of the step motif. When it's opened, the Yale Bulldog is occupying the top step. I'm trying to take the cliché out of clichés. Cézanne's apples were clichés.

Wouldn't you agree with the saying "Nothing is new under the sun"? *Everything* is a cliché.

Almost everything is grist for the creative mill.

Leon Trotsky once wrote that art is a complicated act of twisting and turning old forms that are influenced by stimuli outside of art so that they become new again.

I'm not sure what Trotsky means by "old forms." Does he mean old categories, old ideas—the way things used to be done, old content? The designer's problem has always been to do something with content, old or new, to enhance, to intensify, to dramatize, with uncommon ideas or unusual points of view, *and* to treat these ideas in a practical way by formal manipulation—sensitive interpretation, with integrity and, if possible, with wit. Mies van der Rohe once said that being good is more important than being original. Originality is a product, not an intention.

HARPERCOLLINS COLLEGE OUTLINE

HISTORY OF PHILOSOPHY

Dion Scott-Kakures, Susan Castagnetto, Hugh Benson, William Taschek & Paul Hurley

Comprehensive Outline in Easy-To-Use Narrative Format, Supplements Major Textbooks, Fully Indexed, Bibliography

Stephen Doyle on Humor in Design

Stephen Doyle is the principal of Doyle Partners in New York City. Formerly a designer at *Esquire, Rolling Stone,* and M&Co., he cofounded Drenttel Doyle Partners in the 1980s and developed a distinct design signature and vocabulary combining a neoclassical (or what he calls "modern classicism") type aesthetic with an interest in visual puns. His design of *Spy* magazine in the late eighties, with its multiple type styles and layers of visual and textual information, was highly imitated and became emblematic of the era's magazine design. His work is as much about humor as a communications tool as it is about the formal issues of color and composition. His clients are as diverse as Martha Stewart and the Cooper-Hewitt, National Design Museum (Smithsonian Institution), yet humor remains a constant.

What is the importance of humor in graphic design?

It's a technique to involve an audience. If you design a film, you have a captive audience. When you design a book cover, you are trying to design something that's magnetic—that's going to draw people to it—something that's related to the topic but doesn't give everything away. It should have allure. That's where the humor comes in. If something is nicely wrong enough, it can entice. If something is funny or warm or friendly, then it actually reaches out to people; it begins a dialogue, a two-way street. We try to use humor as a human magnet.

Do you inject some kind of humor into all your work?

No, it is not appropriate to be funny all the time. I pity the woman who married Robin Williams. Also, the work we do is not particularly slapstick-funny, it's not "ha-ha" stuff. More often, we're after charm or light humor—sometimes our design work is a little bit wrong or off-kilter. We're after a double take. We might make something too small, to act insidious, or, then again, too big, to be bombastic. It's that little bit of "upside-downsia" that gives our work a sense of being memorable. It suggests, "We know that you know that we know."

Is humor a strategic tool as well?

I'm interested in humor as a marketing technique as much as anything. We designed some book covers for HarperCollins College Outline texts. These are supplementary college-level texts on topics like psychology and marketing and mathematics. Previously, they looked remedial. They were an embarrassment to own, much less carry around campus. We designed them so that even the guy carrying a precalculus book could look stylish—and smart!

But even if these atypical cover designs are appealing to students, how do you convince the decision makers to buy your ideas?

Every book design project has a couple of target audiences, and they're sequential. First, you gotta sell an idea to your client (the art director, editor, publisher, or whatever). Then, it's gotta break through at the level of the bookstore buyer, and only then does it have the chance to sit on some unsuspecting shelf and flaunt its cover to the consumer audience. How do you convince all these decision makers, when you only come face-to-face with one set? It's the power of the work itself that does the convincing. All the justification in the world, all the literary theory you can stomach, begging, insisting, or threats will get you absolutely nowhere on the decision-making ladder unless the work has some truth or resonance or personality to keep it alive with or without you.

In this particular case, our idiosyncratic approach actually increased sales. The bookstores ordered more books and racked them face out because they were amusing commentaries on the topic as well as good-looking as a series. And they were more powerful for the sheer quantity of them. Our introduction of humor to this genre of books made a big impact on the category, and now other publishers are copying us.

Do you find books are a good genre for design humor?

We don't design a whole lot of books, but we like to do books because they serve as a kind of design touchstone for us. I think what is fascinating about composing a book is that it's a narrative; even if it's just a picture layout, it's telling a story. My design roots are in magazine editorial as an art director. I worked at *Esquire* and *Rolling Stone* magazines, and I'm fascinated with the idea of telling stories with words and pictures. When you design a book, it's not just about graphic design, it's about design and time. It's about sequence and getting from here to there in a considered way. A designer gets to orchestrate the experience from this page to the next. You get to add to the three-dimensional product of the book itself another dimension of time. I love the tactile quality of books. I love the sound of a book hitting the table. It has, after years of magazine design, a permanence that really appeals to me.

Do you see your work as having a distinct Stephen Doyle personality?

"Personality" is a great term, which appeals to me because there really is a common personality rather than a common style with the work that we do. We try to make our work both appropriate to the audience and consistent with our thinking. But—*careful!*—that description also fits a tax return! As Joseph Beuys asks, if your work has no drama to it, who would ever be interested in it? That's where the personality factor becomes an important element. Who wants to go to a dinner party and be seated next to someone who's accurate? Wouldn't you rather spend time with someone amusing?

We're not interested in trends. They're antithetical to getting work noticed. Our job is to stand out from the trends and call attention to the product or the service or the client or whatever it is that we're promoting. Allowing personality into your work can salvage it from being "targeted communication" (which sounds dangerous or boring or both), and it can also rescue your work from being "about design"—that slippery slope of onanism that designers often visit by themselves.

Design students, in particular, are enamored with the trend du jour—

What a difference a day makes! Once everybody has a tattoo, they are a little less risqué. Trends start as something new, but they become mainstream so quickly now, it's hard to tell who is the piper and who are the rats. The ultimate enemy of a trend is trending. It starts out looking different and noticeable, then it buries itself as everybody imitates it. Trends extinguish themselves. And that can leave a student with a dated-looking portfolio.

Let's talk about the work you have done for Champion International paper company's Benefit line of premium papers. Speaking of a wink and a nod, the audience is other designers. Do you have a different set of rules or standards when designing for designers?

Down deep, designers really loathe each other's work. We'll never admit it, but we only feel safe truly admiring the work of the dead. Everybody else, at some level, is the competition. To market paper to designers, we tried to slip in the cracks and send them stuff that didn't really look like design. Our Benefit promotions have no pictures, and there's minimal typography. It's all about color, and, besides, you get good free stuff! Not even a graphic designer can resist free goodies, just so there's not too much design on 'em. We know that everybody throws away booklets, calendars, T-shirts, and refrigerator magnets. Our guiding principle was to develop promotions that people with too much stuff already couldn't throw away.

What we tried to do with Benefit was to remove the hand of the graphic designer so that when you get something in the mail, it's yours—not mine. It is about the exuberant juxtaposition of colors. We overcame language; the promotions do not say Benefit everywhere, but the colors just scream Benefit. I think this is the best identity we ever designed, and there's not even a logo. It's the colors themselves that are Benefit, and the colors change! I think this program is a wonderfully devious way to market to design studios.

From where do these colors originate?

The colors of refrigerators have been changing over the years. Why should it take so long for the paper industry to catch up? Tastes change. Look in the back of your closet! Slowly, but thoroughly, our tastes transform over time to "what's in the air," especially where color is concerned. The Benefit colors are designed by me. Coming up with these colors is very personal, but it is meant to reflect the colors that I see around me. My studio is very respectful when I get out my paints and start mixing these colors up, and that's the crude way that it's done. I paint swatch cards by the hundreds. I swing the hues with tiny variations into grays and yellows and greens. I paint blue swatches, add hints of red, swing through pale violets, and head off into gray. Then the editing and the juxtaposition begins. I try to develop a range with personality, but that is also reasonable as paper: colors you can use, but a little bit off the beaten path. That's Benefit!

Speaking of your romance with color, you have developed a distinctive palette for Martha Stewart's products for Kmart. How difficult has it been to inject your design sophistication into such a mass-market product line?

Difficult? It is a blast! She has just introduced a line of sheets and towels and tablecloths and curtains into Kmart for which we do the packaging and the in-store signage. Martha

Stewart and her team are insistent on not talking down to the millions, and her strategy is working. In one year, her brand has become a billion-dollar business. I think that the work we do for her is very much like what we've been doing for the Cooper-Hewitt, National Design Museum, which is to take high taste and introduce it to the masses. For example, the objective of the book we designed, titled *Design for Life,* for the National Design Museum is to take the museum and introduce it to the people on the street and show them what design is all about. In the same way, working for a mass-market store like Kmart and a high-end product like Martha Stewart, we are acting as translators between high taste and the masses, and that's a job we relish.

Can you be humorous in this realm?

Sure!

There is a photograph in your office of an installation celebrating the seventy-fifth anniversary of women's suffrage. It is the actual text from the Nineteenth Amendment that you applied to the floor of Grand Central Terminal. It says, "The right of citizens of the United States to vote shall not be denied or abridged by the United States or by any state on account of sex." Tell me about the challenge of working within a space like Grand Central and doing something that has such import. This is not about devising identities for high-end or mass-market products.

Can you imagine the power you feel as a graphic designer when you install part of the Constitution in a monumental landmark space like Grand Central in such a way that hundreds of thousands of people passing by stop to read it? This was absolutely thrilling for us. A real career high.

Also, this project curiously summarizes some of the very things that we have been talking about: translating from "on high" to the masses and humor. Even though we are appropriately reverential about the Constitution, and certainly women's right to vote, don't miss the fact that we positioned our type so that people rushing to catch their train were confronted by a massive word on the ground: a very compelling eight-foot-high "SEX"! It certainly worked to pique a little curiosity. After all, it is Forty-second Street!

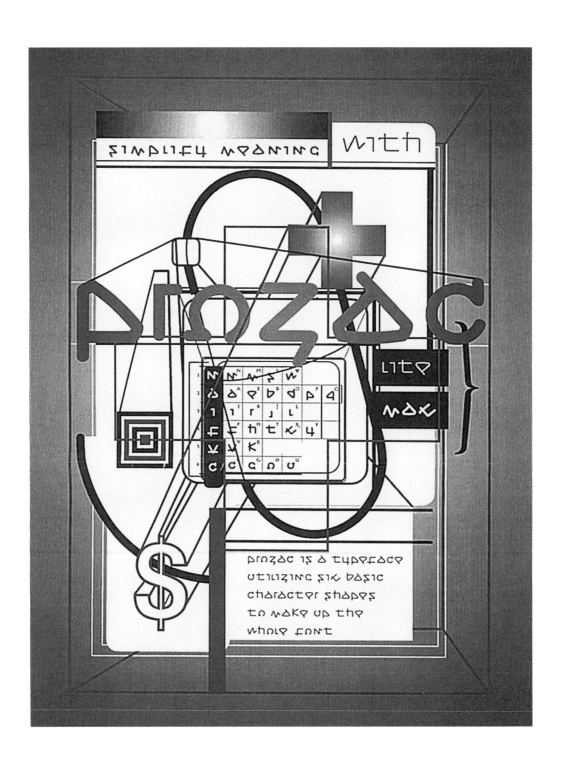

SIMPLIFY MEANING WITH

PROZAC

lite

max

{

$

prozac is a typeface
utilizing six basic
character shapes
to make up the
whole font

20

Jonathan Barnbrook on Experimentation

Jonathan Barnbrook was born in 1966 in Britain and studied at St. Martins and Royal College of Art from 1985 to 1990. He has worked on his own as a graphic designer, type designer, and live-action director, and runs his own font foundry. His most popular fonts are Mason and Exocet released by Emigre Fonts.

How did you get involved with type design?

I got involved in type design because I had no choice; it was an instinctive thing. When I was fourteen I used to draw the names of bands on my school books in the correct typeface copied off their album covers and then invent my own for them. It was the connectivity of visuals and the music that was important, nothing to do with knowing what graphic design was. But when I look at them now, the attention to letterform detail and emphasis on typography in coming up with new logos must have meant that I was instinctively a designer.

Later on, when I became involved in graphic design and started working with page layout, controlling the placement of the elements wasn't enough. It felt like I didn't have full control. I needed to extend the graphic designing absolutely to the drawing of the letterforms as well. It was also a time when the Macintosh thing hadn't really started, and it felt like a lot of the typefaces available did not have the correct voice for contemporary society. So it was also a gut response to define something that reflected the society I lived in and not the typographic models drawn thirty years before that were in general usage. I hope this doesn't sound arrogant. I appreciate and admire some of these fonts. It's just that something more immediate was required.

What was your first attempt at designing a full alphabet?

My first attempt at a full alphabet was an uppercase face that was serif and sans serif in each character. It was called Mulatto. It was designed in 1987 before it was normal to be able to access digital letterforms, and so it involved a lot of drawing and photocollage. It was not the done thing at that time to mix characters in this way, and that was precisely why I did it. Before that, we had done a few exercises in the first year of my graphic design degree where we had to construct the whole alphabet from just the *I* and *o*. Although this kind of project has value, it is a very bad introduction to letterform design because typefaces are about so much more than craft and a laborious aesthetic honing. Life is what typography is really about. The tension of drawing letterforms is really exciting: it is the restriction of the model of the alphabet that everybody has in his head balanced with the significance of the abstract form, the spirit of the time, and the excitement of working with language, which the letterforms directly affect.

Exocet has an inscriptional derivation. Tell me something about the nature of this face.

Exocet was the fifth typeface I designed but the first to be released. It comes from walking around museums and looking at early Greek and Roman stone carving. It was a synthesis of a lot of these letterforms. To me they looked, in a bizarre way, very modern, and I wanted to show that to people. I did a lot of research into this period of letterforms and interpreted them in Exocet. A lot of the early versions of it were much closer to the originals, but it is always important to add something rather than just copy. There are parts in it that do relate to how the original Greek was carved into the stone—like the letter *E,* which was directly taken from how they used to carve the letterforms.

Where does the name Exocet come from?

Exocet is a missile. The typeface was used for the first time in a book called *Illustration Now* and was the first piece of political design that I did. The book was simply an annual of European illustration for the previous year, but it came out shortly after the Gulf War, and the design was a direct response to that and to the first lowering of the European trade barriers. The Exocet missile seemed to be an example of irresponsible arms-selling by the French government. It was sold all over the world to nondemocratic regimes, and so it sort of tied into the theme of the book. I then learned that my home country, Britain, is one of the biggest arms-sellers in the world; maybe I should have named it after one of our despicable exports. The name Exocet sounds very seductive, and my choice of it has to do with how people were seduced by the technology in the Gulf War and completely forgot that real people were being killed in bloody and painful ways. It's strange there have never been any complaints about this name, as there were with Manson. Maybe because people can distance themselves from the responsibility of death that is caused by humans operating technology rather than by humans killing with their own hands. Results are the same either way, and both are unjustified.

Manson. If an alphabet can be controversial, this is it. Of course, the controversy is not based on the cut of the face but the name you gave it. What motivated you to design and name Manson?

The motivation was to add something to culture; this is always the motivation—culture first, money last. You are right that it is not a controversial font (though somebody wrote to me recently and said that he was not allowed to use the font because it looked too demonic), but that is exactly the point of giving it that name. The plan was not to shock, it was to give it a contemporary reference, as it is taken from sketches of lettering from churches and other monumental buildings. I didn't want people to have this cozy view of beautiful letterforms designed with an easily understandable name (like the current name, Mason, which just immediately says stone carving) further enforcing that coziness. Typography more than ever before reflects the pace of change in the contemporary world and the contradictions that exist in it, and it should not be insulated from it. I also had been reading a lot of writing by the Japanese author Mishima where he dealt with the similarity of opposites: pleasure and pain, beauty and cruelty. The Manson typeface is beauty and cruelty combined—let's not forget that the Christian church has a very long history of torture and persecution. There was also just the phonetic sound of the word, it was meant to create a double take: You thought, hmm . . . Manson, it sounds sort of elegant, and then maybe you realized where the name actually came from (the typeface was designed in England, where he is not as well known, with no thought that it would be released in the United States), that it was named after a serial killer, and it would change your whole attitude toward using it.

Naming typefaces has much more weight these days than when it was common to use the names as a sign of immortality or homage.

Maybe it has *less* weight in some ways. Previously, people used their surnames because a typeface could take a decade or so to do—it was a life's work. It has changed in the sense that some of the ideologies in graphic design have complexified, and so it is less unusual to make the name less straight. As you can already tell, the names of typefaces are incredibly important to me. All the typeface designs I do are named only after much thought. A typeface name can be similar to the name of a painting or a good contemporary pop song—it can work on so many levels. It is a specific chance to bring together the wonderful complexity of letterforms with the complexity of language and create a contradiction or illustrate a concept in doing so.

Do you feel that people rejected the name and face disproportionately?

I am really annoyed that people were not prepared to have any kind of discussion about it. I would have expected a bit more sense from the people who complained; they are associated with what is supposedly a creative field. This kind of questioning would have been tolerated in the art world. I was immediately accused of trying to generate publicity or just trying to shock people, and that is the opposite of what I am interested in. People who shock for the sake of it are generally making very boring, empty statements.

Given the response to Manson, would you have done anything different?

Yes, but it would have nothing to do with naming it differently; rather, it would be about the drawing of more characters to take the idea through to a more definite position.

What do you see as the role of any, and especially your own, new typefaces in the current market and milieu?

The role is to question. I don't think about the market. If people don't want to buy my typefaces, I don't care. If people appreciate them and want to buy them, then I am happy for them to do so. I am often amazed how people do use them; they turn up being used in really obvious, crass ways. When a supposedly avant-garde typeface is used on something very mundane with an empty message, it exposes the nature of most graphic design—it is simply about completing the piece of work in an acceptable manner rather than questioning cultural ideologies. My typefaces, on a simple level, are attempts to bring form to the spirit of the time and find a previously unexpressed visual "tone" for saying something.

Does a type designer have a responsibility to the tradition of type?

Yes, but that responsibility can also be to say, "I hate it and I am going to do something else." But you should know it before you say this. My work generally refers to the tradition of type because it is an important learning reference. Typographers absolutely have the responsibility to the craft of type. People should experiment, but they must know the craft first; otherwise, there is no experimentation—there is nothing to work against. Plenty of students and professionals think they are doing experimental type, but they're not—they're just working in a fairly defined contemporary visual language. Experimentation comes first from a rebellion of philosophy, not just a rebellion of style. It depresses me, the number of typographers or font designers I see who think that traditional typographic rules are too boring to learn in pursuit of being experimental. They are missing the fundamental, important things about being a typographer.

How do you see graphic design as having changed—stylistically, philosophically, ideologically—from when you began to now?

In many ways, graphic design has changed very little since the 1920s. It is and always will be about solving a communication problem; it's just that the definition of the problem and the many differing ways of communicating have changed. I think technology has obviously had an effect, both bad and good. It has allowed people greater access to the tools of graphic design, but the education about how to use these things has not happened along with them. People should be fundamentally educated about the basis of technology and typography, which is, first and foremost, that just because you can do something it doesn't mean that it's a good idea. One very positive side is the fragmentation of the industry. There are many smaller design groups and font foundries than there ever have been before. This has produced more diverse work and allowed back-catalogues of typefaces to be released, allowing more particular typography. It is also true that graphic design has taken on the complexities of philosophy in much more mainstream work—ideas such as deconstruction. Despite the world generally turning more toward capitalism, graphic design has opened up to a much wider range of people rather than just big marketing-led design companies.

What excites you most about being a graphic designer?

The chance to communicate something I want to say to people over and above the client's message. This may be the opposite of what people think a graphic designer should do, but it still involves the classic solving of a problem that is the basis of being a good designer. I just identify the problem a little differently. I also like the fact that the work is ostensibly free or at least much cheaper than buying "art." There isn't all the shit that surrounds you when you are an artist: the problems of the canvas as an icon, the absolute insulation that surrounds some artists, where they don't have to explain the work and can produce rubbish without criticism. I do wish, though, graphic design was a little more valued. Working with Damien Hirst highlighted how different it is. You are given a lot more respect for your creativity. There is no difference in whether the work is commissioned or not, as artists do work for collectors or with grants, and often the message can be up to you just as it is with an artist who sets his or her own agenda.

The *Damienhirst* book is a milestone of sorts—a seemingly perfect marriage of content and design. Describe the process of its conception and design?

Do you have a couple of years? Looking back, I find it hard to remember because it was so unstructured. There was no page plan, it just happened organically. There were certain things that Damien Hirst insisted on, such as the pop-ups. I didn't like this idea at first, but I am glad they're in because they give the book a playfulness sorely needed in art books. We did a lot of general talking, though, about the pitifully straight design of most artist's monographs. This is a creative field we are all supposed to be dealing with, right? And yet most of these kind of books fall into a sleepy academic legitimization, with text most people do not read and very little cultural context for the work. It was an honest attempt to bring art book design up-to-date.

What kind of communications did the two of you—artist and designer—have?

We don't live near each other, and so much of it was done by fax. I have to say, Damien Hirst is one of the most open-minded artists I have ever worked with. He doesn't suffer from that dreadful conservative attitude most artists have about graphic design. Instead, he was happy to let me work and generally overlook things. He would even go with something if I believed in it enough. There were a few things, though, that he thought I had got completely wrong, which I had to redo. I didn't mind this at all because I was enhancing his work and he was the only one who knew how it was constructed—it was important not to be precious about the design. We would meet occasionally and go through everything to make sure it was okay. The book constantly changed right up to the end, when we added a few pages while we were at the printer. It is important to be free about these things. Working in film has helped me a lot in my graphics work. It has taught me that you do your best at the time and keep things fluid rather than pinning them down to the absolute degree—rather like working on a shoot and going on what happens on a particular day. I was thinking of working in print in the same way, for pure typography: doing a typographic film of all the relevant information and then using stills as the pages. This opens up all kinds of unconscious layout possibilities from frame to frame.

While overwhelmingly praised for its invention, the book is also something of an excess. Do you feel that you went overboard in any way?

Well, yes. That was all part of it. We wanted to make it extreme—there was no point in just doing this thing in a small way. It was a definitive statement about how far you can take a person's art and enhance it with strong design. If we had held back, it wouldn't have had such an impact. I often try to be as extreme as possible; it is as it should be—an experiment. That is why I get annoyed when certain designers from larger, more commercial companies discredit much of the experimental work, stating that it would never work in the commercial field, then rip it off and water it down for their clients.

Each section was designed appropriately for the different series of works, and so it does change drastically from page to page. You could see each section as a pop song in a different style. I remember just before it was finished thinking how much some people were going to see it as an example of the worst kind of decadence, but I stand by it as an example of how far you could take these things at that particular point in time. Although you have said "excess," it is actually very restrained for my work. If you look at things like the intro pages, they are very simple, they come from the clean, modernist atmospheres of hospitals. There were lots of times when we sat down and "undesigned" the pages, made colors look like they were picked without thought, randomized pictures. I suppose the "excess" part comes from being consciously aware that the pages are manipulated by somebody rather than being "transparent."

I want to go back to your previous comment about ripping off and watering down experimental work. Isn't that the risk of doing work on the edge? You take the plunge, endure the critiques, and then suffer the piracy. Has this happened to you?

As for piracy of typefaces, somebody actually managed to release a pirate version of one of my fonts before I released a legitimate version. I am not so much concerned with the money—as I would then be as bad as the people who do it—although, if I have to operate in the capitalist system, I would expect to actually make some money out of the typeface, which at the moment I don't. What bothers me is that these people have no interest in the ideas of fairness or due credit. I also have to spend a lot of time communicating with people who think I am a large company making millions and therefore stealing a font is a form of rebellion, which is pathetic.

How do you—indeed how does any designer with an iconoclastic viewpoint—remain fresh or, shall we say, ahead of the pack?

If you think about it, people in my position actually are responsible for supporting the status quo. For capitalism to carry on, it must constantly visually evolve so that it can sell people the same thing over again. With the work that I and others do, we constantly feed into this visual evolution.

But there is no conscious decision to be "on the edge." It cannot be a conscious decision. As with making supposedly controversial statements, it can become empty if you worry about such things. I just try to do the work to my potential and do what I think is best. I don't know if I stay ahead of anybody, I just do things in my own way. As for staying fresh, apart from a very nice deodorant produced by a multinational company that exploits low wages in Asia and destroys half of the rain forest in doing so (But hey, if it smells nice and is available when I want it in such nice packaging, too, who cares?), I just take a passionate interest in life, good or bad, and it isn't a problem.

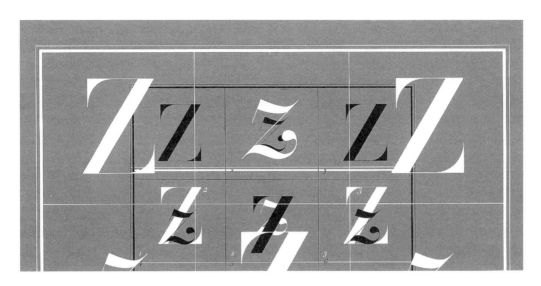

THE TYPE SPECIMEN BOOK OF THE HOEFLER TYPE FOUNDRY No. 1 HTF DIDOT

Jonathan Hoefler on Type Design

Jonathan Hoefler is a typeface designer and an armchair type historian whose New York studio, the Hoefler Type Foundry, specializes in the design of original typefaces. Hoefler's publishing work includes original typeface designs for *Rolling Stone, Harper's Bazaar,* the *New York Times Magazine, Sports Illustrated,* and Condé Nast; his corporate work includes the Hoefler Text family of type for Apple Computer, now appearing on computers everywhere as part of the Macintosh operating system. His work has been exhibited internationally and is included in the permanent collection of the Cooper-Hewitt, National Design Museum (Smithsonian Institution) in New York. The Hoefler Type Foundry publishes *Muse,* a type specimen book appearing periodically and available online at *www.typography.com.*

You began to design professionally when you were still in high school. How did you become a type designer?

I got involved in graphic design through caring about typography and finding that there wasn't anywhere I could do a degree program in type. So I took a year off from college to figure out what I should be doing, during which I worked for the Roger Black Studio on *Smart* magazine and finally at the Font Bureau doing more things related to font design.

Where did this impulse come from?

Some people are attuned to sports or fashion—but one of the reasons is that I've always liked to draw. I've always liked to use computers as well, and do programming. When the Macintosh came out in 1984, it offered me a tool to conduct graphic design in a way that was accessible to me as a teenager.

You were just fourteen. Where did you have access to this?

My neighbor had one. I used to go and feed his cats and use his computer. I could get my feet wet in what was involved with making images. Incidentally, when I was in high school my knowledge of what graphic design entailed probably had more to do with what commercial art was like in the 1930s. I thought it meant doing drawings of tail fins for Detroit. It didn't have to do with typeface design or even the use of type.

In addition to the computer, what were some of your early influences?

Spy magazine was one of the first artifacts that made me aware that typography can be the key ingredient in the design of a publication. I was aware of the way type was being used there more than in any other publication I'd seen.

What about *Spy* excited you?

I don't think of publication design in the 1980s as being particularly spectacular, and this was a magazine that resonated with me on an editorial level as well as on a visual level. It was very stylized typography. The use of Garamond 3, Metro, and Alternate Gothic in a world that, for me, had been Franklin Gothic and Century was distinctive.

I don't want to overemphasize the point that you were a very precocious child. But did you really know the difference between type styles? The subject is often arcane even for designers.

I lived a block and a half from Sam Flax on Twentieth Street, so I bought a $6.95 catalogue of dry-transfer lettering. Initially, that was the only way of accessing information about typography. I went from there to working for a designer who rented space from Push Pin Studios, which gave me access to Seymour Chwast's library, and I got to xerox his 1923 American Type Founders book page for page. I've gradually learned more about typography in its reverse chronology—I mean, digital things and then photo things and then metal things and then typographic things and calligraphic things and so on.

You began as a generalist. When did you turn the corner toward specialization?

I created a promotion piece in 1990 with a typographic thrust—cards that I had printed letterpress, based upon articles I had found in old type catalogues. I had digitized some wood type from these and sent out the promo with the hopes of getting work in book-jacket design or album covers or lettering. People like Gail Anderson and Fred Woodward at *Rolling Stone* responded to it and hired me to do lettering work. At the same time, Roger Black was opening the Font Bureau with David Berlow—they were one of my first clients and I was one of their first employees. I began doing everything that needed to be done there for typeface work, from scanning to some outline drawing to a little bit of design. Those things evolved in parallel when I was first starting. And eventually the work I took on was entirely typographic.

How did you learn to letter?

Just keeping my eyes open, doing what seemed to make sense. I worked very closely with David Berlow when the Font Bureau was starting and learned a great deal from him, not so much about lettering but about type design, about the mechanics of designing a typeface, as distinguished from doing lettering. That was very essential.

What specifically is the difference between lettering and type design?

Well, lettering is for a single application; a typeface is for many applications. The way you go about doing a piece of lettering has to do with its art direction. The way you go about designing a typeface has to do with not knowing how it will be used.

Would you agree that the design you were doing in the early years was based on a revivalist sensibility?

It really depended on the project. Some things I was doing would involve direct digitization of existing artwork; it's very banal but technically useful. One gets a good training in typography by replicating work that's gone by. Some of it was more interpretive in ways—starting from an existing historical design. Like one of the first things I did for Roger Black was a Bodoni revival, without really knowing that a Bodoni revival was a relatively complex project to undertake. First of all, it involved sorting through historical material, finding things that were worth keeping, things that were worth putting aside, and developing some sense of what really were the qualities of Bodoni not expressly found in contemporary revivals of the face. And some projects were entirely new. I've done a number of faces that weren't really grounded in historical continuum—in explicit ways, at least.

For example?

I did a font for the Guggenheim last year that is a set of three sans serifs. It's not specifically based in an existing style, but it is recognized for the low x-height, and so it gets collected with things like Nobel and Kabel. But I hope it doesn't have the feeling of 1930s German typography. I hope it calls to mind the Guggenheim.

That's an interesting point. Within a genre or a family or a style that is noted for or associated with a mid-century modern sensibility, how do you create a type that's functional to its own time period?

I find that really hard to articulate. It's like when I'm asked to describe why I need to design a typeface in the first place. There are a few things that I am very concerned with. One of the things I mentioned earlier is the way type families develop. I don't like to do things that are simply romans, italics, bolds, and bold italics. I'm more interested in doing families of weights or families that evolve in ways that are unconventional—typefaces that can't really be substituted for existing designs. In the case of the Guggenheim font, it was a matter of designing along a weight axis that doesn't necessarily follow the way a face like Nobel or Kabel gets heavier. It does different things. But again, it's a typeface. There are ineffable qualities about these things that make them very hard to justify. A lot of it is simply stylistic appeal.

What faces can you describe that involved pushing aside the historical precedents?

There's the Fetish family of faces. It's one of the more speculative things that I've done. You could say it's a postmodern joke on typography, but it's also a commentary on some of the things that I find curious, not necessarily objectionable, but questionable about contemporary typography. The first design, called Fetish 338, is an attempt to collect all the eccentricities that have in some way come to be associated with classicism. I am trying to take the phenomenon of art direction, which employs some of the aspects of classical typography—swatches and small caps and things from very specific typographic milieus that are divorced from those original functions and used for some other purpose—and to use some of those strategies in a typeface rather than a piece of typography, to see what comes out. And it's sort of a typeface that adjusts itself. It's overly flowered and ornamented, and it's rococo and baroque at the same time.

That's one of the faces in the series. One of them also is a sort of joke on the way typefaces are designed with specific uses in mind. It's a face called Fetish 976. It's used for telephone directories.

Incidentally, are these numbers arbitrary?

Mostly. They come from the fact that every art director I know has a favorite typeface that has a pedigree attached to it. It's always Caslon 540 or Garamond 3. The 976 prefix comes from the "fifty-cent-a-minute" information calls. And this font is designed in the way that faces like Bell Gothic or Bell Centennial are, with one specific application in mind. I think of those as being interesting designs because they both were created for telephone directories and have been used in the last few years in publications in large sizes or even in signage.

So, as quirky as it is, Fetish 976 was designed as a functional face?

It's designed in a way that it aestheticizes the function. It contains many of the aspects of use-specific typography. It has things like ink traps to allow for reproduction in small sizes on bad paper on web offset presses. But rather than using these things functionally, it aestheticizes them. It decides that the theme of the typeface will be the ink trap, and they are used in completely unnecessary ways that seem in some way technical and functional, but are in fact technically ridiculous.

To enlighten the ignorant, what is an ink trap?

In a lot of metal—I suppose both metal photo and digital types—when a typeface is meant to be used in very small sizes, it's necessary to compensate for areas where ink will otherwise collect, a corner, a junction of any two strokes, and so forth. I think one of the reasons why a typeface like Bell Centennial has become so popular in recent years is that it contains these things, which when the typeface is enlarged to 72 point become interesting. They become stylistic attributes as opposed to functional ones. So in the case of this design, I have taken a font that is obviously not intended to be used informationally in 6 point and applied to it these strange structural elements just to see what would happen, and I think the result is interesting. Unexpected things happen as a result of these two aesthetics colliding: on the one hand, the very baroque and overbaked, and on the other hand, the very specific and technical.

You call this a "speculative" typeface. Do you mean experimental?

I wrote a big manifesto about this in the first issue of what I hope will be many issues of *Muse,* my specimen book, really trying to undo the word "experimental," which I think is bandied about too much in typography.

"Experimental" tends to be an alibi sometimes. Unfortunately, it has become so married to "unusual." An experimental typeface these days tends to be one that does not look like a book typeface. It becomes a way of foreclosing the whole discussion. I read an article on one of the faces submitted to Neville Brody's *Fuse* in which the designer said that it can't be evaluated in traditional terms because it's an experimental design—which I think is a cop-out. It's either a work of design or it's a work of fine art. If it is both, I am more interested rather than less. But to make no distinction between typefaces that can be used for conveying words and typefaces that can't, muddies the field.

To get back to your speculative work, how do you define that? Is Fetish 976 a face that you feel can and should be used?

Oh, absolutely. I make no bones of the fact that it's a novelty. It doesn't have the versatility of the more sober text faces and display faces I've done. But it's certainly usable.

So, one might criticize the typographer who screws up in using the typeface? Do you see your typefaces used in ways that you would never want to see them used?

It's a sword that cuts both ways. Obviously, I'm disappointed by things that I see sometimes, and people use my work in ways that I don't think are very attentive. On the other hand, people also use my faces in ways I never expected, and it's a delight to see. The thing that I am most suspicious of is a typeface designed in a vacuum, when someone makes the font with no idea whatsoever of how it might be used.

What do you use as a proving ground? Do you use your faces in their own typographic environment?

Well, I have two main criteria in designing a typeface. First of all, I don't want to design any faces I can't imagine using myself, which is why I've obviously strayed away from certain aesthetics. Second of all, I have my clients. Most of the work I do at this point is commissioned, and I enjoy it that way. The concerns of readers are, I think, paramount, and obviously art directors are there to safeguard those concerns.

Do you go the conservative route?

Absolutely. I'm working on a new series of faces right now called Knockout. It began life as an update of Champion Gothic, one of the first type families I designed for *Sports Illustrated,* and I am now doing this new set of versions for *Sports Illustrated.* In this typeface, I am trying to both make something that is functional in a very bulletproof way—a designer who needs to do a chart can pick one of the faces and use it safely without having to think about too many things—yet also imbue it with enough character that it becomes interesting in display sizes. There are things about the style of these letters that resonates with me and that I hope comes through in both their very sober applications and their very avant-garde applications. And, certainly, I try everything before it goes out the door. It's less about quality assurance and more about enjoyment. I love playing with fonts when they're done. That's the whole point of doing them in the first place—to have them.

"Knockout" derives from boxing terminology?

The whole boxing theme came about when Champion was designed. It's a face in six different widths, and there's no real morphology that's been adopted for describing weights in that way. If the variation is in the thickness of the stem, you might say it's light, medium, bold, extra bold, whatever. But in various different widths, there are a handful of terms like "extended," "condensed," "compressed," that are not used in a uniform way. So we decided to use our own system, which is to adopt the names of the American Federation of Boxing weights. In Champion they proceed bantamweight, featherweight, lightweight, welterweight, middleweight, heavyweight. Knockout is an improvement upon that. It goes from flyweight to sumo, and so it's an extension of the same idea. And each of these nine different ideas—flyweight, bantamweight, featherweight, lightweight, welterweight, middleweight, cruiserweight, and sumo—comes in different leagues as well. So there's, for example, junior welterweight, full welterweight, and ultimate welterweight.

What is your basic attitude about reprising typefaces?

The *Rolling Stone* faces are a good example because they're not explicit revivals for testing designs. The whole family is slab serif. Obviously, it's designed along nineteenth-century lines, so it looks like something from Stephenson Black and something from Herb Lubalin. It's got a very specific style to it. But that family of designs includes, in addition to the four Victorian styles—the Egyptian, the Gothic, the Latin, and the Grecian—a set of italics for all of them, two of which, the Latin italic and the Grecian italic, never existed historically. They're mythical. And the project for me, of creating a Latin italic or a Grecian italic in ways that are historically sympathetic yet entirely new, is part of the sum of the typeface. It's a way of reinventing or reworking something–"rephrasing" is probably a good way of putting it—in a way that's unique, and not merely rehashing what's gone before. It's also an incredible challenge. Finding ways of doing these things is what a lot of typography has been about for the last hundred years.

You have to immerse yourself in the historical precedents. How do you do it?

I buy a lot of books. I'm also a member of ATypI, and I've gone to its annual congress for the last nine years. When I began going, it was peopled largely by German manufacturers of typesetting equipment, as well as calligraphers, stonecutters, sign painters who work in gold leaf, Web designers, font hinters, and computer programmers. All these disciplines bring their own interests to bear in the design of typography, and the best thing you can do is be part of it.

Your Apple face is one that comes with all Macintoshes. That's a huge responsibility. How did you come to work with Apple?

In 1991, I met an engineer from Apple, who explained that they were working on a new technology for type, which ultimately became called TrueType GX. It was an attempt to automate a lot of the aspects of typography that are tedious: ligature insertion, smart quotes, things like that. And because my typeface Hoefler Text had a broad enough character set, since it was steeped in classical typography as opposed to digital typography—it had small caps and swatches and ligatures and old figures and all these sorts of things—it seemed a good candidate for inclusion in this project. There was a good synergy between the interests of the designers who were involved—I was one, Matthew Carter was another, the Font Bureau, and Bigelow & Holmes—and the interests of engineers in line-and-layout technologies, people like Dave Alstadt, who is one of the fathers of the technology, and Eric Maeder, both of whom brought their interests in language and their interests in technology to bear upon the work they were doing. The font for Apple Computer was a challenge in part because of its size and in part because it had to do more with satisfying engineers than with satisfying art directors, who bring a very different set of notions to the table. The engineers are not as interested in the style of letters as in the way in which they're used, the way in which they're encoded, and that was a good challenge for me as well.

There were some wonderful scenes. I was talking to one of the engineers about the way small caps are used, and saying, "Small caps *are* used; remember, all caps are distracting in postal codes or in introductions or in acronyms and so forth." And he asked what one does when setting in italics for small caps. I couldn't really find an answer besides using roman small caps, which is what Bruce Walters might have done and what Updike might have done. He asked for "italic small caps," but there simply hadn't been any historically—or there hadn't been until the digital age—so it didn't really seem worth doing them. But I couldn't find an answer out of the argument, the semantic argument "What do you do if?" except to draw them. And the result is something I would never have thought to do myself, which is now my favorite part of the typeface—the italic small caps.

In terms of your own work, give me a good example of what you consider problem solving versus window dressing.

Well, I don't intend to take on the job if it's window dressing. When I get a call from a client who says, "We want our own typeface," my first question is usually "Why?" And unless I can get a good answer, I am skeptical that the job will ever take flight, and most of them don't. A lot of it is vanity: The competition has their own typeface, and so an art director at another magazine wants one, too. If there isn't some overarching reason for me to invest the time that I put into a typeface, I don't want to do it. But if someone comes to me and says, "We need a family of sans serifs that can be used in large sizes and can be used for unusual layouts where some words might be long and they can be condensed mathematically" (as was the case for *Sports Illustrated*); or if someone says, "We need a family of faces built on the same set width so we can recycle our layout from one font to the next" (as *Rolling Stone* did); or "We need a modern typeface like Bodoni or Didot that can be in very, very large sizes and very, very small" (as *Harper's Bazaar* did), those are the intersections of the technology and the aesthetics that I think are exciting and worth exploring.

And how did you learn?

Trial-and-error, mostly.

What is your learning curve?

It's ongoing. There's not a typeface I've ever finished that I wouldn't revisit. If I had the time, I'd redo them all.

But does that mean the face is flawed?

I don't think so. If I get complaints about a typeface, obviously I'll fix it, but that's yet to happen. I think it's more that I, as I think all type designers do, bring different interests to bear upon typefaces, and those interests are ever-broadening.

As you're talking about changing this and that in the typefaces that you do, it suggests that every typeface, even our most sacrosanct typefaces, can do with a little adjustment. Would you say that's true?

Well, part of the question is, what are the sacrosanct typefaces? If someone said, "You can never improve upon Garamond," what does he mean? The metal punches made by Claude Garamond in the 1930s, or the Garamond revival they know from prototype, or any of the sixty Garamond revivals made digitally? What is that essence of Garamond-ness that is so ideal, so Platonic, and so untouchable? There really isn't one. There are aspects of every typeface that are exemplary and worthy of study, worthy of emulation in fact, but there is no perfection. There is nothing that is insurmountable.

How do you feel about the sheer number of type designers who are one-hit wonders?

I think it's great. Cheltenham is a one-shot deal. Bertram Grosvenor Goodhue was an architect who had an idea for a font one day and made it, and it's been one of the most enduring typefaces in history. Bruce Rogers did one, or two if you count Montaigne. A lot of the totemic figures in type history have been the one-shot people. And for the most part, they have not been typographers. Caslon was a gunmaker. Baskerville sold Japan ware. Typography was an ingredient in a larger commercial enterprise for all of these people, and they did some of the most enduring things. So I am delighted to see a typeface by someone I have never heard of before.

How do you respond to those who say there are enough typefaces; we don't need any more?

I think that's kind of a dumb question. I don't think anybody would say there are enough novels. So I don't really see a reason to talk about that. But at the same time, as I was trying to say earlier, I don't think more typefaces for the sake of more typefaces is a good thing.

How do you feel about the more eccentric things that are being described as experimental or quirky or weird?

Some of them are great. Some of them aren't. Anybody who has a strong idea about something and can make it manifest in typeface usually has something to say, and if the final result is something that's interesting to designers and to readers, then all the better.

Does it go back to what we were talking about earlier? Does it have to work in the real world?

I don't think it has to have any kind of fealty to the historical continuum to be good. Whether it works, who knows? Obviously, I'm partial to typefaces that can be used by designers and read by readers. But you know, everything is different. A lot of contemporary typefaces, I think, are basically lettering shoehorned into a font. They don't necessarily have a shelf life that goes beyond their one use, but that one use may be enough.

Now you're at the ripe old age of twenty-seven, having done more than most people at forty-seven. What do you want to do that you haven't done?

I'm not really sure. I feel that a lot of the things I do right now are either the very conventional faces like Knockout or the very speculative ones like Fetish, and it's very hard for me to unite those two interests: to do a face that is a critical experiment but also produces a face that's versatile in a way that the more traditional things I've done are. I'd like to get closer to marrying those two things, and I have a few ideas in mind how it might happen, but I really haven't had a chance to explore it, certainly in a commercial environment. In part, my catalogue/magazine *Muse* and the retail business are ways of funding that work and being able to take the time to invest in a typeface that may not be used by anybody.

THE CRUISE

LIKE A HOLE IN THE HEAD

A NOVEL

JEN
BANBURY

JACK LONDON

Michael Ian Kaye on Book Jackets

Michael Ian Kaye is the creative director of Little, Brown and Company. Formerly the art director of Farrar, Straus and Giroux and an associate art director at Penguin USA, he has designed many books and many more book jackets, working with clients such as the Dial Press, Ecco Press, HarperCollins, Houghton Mifflin, Knopf, W. W. Norton, Random House, Simon and Schuster, and Scribner. Kaye has also designed several issues of *U&lc* for International Typeface Corporation. He is currently art-directing and designing the *AIGA Journal of Graphic Design*. He is the recipient of the 1997 *Literary Market Place* Award honoring excellence in book publishing for individual achievement in design (book jackets and covers). Kaye graduated in 1987 from the Allen R. Hite Art Institute at the University of Louisville in Kentucky and now teaches at the School of Visual Arts in New York City.

Why did you choose book jackets out of all the possible genres of design?

It kind of chose me. Since my first job was in book publishing, my first opportunities to design and conceptualize designs were on book-related projects, both book interiors and book jackets.

What about designing a jacket is more challenging than other forms?

Extracting a single image or concept from a four-hundred-page text is an essential part of the process. Many other forms of design do not require this interpretational instinct. It is important to me that my book jackets not only reflect the subject and tone of the book but are true to the artistic spirit the author has intended. This sometimes happens through my interpretation of the text but more often as a reaction to the text.

The jacket has always been treated as a separate, even unwanted, appendage in book design. How do you relate the jacket to the book?

I question "unwanted," but perhaps I'm slightly biased. Originally, book jackets were developed for the sole purpose of protecting the book and slowly evolved into the marketing tools that they are today. But just as the case materials are chosen thoughtfully by designers in order to reflect the mood, tone, or theme of the book's text, my designs are based on similar cues. I hope designing with this sort of sensitivity and appropriateness makes the book jacket not only relate but become integral to the book as an object. If it weren't for the expense, book publishers today would probably protect all their book jackets with an acetate covering (a book-jacket jacket) in order to prevent spoilage from handling. Maybe I'm dreaming.

How much of jacket design is a marketing issue, and how much an aesthetic one?

As a designer, one must always consider the market to whom he or she is communicating and the visual cues to which they respond (rarely the same as those of the designer). I'm not sure why marketing issues and aesthetic ones are considered by so many designers and design types to be mutually exclusive, or that one has to be sacrificed for the sake of the other. Perhaps the reason is that people all too often confuse aesthetic issues with those of self-expression. The inclusion of self-expression into the design equation is what really complicates matters. So many times we hear "how much _____ (fill in the blank with a quirky design idea: backwards type, itty-bitty type, black-on-black type, et cetera) can I get away with?" If we are getting away with something, at whose or what expense? Since eliminating self-expression from the equation is not desirable or possible, I try to be equally responsible to all concerns. For me, it is the design process that is the act of self-expression, not any given component.

Do you believe in the ten-foot rule? Should a jacket be a miniposter?

Any designed surface should be considered a mini- or maxiposter. Some surfaces should shout, and some surfaces should invite you in. Their functions are all the same: gain attention and inform the viewer. The only variables exist in the complexity of the information that needs to be communicated and the ego of the designer.

The conventions governing jacket design, the taboos and rules, can be daunting. Best-sellers must look like best-sellers. "More commercial" is a mantra for publishers. How do you circumvent these regulations?

Learn from the past, both the successes and failures; note the signals to which people respond; be aware of the present and the context within which things will be seen; and design for the future. Hokey, I know, but it's true. For me, design is an outlet. Each project allows me to use all prior knowledge and experience I have gained through seeing and being. When someone asks for large type, for example, is that what he or she really wants? Nine out of ten times, no. Readability, yes. A sense of importance, yes. Clarity, yes. The science of seeing negates so much popular belief where design signals are concerned, and I see it as my job to reeducate and help nondesigners embrace the ideals of good communication.

Okay, very good sentiments. But how often have you been asked—or, rather, ordered—to render a design cliché because it is presumed to represent a certain audience type?

I'm never really directed conceptually to target a specific market, but I do get asked for visual clichés; big type, foil stamping, embossing, etcetera. In these cases, I know the concern is readability and that the book feel important and special. These are things that can be achieved without succumbing to the hackneyed tricks of the trade. At times it's also fun to play with these materials and invent new ways to use them—teaching an old dog new tricks.

When you started doing jackets, who were your models? But more important, what were you trying to change or rebel against?

When I began designing book jackets, the trend was to decorate: commission fancy art and embellish; choose decorative typefaces that speak to the art not the text; when the art is too busy, place a colorful panel or two or three to aid in readability. Conceptually driven design had very little shelf space. This was the image-driven 1980s; "it looks like it relates" was good enough. This was my training ground, where many of my formal skills developed, and, for a brief time, I was a contributor. As I grew into myself and gained a broader information base, the ideas began to drive the work and there was less room for embellishment. This continues to happen as I develop a stronger sense of self and confidence in the work that I am doing.

And your models?

My models are varied: Renaissance painters for their strong sense of geometry and grid, the Hudson River school painters for their amazing compositional skills, the surrealists for their irony, the abstract expressionists for their energy, the early modernists for their clarity, pop artists for their in-your-faceness, and conceptual artists for their thoughtfulness.

And designers? Is everything rooted in fine art—no applied artists, commercial artists, or graphic designers?

I must say that where my influences are concerned I do not really distinguish between fine and applied artists. I am much more conscious of the ideas behind and the structure that supports these ideas—the vehicle is not as important to me. Obviously, I'm skirting the issue of names, not because there aren't any but because there are too many. I fear this sounds elitist, which is not my intention, but I truly believe that the experience of walking on a darkly lit, abandoned street in Brooklyn has the same power to influence as standing in front of the work of a master painter or turning the pages in a well-designed book. The question of heroes is entirely different.

You started your career doing jackets that were like paintings or posters; now you've become more minimalist in approach. Why have you turned down the volume?

I think that I have increased the volume or at least uncluttered the airwaves. Minimalism is extreme, and as a designer of product, I'm not quite sure this is attainable, since so many of the elements are beyond my control. I have become much more sensitive to the elements I choose and how I use them. My newer designs are more conceptually and formally driven and less decorated.

Describe your most satisfying jacket and your most difficult.

An Underachiever's Diary by Benjamin Anastas is very close to this minimalism of which you speak and is also my favorite to date. Rarely is one provided with a subject so appropriate and verbiage that aptly lends itself to be set in black 12.5-point Helvetica type placed title flush left and author flush right on a common baseline three-eighths of an inch from the bottom trim on an all-white field.

The Farrar, Straus and Giroux (FSG) fiftieth-anniversary poster is by far the most difficult project I have worked on. I commissioned forty-nine designers, illustrators, and photographers, and myself, to create one artful fish (the FSG logo consisted of three fish) to be incorporated into a commemorative poster. Among these artists were some heroes and many peers. Never has a more daunting task been defined: Combine fifty pieces of disparate art and their respective credits, and the names of fifty literary stars—Nobel Prize winners, etcetera—on a single document that will serve as the announcement for an exhibition at the AIGA. Pressure, or what? Weeks were spent solely focusing on organizing the material in a cohesive fashion. Grids didn't help because all the art involved different sizes and shapes. No art could be used larger or smaller than others for fear of insulting. An overall concept seemed impossible because within each piece of art a concept already existed. An elegant arrangement seemed the only option. Weeks of moving elements around on the page were to no avail. What resulted was an elegant typographic border of names surrounding an arrangement of the art meant to echo a nineteenth-century zoological print but also taking the shape of a large fish whose tail appears as an inset on a board from an old leather book. I'm still not sure if I like it.

How has book-jacket design changed since you entered the field?

Book jackets have become more thoughtful, slightly reverential to the thinking that was going on in the sixties concept-driven stuff. Decoration is taking a backseat for the time being. These things come and go in cycles that somewhat parallel those of the art world.

BENDAY

POTLATCH PRESENTS A FILM ABOUT THE WORLD'S GREATEST DESIGNER

A RIGHTEOUS PRODUCTION WRITTEN AND DIRECTED BY DANA ARNETT AND BOB RICE
STARRING KYLE COLERIDER-KRUGH PRODUCED BY KATHLEEN URSULA ROONEY MUSIC BY EVAN CHEN CASTING BY JANE BRODY
DIRECTOR OF PHOTOGRAPHY GARY KATZ EDITED BY SEAN BERRINGER POST PRODUCTION SUPERIOR STREET

Potlatch

Dana Arnett on Design and Film

Dana Arnett is a founding principal of VSA Partners, Inc., in Chicago. Arnett and his firm have been recognized globally by over thirty of the top-ranked competitions and professional magazines for their work in the areas of design, filmmaking, and new media. Over the last four years, much of Dana's focus has turned to filmmaking and brand/image positioning. And more recently, he has participated as a presenter at the Smithsonian Institution's Graphis Series, received Gold Medals from the Art Directors Club and Broadcast Designers Association, and placed Best of Show in the AR100 four of the last five years with the Chicago Board of Trade Annual Report. Among VSA's clients are Capitol Records, Coca-Cola, Kodak, Warner Bros. Records, Harley-Davidson, October Films, and Chronicle Books.

As a designer who is primarily known for print work, why did you turn to film?

I think it started long before I ever got into print design. I started turning to film by going to the movies. But, to answer your question more directly, I think I simply hit a threshold with the main focus of my creative work being print. Film gave me an outlet at that critical point in my career when I needed a greater challenge. It allowed me the means to expand on my secondary interests of theater and music.

What aspects of your graphic design background and training have helped you in your film work?

Storyboarding and writing. I have always thought of the best design as being nothing more than solid storytelling: great words combined (the right way) with great pictures. I sketch almost all the scenes we shoot. And I work intensely with my cowriters, actors, and the DP [director of photography] to ensure that the words become natural dialogue. What graphic design doesn't teach you is the art of dialogue. Collaboration is the essence of filmmaking. That is in fact why a film is referred to as a "production." The process is dependent upon the director's and producer's ability to manage people and resources every step of the way. The bulk of your collaborators are generally unionized, working on the clock, with the complete assurance that the director and producer are focused on all aspects of the creative and mechanical integrity. This is indeed the basis for your team relationship during the making of a film. The liabilities of doing things right, on time, and with precision are elevated because you get what you shoot.

But in essence you were really starting from scratch?

I really had to start over when I first started making films. I had to learn a whole new protocol and set of rules for working creatively. My DP told me that the reason I have succeeded so far is that I haven't been afraid to ask questions—the smart or dumb kind.

Having no formal or academic training in this medium, I have relied heavily on the support of my lead crew members to help train me. A lot of the collaborative lessons I learned as a design director transferred over to film—most important, my comfort in leading and nurturing a team of people. A long time ago, my partner Bob Vogele taught me that people will support what they help create. All individuals from the gaffer to the craft service person should feel they can contribute and are contributing. Like a design assignment, a film project will be most rewarding when people feel they have contributed to something that is rewarding. The best things I've ever collaborated on have had that sense of reward.

How much more difficult is creating a cinematic narrative than a flow of print pages?

When I began working in film, I quickly learned the larger and more complex sides that surround motion-picture production. Film is as much about managing people as it is about creating great scenes. When the camera is rolling, you're forced to articulate far more than you're accustomed to addressing at the drafting board. From movement to sound to light to cover shots to edit capability, you're forced to spin a lot more plates. For the most part, you are never shooting scenes in order. This forces you to keep the continuity of the entire film in perspective at all times. Whereas in print, the two-dimensional reference is always in front of you. When I talk about plate spinning, I'm simply referring to the demands of shooting a long-format piece. Along with the constant reprocessing of the full-length piece comes the here and now aspect of prepping scenes, reviewing the script, rehearsing, ad-libbing, blocking the movement, directing the technical aspects, et cetera, et cetera. I find it far more demanding and exciting to face this type of challenge.

Describe the nature of your films.

Human and situational. I am most interested in how my films express the living experience. I look at film as an opportunity to widen and enhance a person's experience through dialogue, story line, and venue. Like most filmmakers, I want my work to strike the viewer in very intense ways. In *Ben Day,* we were able to create a tremendous dynamic through little more than just great acting and a compelling short story. When I see these huge productions with grand special effects, it tells me what I do and don't want to do with my films. I like telling simple stories with great actors.

What was the impetus to make your first film, *Ben Day*?

Potlatch Paper Company, our underwriter, wanted a video paper promotion—you know, something that they felt could tell their story and excite their customers. They definitely thought we were going to come back to them with some cool paper film. We convinced them, through some very intense coaxing, that their money was better spent by making a deeper connection with their audience. After all, here we are three years later still talking about *Ben Day*. Would we still be talking about some video that touted the enamel surface of a paper grade? I don't think so. We attempted to personify, through a great short story and a very likable character, what it's like to work as a commercial artist. It was important for us to make that deeper connection to what we do as commercial artists by living out the experiences through film. Ironically, most of the stories are actually subtly tweaked real-life experiences that my cocreater and I had experienced throughout our own careers.

Ben Day **is a dark comedy. Is that the direction that you want your films to take?**

Regardless of the direction my future work takes, there is one goal that I will always focus on: that is, to captivate an audience. I will always view *Ben Day* as a stepping stone. At this early stage of my filmmaking career, it's too soon to predict a future direction for my work. Most filmmakers start out by tackling subject matter that is familiar to them, telling stories they are comfortable with and confident in directing. *Ben Day* was just that for me.

You have also produced minidocumentaries. Do you see yourself as somehow wedding the satiric and documentary form?

That's a great question, especially because I have tremendous affection and respect for satiric-style documentaries like *Real Life, Waiting for Guffman,* and *Spinal Tap,* to name a few. All have masterfully bridged the best of both styles. I do love the way humor can be used to tell a serious story. When done well, juxtaposing the two mediums creates this amazing twist. It pits nonfiction against fiction and plays to the side of human nature that delights in confrontation. In many ways, *Ben Day* fused elements of both.

Being a news junkie and ardent fan of comedy, I will probably try my hand at exploring the notion of blending both these styles. Many films tread a fine line between truth and fiction. Members of society are very much conditioned to believe just about everything they see and hear in the various media. I'm sure millions of people out there think that Oliver Stone's *JFK* was a true story.

Now that you are involved with film, has graphic design lost any of its appeal as a communicative or even an expressive medium?

I love doing almost anything that poses a tremendous creative challenge. I doubt that I'll ever grow tired of design. I'm finding out the hard way that it's very hard doing both. I didn't get a lot of sleep in 1997 running a design firm and shooting films.

Has any of what you learned in film been transferred to print?

About the only thing I can measure is my desire to do more book design. Film is an escape for me. It takes me away from all those corporate communication managers and somewhat overly inflated brochure assignments. You can build a book in some of the same ways you build a film, taking each chapter like a theme and building a complete story through literary purpose instead of through corporate purpose.

Your print work for Harley-Davidson toes the line between corporate style and personal expression. Do you have the desire to veer more toward the latter?

First of all, I'm a rider. Being an avid participant in the lifestyle side of motorcycles has biased and hopefully enlightened my approach to any given design assignment for Harley-Davidson. I probably would have been fired years ago if Harley thought my work was about me. Willie G. Davidson, the great-grandson of the founder, refers to the passion of motorcycle individualism and customization as folk art. Maybe I'm just a folk artist.

I think most "true" artists, fine or commercial, will answer to a personal voice when facing a creative challenge. After all, we're not making toothpaste here. Personal expression, in most cases, is the one and only way we define and separate ourselves from other creatives. When the expression has value, people will follow.

Given your own career path, how do you see the definition of graphic design changing in the future?

I think I got my first real sense of the meaning of graphic design when I realized it had the power not only to communicate, but also to effect change. The term "graphic design" may change and may already be obsolete. Given the rapid advance and enhancement that technology has brought to this medium, we really need to broaden the basic modifier of "graphic," before we further pigeonhole our profession. It starts by accrediting our design education system and informing the world about the broader sense of what we do. If only we were as disciplined and committed as architects have been at upholding the standards of their profession, we may never have had to ask this question.

Will designers have to be involved with motion and sound in the future?

The digital workstation has already provided this opportunity. The future really happened many years ago when addressing this question. Just look at the work of Saul Bass or Ray and Charles Eames, they each used sound and motion in their work. They just seized the bigger opportunities of design sooner than most of us.

Chris Pullman on Design for Television

Since 1973, Chris Pullman has served as vice president for design for WGBH, Boston, which supplies about 30 percent of the PBS prime-time schedule. He and his staff are responsible for the visual personality of WGBH as expressed through its on-air titles, credits, and animation; promotional and sales support; classroom materials; and interactive media. From 1982 to 1987 he was also responsible for the numerous trade books, publications, and products the station creates in conjunction with its programming.

You have been at WGBH since 1973. Was there broadcast in your life before this?

No. In fact, when I started at WGBH in October of 1973, I didn't even own a TV.

What is the difference in working for public television versus network?

The main purpose of public television is to bring ideas to an audience; the main purpose of commercial television in this country is to bring an audience to an advertiser. From day one, television in the United States was conceived as a marketing medium. There was no alternative to commercial television until 1967 when President Johnson passed the Public Broadcasting Act, which provided a small annual appropriation for alternative, commercial-free broadcasting. This is a very different history than in almost any other developed nation—including England, Japan, Germany, Sweden—where television broadcasting began as a government-supported public service and has only relatively recently had commercial services added to the mix.

The key distinction between commercial television and public television is that they have very different missions. This affects the design environment in many ways. The most obvious is the content. If you get right down to it, on commercial television the only reason a program exists is to keep the target audience watching between commercials. The more people who watch, the higher the rate the network can charge for commercial time. All the other choices—like content, quality, and cost—need to support that equation. While audience size is important in public television—why *wouldn't* we want to reach as many people as possible with an idea or insight?—it is not the primary goal in determining which programs we make or how the content is treated.

Of course money, in the form of available funds, is a major issue as well. How does design figure in the quest for audience size?

For the networks and the cable services, the stakes are very high for audience size and loyalty, and so huge budgets are spent to attract audiences. A&E [Arts and Entertainment network] spends more on promotion than PBS does on programming, yet they reach a fraction of our audience. And the handmaiden of big budgets is fancy technology. In a commodity business like commercial television, differentiation is the key. Being the first commercial or promotion to trot out the latest effect is a big deal—today, it's drifting type, shaky cam, and white-flash transitions. When you go to the annual Broadcast Designers Association conference, the networks and the cable channels dominate the latest and greatest. In many cases—like local news, the backbone of network television—technique has to substitute for content.

Are there differences in the kind of design being done for commercial versus public television?

In commercial television, news, advertising sales, and network or local branding and promotion are the biggest sources of design work. While we deal with these too, a sizable chunk of our work is devoted to designing educational supplements to our programming in print and interactive media. News and sports are less important in public television than formats such as documentary, performance, and children's programming. While news and sports are the most graphic-dependent genres in television, they are also the most grueling assignments. At the networks and local affiliates, you see bullpens full of "news graphic artists." If the goal were to help people understand things and use the power of visualization to explain things, I'd say fine. But in most cases they're producing short-order, over-the-shoulder PaintBox images of bombings and domestic violence done in graveyard shifts with no psychic payback.

There is hardly anything I work on that doesn't have some valuable social or educational underpinning. Precious little on commercial television does. It is easy to get snobby about it, but in the end, whether you would be happy working at the networks depends on what your personal values and interests are. I wouldn't.

What is the extent of your involvement—print, advertising, on-air ID, program graphics?

We do them all, and that's one of the great things about being a designer in this environment. While our main product is television and radio programs, by tonnage the bulk of our work ends up on paper. As with any product, we raise money to make it (involving proposals and sales materials). Once we have the funding, we make the program (titles, credits, technical animation and maps to explain things, packaging for distribution). Then, we promote the show to get an audience (on-air promos, advertising, press materials, posters, gimmicks, and T-shirts). We also work on a huge category that few people know about: educational outreach (teacher's guides, classroom materials, books, and periodicals) to extend the life of the program. And since the early 1980s, we have been designing content for interactive media: first videodisks, then CD-ROMs, and now the Web.

You were responsible for the *Masterpiece Theatre* intro, an icon of public television. How did you conceive of it?

Masterpiece Theatre had been on the air for a few years when I got to WGBH. The title sequence, or "open," that's on the air now is actually the third one I have done. The first was a Union Jack waving in slow motion that resolved to the logo. But as the series got more international and not just British, the notion was to stress the literature-into-film angle.

We discussed many ideas but agreed on the notion of a stately cruise through the quintessential paneled library—possibly the library of Alistair Cooke, then our erudite host. The music was already well established for the series (J. J. Mouret's Rondeau from *Symphonies and Fanfares for the King's Supper*), and so the structure of the shots responded to the structure of the theme.

We spent many weeks wheedling first editions of George Eliot and Charles Dickens from friends and relations—I scrounged the bulk from the rare book library at Princeton—and finding the appropriate nostalgic props. The open was shot in three scenes in a garage in New Jersey using the (then) latest gimbal-mounted "snorkel" camera, which could snake its way very intimately through the artifacts. The piece starts on the spine of a leather-bound volume and resolves on a title-page cartouche, which now serves as the logo for the series.

The present open is a 1993 update of the library idea, incorporating modest special effects that bring to life a few of the framed pictures as the camera sweeps past (this time adding a computer-based, motion-control 35 mm camera as well as the gimbal-mounted setup). The whole thing is meant to set the tone for the series and evoke fond memories of episodes past. My guess is that we will need to do another refresher in a few years.

Does being a graphic designer in television necessitate that you are very well versed in the medium?

I think it's the same in any medium you work in: the more you know about its special biases, the better you can design for it. For just about everybody on my staff, it's been learning by doing, but shortly after I got to WGBH, I began to realize the inherent weaknesses and strengths of television as a design medium.

The most obvious drawbacks include the single format (everything you do has to work in a four-by-three-inch rectangle); edgelessness (whereas a lot of the action on paper happens in relation to the edge of the sheet, in television—with differing set shapes and transmission loss—there's no reliable edge, making the middle the best place to be, especially for text); and almost completely unreliable color rendering (comparable to today's hassles of color matching on computers). But the biggest difference is that TV is an incredibly low-resolution, flickering medium, which makes it a very bad place for type, among other things.

Still, television brings some powerful advantages to the designer. Sound allows an alternative to typography for delivering verbal information—and many feel that the audio portion of television is more powerful than the video in delivering information and emotions. Motion can overcome low resolution by allowing zooms and pans to rapidly change the scale of elements and control point of view. And, of course, the medium being time based and linear (therefore difficult to interrupt, unlike interactive media), the producer/designer (rather than the reader) controls the pace, duration, and delivery of a message. For the designer, storytelling is the game. Choreography, rather than composition, is the essential skill.

Like every other medium, television is good at some things, bad at others. Look at the plethora of 911 shockumentaries, which happen to be something that television is really good at (emotional, immediate, cheap). Long, reasoned arguments without obvious pictures—like explaining the healthcare crisis or social security reform—are hard for television to deal with. As McLuhan suggested, there are whole areas of content that specific media cannot express well, and therefore, gradually, the dominant medium in a culture—television now being ours—will begin to determine what we even *can* think about. This is sort of scary but true, I think.

What was the most challenging on-air project that you worked on?

The opportunity I found when I arrived at WGBH was to help define an on-air personality for WGBH in Boston. We built on an identity package developed by Chermayeff & Geismar just before I arrived, and over the next five years we were able to personify the station's eclectic energy and confidence through endless variations of our channel digit. We learned the business of designing for television while building an affable, unpredictable institutional persona.

I'd say *Vietnam: A Television History,* from 1983, was one of my most immersive and challenging projects. It was the first project where I was truly part of the production team, responsible for the title sequence as well as all the internal informational graphics (mostly maps). As with most of our shows, a series identity is developed that informs the title sequence and is applied to a host of promotional and educational print materials that support the series. This particular series was important because from it flowed a long line of historical documentaries including our history strand, *The American Experience.*

In the early eighties, when this project was developing, Vietnam was a very tricky topic: too close for comfort but badly in need of talking through. And most of the key players were still around. Each show started with a tease of a minute or two that set up the issues of that program. I felt strongly that it was wrong to make a big heroic title sequence built out of the best shots from the whole series. The images were so strong and so authentic that I felt they should stay inside the program. Instead, I thought that the title should be a brief, enigmatic swinging door between the tease and the episode.

Mickey Hart, percussionist for the Grateful Dead, had agreed to do the sound for the series (he had previously created many of the sound images for the movie *Apocalypse Now*). I consequently developed an idea that could take advantage of his ability to evoke the sounds of that era, especially the archetypal aural image of the helicopter. I envisioned a point of view of a chopper flying low over the jungle and the words "Vietnam: A Television History" swinging by underneath. I practiced the move on a foam-core model, then photographed it with a Nikon and used the photos as the basis for a storyboard.

At the moment, computer-aided animation was in its infancy (and very pricey), but I felt it was the right way to create such a surreal landscape. I wanted it to be suggestive but not overly descriptive, with the letters, like an illuminated landing strip, coming out of the darkness below the camera. I convinced Computer Image (a fledgling New York shop whose principals have gone on to create virtual theme rides in Vegas) to accept the project for our measly budget, and they began doing motion tests.

Meanwhile, I drew a diagram of what I thought the sound dynamics should be and passed it and the storyboard on to Mickey Hart. He produced a strange mélange of Western and Eastern sounds mixed with the iconic sound of choppers thundering past. The sound and images mixed beautifully (that makes it sound too easy: like all these motion projects, it was agonizing to get it right). As the flickering orange and green streaks rush by below, like tracer bullets in the jungle, it still gives me a chill to watch it.

Is this the work of an individual with a vision or a collaborator?

TV-making is very complicated and inevitably collaborative. You are dependent on many other people to help realize a vision, but somebody has to *have* that vision in the first place. In the case of a program, it is usually the producer's vision. But as you get down to the smaller bits or even holistic issues like look and feel, the designer can play a very crucial role. One typical role is to be the visualizer, the person who is able to help everybody else "previsualize" how something might be: how a structure could express itself, how an abstract concept (antibodies at work) might be visualized, how a series of video events can be held together by a common visual vocabulary. The designer also contributes the text-on-screen specs (typeface, color, scale, behaviors) for titles, credits, IDs (identifying who is speaking, for example), and other messages like book and video offers and, in our case, underwriters.

But after having the idea, you have to have the social skills to be able to get all the troops marching in the same direction and not lose the core vision in the inevitable consensus building and technical compromises. And a lot of times you can't touch the tools, relying instead on your ability to verbalize what is wanted.

What else differentiates print design from television?

TV is the ultimate ephemera. Poof, it's gone. But TV has incredible reach relative to most things that are printed. For example, 9 million people a week watch *NOVA,* our science series on PBS. *Time* magazine reaches 4.1 million a week; *USA Today* reaches 2.1 million; the *New York Times* Sunday edition reaches 1.75 million. We recently calculated that the four-hour biography of Truman on *The American Experience* reached fifteen times as many people (15.25 million) as David McCullough's runaway best-selling book (1 million). And seven times as many people watch PBS each week (102 million) as use the nation's public libraries (15 million). TV is where the culture is, for better or worse. So, if you are interested in influencing a lot of people where they are, TV's your game.

TV is also incredibly expensive. It takes $5–$7 million to produce an hour of *NOVA.* Then we hear about NBC plunking down $13 million per episode for *ER.* Usually, the more expensive a thing is, the less it can be controlled by a single vision and the more likely it is to be watered down. But that will change as production tools get cheaper and distribution channels proliferate.

TV is linear and is only good at certain things. TV is good at giving an impression, expressing an emotion, interesting you in something, amusing you, but not too good at making information stick. TV is real time, you can't skim it; and one-shot, it's hard to refer back to. TV is four-dimensional not two-dimensional. As I have said, in print the key skill for a designer is composition; in TV it is choreography. TV is an inhospitable medium for typography because of its low resolution and bias toward sound and pictures.

Recent changes in technology and, to some extent, taste have made it much easier for text be a dynamic character in a video event; so interesting things are starting to happen.

TV is generally designed by different *kinds* of designers than those who design print. At least until recently, most designers in television came from advertising, post-production (editors or PaintBox artists), or engineering backgrounds. Few had a "classical," typography-centered design education. But how many schools, even today, get involved with motion or screen design if it isn't for the Internet?

With on-air projects you are part of a team. Have you ventured at all into directing?

In television, "directing" means something different than it does in the movies. In television, the director is the person who has to get everybody else to realize the vision of the producer. This is essentially the opposite terminology from the movies, where the director is the creative lead. So I take the sense of your question to be, have I ventured into being a producer?

Yes, a few times. On something like a titles sequence or show open, the designer is really the producer. In fact, for the last *Masterpiece Theatre* open, I hired Richard Greenberg to "direct" the motion-control sequences because I knew he knew how to talk that talk.

Then, in the early eighties, I took six months and wrote (with Austin Hoyt, a producer at WGBH) a treatment for an NEA-proposed series on design. Had it been selected, I would have been the producer/designer. Instead, Spiro Kostof got the grant and did a very different, architectural survey.

Is design for television open-ended? By this I mean, whereas there are limits to print design, do you see TV as consistently providing new areas to explore?

The thing that is really "open-ended" about TV is that it is motion, it is sound, and it is electronic—and soon digital. The smart guys say that TVs and computers will merge, producing one simple appliance for access to communications. For example, they say we will begin to disregard the difference between TV and the Internet.

Right now we are in the middle of learning how to write for this sort of hybrid media. As we plan a big project, we are thinking about the way the core content—like a series on the great engineering feats of the ancient world—can be best expressed in the various distribution modes we have available: linear television, online media (even linked directly to the broadcast), offline interactive media, and the many print applications that are still often the best way to reach a large audience with a stable, universally accessible format. Each of these media will have its own special strengths, ways of expressing certain ideas well and others poorly. Producers and designers need to understand the differences and how they can work in concert to present a subject coherently.

To some extent, what we call print is involved in this same digital evolution. After all, the Internet is mostly print now and will be for a long time. Designing for a particular medium will become less common than designing for hybrid media where the delivery system (paper or screen) is variable. "Rule-based" design will let the content adjust itself and its form to fit whatever "output device" is handy. This will be a weird experience for most designers since the end appearance will not be under their control. The design problem will not be one of finding the right layout but will involve a more overarching notion of organization and hierarchy applied to a given set of content.

Will you remain in this area of design or seek out new challenges?

This is a big conundrum for me. Next October, I will have been here for twenty-five years. In 1973, I said I'd give it three to five years. A number of times I have asked myself, Is this the time to try something else? But every time, I find that I can't think of a more interesting place to be. In a moment when the whole design profession is opening up from its long, solitary, and static association with print, an environment like WGBH presents a natural place to experiment with the communications potential of these new media because they are all right here.

Of course, I sometimes yearn to design a nice book with my own hands, take a sabbatical to paint or write, or produce a documentary of my own. But the harder question for me is how to take full advantage of the opportunities a place like this offers and not get bogged down in the day-to-day, short-term problems that need solving before 5 P.M. For right now, this seems like a good effort to be part of.

デジタル文様事典シリーズ

デジタル
エスニック
文様事典

ホセ・コンデ

河出書房新社

Jose Conde on Design in Japan

Jose Conde was born and raised in Independence, Missouri, a suburb of Kansas City. His mother is Irish-American; his father was born in Cuba and moved to the United States to attend high school in Florida and later the Art Center College of Art and Design in Pasadena, California. He was an industrial designer for Ford and Raymond Loewy before going out to work on his own. Conde came to New York to attend Parsons School of Design, graduating with a B.F.A. in 1985. His first design job was working in the corporate and magazine art departments of the *New York Times* while he was still a student. Also prior to graduation, he started working for Paul Davis; he stayed for five years before moving to Japan for the first time. Upon returning, he was corporate art director for Rizzoli for about two years and freelanced for another. Then he moved back to Japan, where he has lived and worked since. Now, after considerable success and mastery of a difficult language, he and his wife/partner (who is half Japanese) have decided to pull up stakes and move to South Africa. The question on my mind was, Why leave the comfort of his own world for the challenges of not only one decidedly foreign country, but two?

Why did you decide to live and work in Japan?

While I was a student, I got very interested in ukiyo-e prints, and although at Parsons there was only one course on the subject, I bought every book I could get my hands on and studied it earnestly. Paul Davis had been to Japan many times and had quite a large number of books on contemporary Japanese design. He was always telling me stories about different Japanese designers and showing me their work, and so through him I got a pretty thorough education in contemporary Japanese graphic design and illustration.

Many of the designers would stop by his studio when they visited New York. Actually, Paul was one of the first American designers (the first illustrator) to have a major show in Japan. He was one of two Americans (the other being Lou Dorfsman) who participated in the graphic design exhibition *Persona* in the early sixties. This was a watershed moment for postwar Japanese design, and Paul's influence is very clear in the work of a lot of Japanese designers/illustrators from that time, notably Yokoo Tadanori.

The summer I graduated, I took five week's leave from Paul Davis Studio and went to Japan to attend a design seminar that Parsons organized. Just about every major postwar Japanese designer made a presentation: Yokoo Tadanori, Ikko Tanaka, Shin Matsunaga, Shigeo Fukuda, Kazumasa Nagai, and more. It was fascinating, but I do remember thinking at the time that it would probably be the first and last time I went to Japan. This was August 1985; the yen was trading at 250 to U.S. $1.

Japan is not an easy place for an American to practice visual communications. How did you break in?

Davis had a major exhibition at a Japanese department store in 1987, and when he came back he told me about a Japanese friend who had a design/marketing firm that had many international clients and was looking for a "foreign" designer/art director. I jumped at the opportunity and moved to Tokyo for the first time in the final days of 1988. I had a one-year contract. This was the height of the Japanese "bubble." The yen was trading at about 140 to U.S. $1.

At the time, I thought my stay in Japan would be limited, and so I never bothered to learn the language much beyond how to order my own beer. I was having a good time, but I wasn't that happy with the company I was working at. I gave some thought to looking for another job in Japan, but that would have been a slap in the face to my boss and would have reflected badly on Paul, I thought (such matters are taken seriously in Japan). And so, when I got an offer from Rizzoli to return to New York, I took it (although I did stay four months beyond my contract).

But you went back to Japan, and this time for a much longer stay.

The trip to Japan I took with Parsons in the summer of 1985 was put together by Kiyoshi Kanai, a Japanese designer who lives in New York. I ran into him on the street one day in the spring of 1992. He told me how he was helping Parsons set up a "sister" school in Kanazawa, Japan, and asked if I would be interested in going there to start the graphic design department. It seemed like an interesting project. I was interested in design education and I enjoyed Japan. My wife, whom I had met while working in Tokyo, was born and raised in Japan and was happy to return, and so I accepted the offer.

We moved to Kanazawa—a historic, very beautiful city on the western coast of Japan—in early 1993 and stayed for two school years. I really enjoyed the time we spent there, but teaching full-time was not for me, and so when my contract was up we moved to Tokyo and set up a design studio. That was in early 1995, and the yen was at 85 to U.S. $1.

Are you fluent in the language?

I had been in Japan for about one month when, feeling a little cocky about my Japanese, I went into a neighborhood store and asked the woman behind the counter for a bar of soap. She disappeared for what seemed ages only to reappear carrying an armful of condoms. I don't have such problems anymore.

I am not fluent, although I can speak pretty well, I guess. When I decided to set up my own studio, I consciously decided to have a "Japanese" studio; that is, a studio whose primary language of business would be Japanese and whose clients would be Japanese. It wasn't a business decision—in fact, it would have been a poor business decision—I just felt it didn't make sense to be in Japan and speak only English and do only English-language jobs. I could get much better work in New York if I wanted to do that. So, the first thing I did when I moved to Tokyo was to spend a year studying Japanese intensively. It was a painful year, going back to school full-time and trying to work in whatever time I had left over.

The result of my year (and countless other hours of study) is that even though I can't describe myself as fluent, I can function fine in Japanese. I can read pretty well, too, although my writing still lags behind. My business partner (and wife) is native-fluent in English and Japanese; my assistant is Japanese and speaks only a little English.

Despite the Japanese penchant for things American, how do you practice design in a country that is in so many ways decidedly foreign?

This is a difficult question to answer. We Westerners like to speak of the Japanese passion for things Western, but I think it is really difficult to use the strict term "Eastern" with regard to the Japanese. Or to put it in other words, I think it is easy to claim that Americans are definitely Western, but not so easy to claim the Japanese are absolutely Eastern. I can imagine a lot of people scoffing at this, but where does one draw the line between the two? The average Japanese art student can distinguish between Rauschenberg, Rosenquist, and Warhol, but has no knowledge of the great ukiyo-e artists or potters or calligraphers. The most popular songs in Tokyo are the most popular songs in New York. My assistant, who is in her early twenties, tells me of not realizing that McDonald's and Disneyland were not "Japanese" until she was in her teens.

I remember well the first evening I spent in Japan. When I got to my hotel room after a twelve-hour flight and two-hour bus ride from the airport, and went into the bathroom to wash my hands, I found that the hot water came out of the blue-colored tap. I remember thinking deeply about what cultural influences could produce a symbol for hot water that is completely the opposite of my own culture. "My God! I'm going to be in for some shocks while I am here," I thought. Of course, in the next bathroom I went into I found that the hot water did indeed come out of the red tap. "My God! Both countries are fucked up!" I thought.

Do you find that Eastern and Western sensibilities clash?

Admittedly, there are tastes that are distinctively Japanese. I am just not so sure these can always be conveniently labeled Eastern. I think Japan and America are certainly very different. I think part of this difference has to do with our religious traditions: on the part of America (in the broadest of terms), our Judeo-Christian values and the strict division of almost everything into a good-versus-evil dichotomy (or, if you prefer, good/bad or maybe modernist/postmodernist); on the part of Japan, their Shinto/Buddhist values or, really, lack of clear values and religiousness. I see a manifestation of this in the field of criticism, for instance. In America, for every genre of art—and for many fields of business as well—there is a corresponding school of criticism, and these critics often wield a lot of power. In Japan there is *very* little criticism. In graphic design, it is basically nonexistent.

But I believe these religious influences are largely atavistic, on both sides. Contemporary America and Japan both share the culture of consumerism, which in fact makes them quite similar in many fundamental ways.

How do you do business in such a foreign country?

Much that is difficult about doing business in Japan is the same in America: corporate bureaucracy, company politics, poor management, et cetera. Others are a source of amusement as well as frustration: the tossing of "What do you think? What do you think?" around the conference table about a dozen times until everyone is pretty sure what the others think and it is safe to reach a consensus.

I will add that I have a great aversion to dogma and tend not to be confrontational. Some Japanese have described me as "Japanese-like" in nature. I do not like to boast, raise my voice, or argue—characteristics perceived to be typically Western. I am neither tall nor short, not particularly muscular, and my frame is medium, which serves me well in a country that often sells clothing in one size only. In this sense, I am aware of the fact that the Japanese rarely perceive me as a threat.

When having a meeting with a client, my silence will sometimes be misinterpreted as consensus. And the objective of most meetings is to reach such a consensus. Quite often, the client will be taken by surprise when I eventually come around and explain exactly why I disagree with this or that. There is a moment that is unique to Japanese business: the careful selection of words, the precise timing of the comments, and the seemingly endless going back and forth until someone finally, finally carefully rolls the ball past the goalkeeper—no powerful shoots or unexpected kicks, no forced entry—and the game is won without anybody feeling like a loser. Sometimes I find myself losing track of the score as the meetings drag on and on, and then I have to resort to using blunt language, but I am forgiven for my bluntness because after all, I am a foreigner.

It has been only in the past year that I have come to understand those subtle moments when the Japanese are saying yes, yes, yes and are enthusiastically shaking their heads up and down, but they actually mean absolutely NO!

Who are your clients?

I have an eclectic mix of clients. I have been doing books and book covers for Japanese publishers, promotional and simple exhibition graphics for an interior design gallery, department stores, a Japanese and Chinese font-software company, promotion for magazines. And I have also been doing a handful of projects a year for various American book publishers.

How do you find work?

One of the big differences between working in Japan and the United States is finding work. In the United States, or at least New York anyway, I think it is relatively easy to find work. People are always looking for something new or someone new, and we tend to accept that as part of the business. Especially if you are pitching your work to an art director, most are happy to look at your work. In Japan, you would rarely approach someone without an introduction from a third party (even a remote one), and this is one of the big differences of doing business here. And the reverse is also often true: one is rarely approached just out of the blue.

To help with this difficult point of doing business, there are people in Japan who call themselves "planners" or "coordinators" (they use the English words). In America they would probably be called agents, although they work a little differently. Basically, they are professional networkers. In Japanese you would say *kao ga hiroi,* "their faces are wide," meaning they know a lot of people. They provide the necessary introductions between designer and client. We have worked with a number of coordinators. Sometimes they provide you with access to jobs you would not otherwise have access to; the downside is that they can be vague about the terms of the job (a Japanese tendency) and often insist on making the presentation and dealing directly with the client (although sometimes this is a plus).

Do you feel any connection to the Japanese design community?

Not really. I do have friends and acquaintances who are designers, but being busy with work and with a young family, I don't have that much time for socializing.

There are a few professional organizations, which I have not joined. There are no egalitarian organizations such as the AIGA that anyone can join. You must be recommended for admission, you must be voted in by the other members, and you must pay a large fee. I could probably arrange for the recommendations and politics for entry, but I don't have much interest. Although I have much admiration for the members' work, I am critical of the activities of the two largest graphic design organizations.

There are a few other foreigner-run design studios in Tokyo. Most seem to focus on doing English-language work. Although I've never met him, Helmut Schmidt has a successful studio in Osaka. He was a student of Emil Ruder and has a distinctive Japanese-Swiss style. He has done the graphics for a number of quintessential "Japanese" products. His work deserves to be better known.

Are the Japanese accepting and welcoming of a foreign practitioner?

I think I am greeted with ambivalence. Why do you want to live in Tokyo when you could live in New York? is the most common question, often asked with a suspicious tone. I know I am something of a curiosity, and I know this has helped me to get some jobs. People like the novelty of working with a foreigner, or they believe that as a foreigner I can provide them with a fresh, unique point of view (which is often true, I think). But for every job I have gotten for such reasons, there was another job I lost because someone didn't want to work with a foreigner—thought it would be difficult or a hassle.

There is also the common prejudice that a foreigner cannot "handle" kanji (Chinese characters), which is a joke. Certainly, using kanji well is difficult. Japanese mix four types of characters (kanji, hiragana, katakana, and romaji) and a lot of punctuation, which adds to the challenge. But there is no secret passed through the blood of one's ancestors. Good Japanese typography requires time and effort and study, as does good English typography.

On the other hand, relationships in Japan are usually long-lasting. Many businesses have built their images around one designer. For instance, there are a half-dozen magazines whose every cover (a couple of them weeklies) for the past ten years or so have been done by the same illustrator. I can't think of a comparably visible equivalent in the States.

How have Japanese aesthetics influenced your work?

I really don't know if they have influenced my work in any way that shows clearly. Before I had ever gone to Japan, people said that I had a "Japanese sense of space" in my work. I don't have a strong style; I am attracted to the problem-solving side of graphic design and to the craft side. I am very interested in Japanese craft, particularly the mingei movement that developed in the first half of this century around the work of the potters Bernard Leach and Hamada Shoji and the writer Soetsu Yanagi. Their concept of the "unknown craftsman" has been a source of inspiration. I also get a lot of inspiration from traditional Japanese and Chinese calligraphy. I am fascinated by the style of calligraphy whose beauty lies not in the flowing quality and harmony of forms that we normally associate with Asian calligraphy, but in the contrast of different forms and stroke-weight and the purposeful interruption of flow (a medieval Chinese grunge, perhaps?). I am fascinated by calligraphy written in such a simplified style that it is impossible to read today except by the serious scholar. I am fascinated by archaic Chinese characters, arrested in their metamorphosis from pictograph to ideograph. You quite often see these characters used on shop signs—it would be as if a shop in New York wrote its name in Phoenician. Such calligraphy has helped evolve very different ideas about legibility. I have incorporated some of this inspiration into my work, but mostly in subtle ways: typography that loosely takes its form from archaic characters, for instance. But my work is decidedly uncalligraphic. The influence is largely spiritual—the influence anyone would feel in the presence of great art.

Nicholas Callaway on Book Packaging

Nicholas Callaway is the founder and president of Callaway Editions, one of the most design-savvy book packagers in America. His books include *Madonna: Sex*, *Ferrington Guitars*, *Cyclops* by Albert Watson, and *LaChapelle Land* by David LaChapelle. After receiving a B.A. from Harvard in 1975, he became the first director of the Galerie Zabriskie, in Paris, France, which specialized in nineteenth- and twentieth-century photography. He researched and curated the exhibitions; mounted, framed, and installed the shows; managed the bookstore; wrote, edited, and designed newsletters, catalogues, and exhibitions; handled media relations; managed the artists; and became a general advocate for art photography in Paris in the late seventies. In 1979, he returned to New York to publish books. Despite publishing successful books, Callaway was initially undercapitalized. Forced to rethink his operation, he turned from publisher to packager—developing content, finding talent, designing, and producing. Each book is then published by a larger (and usually different) publishing partner. Callaway's books are exemplary marriages of content and design.

Judging from your books, from Georgia O'Keeffe's flowers to Madonna's sexuality, it's obvious that you have eclectic tastes. Can you describe these tastes or passions?

Words and pictures, both still and moving, that have the ability to inspire or astonish. I have learned to segregate my personal passions from my tastes as a producer. Professional: the arts, especially the useful ones, design, photography, fashion, children's entertainment, popular culture, golf. Personal: Greek revival architecture, ancient Egyptian civilization, Tibetan sacred texts, medieval music, golf.

As a book packager, you are reliant on publishers to support your projects. How do you decide what is publishable?

Ideas come from many different sources: extraordinary artists I admire and seek out (Irving Penn), newspaper clippings (David LaChapelle), Page Six (Madonna), a wooden pull-toy found on a search for a gift for my then-infant daughter (Miss Spider). Once we fall for someone, then it's a question of trying to start a chain of enthusiasm that begins with our copublishers. It's a difficult and exciting challenge to convey your vision to someone who often doesn't yet see it.

The graphic design of your books is one of their defining characteristics. What are your design preferences?

I try to get inside the subject and divine what it wants to be in its designed form. We try to have no design preconceptions, and I enjoy the fact that we live in an age that has such an astonishing array of styles. I am equally fond of our Stieglitz and Madonna books, and they are not as different as many people might think.

Madonna: Sex was quite a controversial book, and not only because of its content and Mylar covering. Fabien Baron's design ushered in the trend of book as object. What was the challenge in making this book?

Madonna, Fabien, and I wanted to make a book/object that would look and feel unlike any other book ever made, beginning with how the book was approached by the consumer. It needed to be sealed in a way that would protect the innocent (we thought of diary locks), and we wanted an opening device that would require penetration, as it were. The Mylar bag (made by a body-bag manufacturer) idea came from vacuum-sealed peanut packs you get on airplanes. We had hoped to vacuum-pack it so that it would be stretched tight across the aluminum cover and would make a whooshing sound when opened. That turned out not to be possible. We wanted lavish, sensuous printing in both black-and-white and color, but we faced seriously short deadlines.

From this, shall we say, novel and novelty approach to the high classicism of your **Alfred Stieglitz: Photographs and Writings** (1982), you have covered many design methods. How did this come about?

The planning for the Stieglitz book had begun in 1946, the year he died, when O'Keeffe gathered together his entire archive, donated it to five American museums, and decided to publish a book that would do justice to the greatness of his work. Nearly thirty years later, I met her at a Harvard commencement when she was given an honorary degree. I anonymously handed her a peony, which she kept with her throughout the ceremony. A year later, at the age of nineteen, I wrote to the famous recluse when I was planning a trip to photograph in the Southwest, telling her I had given her the flower. I received a letter a few weeks later, saying she had always wondered who gave her the peony. I spent several days with her that summer. Eight years later, a week after I returned from France to start my publishing house, I took the $300 I had saved and went to see her, asking if I could publish her memorial to Stieglitz—despite the fact that I had never published a book before. Three years later, it was issued. The express intent was to set a new standard of printing fidelity to the original. The book was on press for six months; every picture was press-proofed before printing; paper was specially manufactured by Mohawk to the right color and tooth; each picture was printed split-fountain, dry-trap on a one-color press in three-hundred-line tritone to match the color and tonal range of the original.

Stieglitz was an exercise in understatement; **LaChapelle Land** (1996) was over the top, a tour de force of image and package. What were some of the concerns with this book?

We wanted to see how over the top we could make it: full bleed from beginning to end, glossy inks, glossy paper, with gloss varnish. David wanted to have a billboard effect for the outside, and I thought of the great Japanese poster artist Yokoo Tadanori. So I wrote to him—he and David never met during the process—and he agreed to create a collage that double-distilled David's work by putting together into a seamless whole as many of the elements that appeared inside the book as possible: *Sergeant Pepper* meets tantric monopoly. When David saw his computer-rendered rough, he astutely said that computers aren't cool anymore, that what he missed was the handwrought, rough-cut feeling from Yokoo's early work in silkscreen. I wrote to Yokoo, asking him if he ever did silkscreen anymore. He came back two months later with the amazing thirty-color hand-pulled silkscreen we used for the box. It seemed like the perfect yin, and so we asked if he could do yang for the cover inside. He did. The next challenge was to get the feeling of thirty-color silkscreen in offset process color. We convinced the printer to do twelve colors for the price of four.

Your marriages of design and content are usually very successful. What made you decide on the matchup between David Carson and Albert Watson with *Cyclops* (1994)?

I had admired David Carson for a number of years, since *Beach Culture,* and we had talked about working together on several projects, but it was Albert who first suggested David, feeling that he would provide a "rock 'n' roll" counterpoint to the graphic monumentality of the photographs. I would say that the final result was art-directed by the two of them in equal measure.

***Ferrington Guitars* (1992), designed by Skolos/Wedell, marked, at least in my mind, the beginning of what I'd call the "overall package" in book production. How did this book come about?**

I met Danny Ferrington at Linda Ronstadt's house while photographing one of her O'Keeffe paintings for *One Hundred Flowers* (1987); he was working as her personal assistant. I was so taken with the combination of his native genius and his endearing charm that we decided to do a book on the spot. It took five years. Halfway through, the CD revolution was taking the industry by storm, and I said to Danny that it would be a bit like coitus interruptus for the viewer to be able to see all these beautiful guitars, but not be able to hear them. After all, a guitar—any musical instrument—is both latent and mute until it is brought to life by the musician. So, we decided to produce an album of original compositions written and performed specially for the book.

How do you work with designers? Do you give a long leash? Do you impose constraints?

We made many trials with different designers on the guitar book until I remembered a series of extraordinary posters created for an audio company by a team of whom I had never heard—Nancy Skolos and Tom Wedell—and they were perfect, seamless: she the designer, he the still-life photographer. I said we wanted a book that would not just show instruments, but in every way symbolize and express and be music. They nearly killed themselves doing it, but it fulfilled our idea. In many cases, we provide creative direction and criteria—price point, trim size, overall look—and then leave it to the designers to stand or fall on their own. This means we often go through several designers before we find the right marriage of content to form.

Who are the best book designers?

The best book designers are those who deeply understand the unique expressive possibilities of the book's printed page, whether or not they do the bulk of their work in books or not. That being said, good design is good design, and often we try to entice designers from other media to bring a fresh eye to book design. Most designers long for books, even though it doesn't pay well, and don't have the opportunity to work on good ones; so we have a large talent pool to work with. And we need more!

Do you think that design makes a significant impact on the consumer's enjoyment of the book?

Absolutely. It is a fact still neglected by the majority of publishers, in contrast to most other consumer goods, from fashion to cars to computers to electronics.

Let's talk a little about the Miss Spider series by David Kirk. In a very competitive children's book market, what was it about this project that caught your fancy?

David is a visionary and a genius of an artist. I knew it the minute I saw one of his toys. I was a new consumer in the toy market, searching for Christmas presents for my daughter's first Christmas, wandering the aisles of Toys "R" Us, appalled by the bad design, cheap manufacturing, and ugly packaging. I went to Mythology (now closed), an offbeat store on the Upper West Side of Manhattan, and was dumbstruck by a wooden pull-toy called a Sneaking Baby Alligator. Everything about it was original, clearly the result of a single, and singular, creative mind as opposed to a marketing committee. It was brilliant, with a strange palette, beautifully engineered, and in a box with a painted label that stimulated the child's imagination by placing the three-dimensional toy in a little story context. It was also an immediate, huge hit with my daughter. I wanted to find out who was behind this "Hoobert Toy," so I called the company and asked to speak to the president. It was David Kirk on the line, and he said, "That's me." I told him how impressed my daughter and I were with his toy, and asked who painted his packaging. He said, "Me. I used to be a painter before becoming a toymaker." I asked if he had ever thought of illustrating a children's book, and he said he had indeed. It was called *Miss Spider's Tea Party* and was about a lonely spider's quest to make friends against the odds. "Do you have a publisher?" I inquired. "Yes," he said quietly. Not knowing what to say, I blurted out, "Well, are you happy with your publisher?" He said that he wasn't because he had been paid a tiny advance and then his editor orphaned him by going to another house, and he had never heard from the editor again. I asked him to send any materials, and it was a moment I will remember all my life because I knew that he was literally a visionary—no hesitation, no searching; the most exquisite, fully formed line renderings of a world that existed only in his imagination.

How would you describe Kirk's vision?

I describe it as David's toll-free number into the collective unconscious of children. When I later saw his oil paintings, I was equally dumbstruck by their beauty and their technical mastery. This was no illustrator; it was a great painter transcribing his fantasy world. I called him and said that it was one of the most amazing children's books I had ever seen, said that I would not want to interfere in a publishing relationship that was working, but since this one was not, why don't we go to David's original publisher together and see if we could buy him out? I offered him an advance four times what he had been paid. This was more than David had ever made in a year, and so he was pleased. We went to the publisher, who let him out of his contract. Four years and three books later, Miss Spider's books have become the biggest-selling nonmovie, non-TV children's picture books of our time. David and I are partners in a family entertainment company, Callaway & Kirk. Four new books are in the works (no bugs), three more Miss Spider titles, two computer-animated feature films (one starring Miss Spider) for Universal, a learn-to-read CD-ROM with Scholastic, and many toys.

Do you see the children's book field as expanding or contracting, creatively?

From a field of approximately five thousand children's books published each year, there are about ten I find interesting. I don't see it expanding creatively, especially in relation to the enormous creative potential. We are trying.

What is the future of books and book design?

The technologies related to creating images, design, prepress, and printing are all getting better. Creativity and excellence are as rare as ever. Books aren't going away, but their place will change.

"You're some tomato.
We could make beautiful Bloody Marys together.
I'm different from those other fellows."

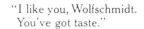

"I like you, Wolfschmidt.
You've got taste."

Wolfschmidt Vodka has the touch of taste that marks genuine old world vodka. Wolfschmidt in a Bloody Mary is a tomato in triumph. Wolfschmidt brings out the best in every drink.

George **Lois** on Advertising

George Lois, a child of the "creative revolution" of the 1950s, was the father of the Big Idea in American advertising during the 1960s. Papert Koenig Lois, which he founded in 1960, was the "second creative agency" in the world, challenging Doyle Dane Bernbach's hegemony. Lois's iconoclastic campaigns for Xerox, Wolfschmidt vodka, Coldene, Maypo, and scores of other products were among the most memorable of their time and have rightly earned their place in advertising history. Lois is a critical mass of cultural and political forces, an aficionado of art, and a left-wing activist who has used his skill at propaganda in the service of promoting social causes and political candidates. He has a street-smart way of direct, no-nonsense communication, seasoned with a strong sense of wit, humor, and biting satire. Advertising, he believes, is not about forcing people to acquire unnecessary merchandise; rather, it is a medium that informs, entertains, and, if executed with intelligence, has the power to alter behavior for the better. Lois is not cynical about what he does. He uses the intuition he brings to advertising to sell controversial ideas. Among his many acts of intervention, the most lasting has been the conception and design of *Esquire* magazine covers from the late sixties to early seventies—graphic commentaries that are today among the most memorable icons of this unsettling social and political era. At age sixty-seven, he has been the principal of Lois/USA for over twenty years and continues to be an exemplar of the Big, and smart, Idea.

You were raised in New York. Your parents were Greek immigrants. Your father was a florist, and you were his delivery boy. How did you become interested in graphic design? And why advertising, in particular?

When I was still in elementary school in the Bronx, I was more excited looking at a Cassandre poster than looking at a Stuart Davis painting. Also, I could draw very well, and I was very precocious about the history of art. For example, I had a postcard of a Cycladic idol from 3500 B.C. that I kept next to my bed.

What inspired you to go to art school?

When I was twelve I had a terrific art teacher, Miss Ida Engel, who asked me if I had enough money to go on the subway. I said, "Yes, ma'am. Why?" She said, "I want you to be at the High School of Music and Art by eleven o'clock to take the entry test." She gave me a portfolio, which she bought for three or four bucks—a lot of money then. Inside were about eighty of my drawings that she had saved over the past three years at P.S. 7. She insisted that I take the test. I was accepted.

Did your father encourage you, too?

No. In fact, my father was very concerned about me because I was drawing all the time, and it wasn't too manly. Every day I would go out and get the newspapers for 2¢ apiece, bring them into my father's store, and draw every paper's headlines three-dimensionally. I don't know what drove me to drawing, but I was sure I had invented perspective. I remember looking out of my window and a building was here and a building there and there . . . and from my eye, from where I sat in my window, I looked down the street, and you had to be an idiot not to see the perspective going off into a vanishing point. If I lived in the thirteenth century, I would have invented it before the Sienese!

And your interest in graphic design?

There were teachers at the High School of Music and Art who came from the Bauhaus. I would design with that sensibility but always put words into my work. I really had a designer's mentality. I remember doing a poster in my first year, on Switzerland. I got a photograph of the Swiss Alps, then took yellow paper and cut holes all over, making mountains out of gigantic slices of Swiss cheese. I was always looking for visual ideas.

What was going on in advertising at that time that made you want to enter the field?

Paul Rand was God to me then. Still is.

You were still in high school and you were familiar with Rand. But more important, you knew exactly what you wanted to do with your life. Did you go on to an art college?

I went to Pratt Institute in Brooklyn. All during high school I worked in my father's store day and night. After I graduated, I continued going down to the flower market with him at four o'clock in the morning. Then, on September 4, my father came into my room and said, "George, it's four o'clock; you're going to market." I said, "I can't go today, Papa." He asked why not and I said, "I'm starting college today." That's how I told my father that I wasn't going to take over his store. I'm sure he was shattered, but he didn't show it to me.

Was college as rewarding as high school?

The first year was terrible because it was foundation year, and they didn't teach the foundations of design nearly as well as they had at Music and Art. Or maybe by that time I was too sophisticated. Most of the teachers didn't know what they were doing. I was kind of a maverick, anyway. In the second year, I took a class with Herschel Levit. He was a great teacher. He talked about music and dance and food, and we'd ooh and aah over Rand's work. Mr. Levit would give an assignment, and I'd come in with six finished ones while everybody in the class was struggling to get one done. However, I didn't go to other classes except for the life-drawing class. Finally, Levit came to me at the beginning of the second term and he insisted, "George, you've got to get out of here." And he gave me Reba Sochis's phone number.

Who was Reba Sochis?

Reba had a design studio. She and Cipe Pineles were the first women art directors in the field, and she was the first woman in town who ran a studio with thirty guys working for her. She was a wonderful designer and a great typographer with a light touch. And at the time she needed a young talent.

This was your first job and you didn't even finish art college. What were you working on at that time?

Promotion pieces, packages, and very fancy boxes for things like Talon zippers. Incidentally, she had a policy that when you did comp lettering, you had to letter with a brush and you had to letter every word of copy, whether it was 72 point or 8 point. Boy, if you didn't learn there. . . .

You have always had strong political commitments. Did your leftism, like your passion for art and design, develop during this period?

Reba and some of her friends were a big influence on me. I'm a humanist, with some communist in it. I hate the unfairness of the system and the continuing injustices in America. I care about the working class, about the working man. I've always had that thing in me, you know—fighting for Ruben "Hurricane" Carter [Lois organized a campaign that helped get the former boxer's murder conviction overturned], giving papers out in front of factories and guys all cursing at me. Reba crystalized it for me, and many of her pals—Paul Robeson, W. E. B. DuBois, and Alger Hiss—became my friends. I agreed with everything they talked about: human rights, racial injustice, the First Amendment, and the right-wing attack on our basic freedoms. McCarthyism was a terrible stain on American history, a terrible time for America.

Given your political leanings, did you see any contradiction in being an advertising and promotion designer?

You mean selling capitalist goods? No. To me it was always communicating, designing, convincing.

From Reba Sochis's studio you were drafted into the army, served in Korea during the war (where I understand you were busted in rank), and returned unharmed to New York at age twenty-one. Then you went to work at CBS television for the legendary art director William Golden. Was this a detour on the road to advertising?

In those days, if you were in advertising, it was basically a schlock industry. You had to work at a fashion agency to do anything of any quality, but they didn't have ideas. They merely made everything look good. I wouldn't have lasted a day. CBS was not quite an advertising job in that sense. I went to see Lou Dorfsman [art director for CBS radio], who introduced me to Bill Golden. He had been looking for a new designer for a few years, but I was given the job immediately.

I was a month out of Korea and working at a dream job for a graphic designer when the FBI paid Golden a visit and told him I was a communist, obviously trying to get me fired. Bill told me not to worry about it and to go upstairs and see his boss, Dr. Frank Stanton [the president of CBS television], who asked me some questions, including, "Is it true you're a Korean veteran?" I said, "Yeah." He said, "Well, don't worry about it, just go back to work." CBS was a bastion of liberty in those days. They gave work to the artist Ben Shahn, whom the FBI hounded. And, finally, Edward R. Murrow helped put the knife in Joe McCarthy.

What kind of work were you doing at CBS?

If Frank Stanton and William Paley [the chairman of CBS] gave speeches, they would lob the text at me, and I would design a beautiful book. Beyond creating letterheads, logos, and promotional pieces for their programs like the great *Playhouse 90,* I did hundreds of tune-in ads. I did the first *Gunsmoke* ads, the morning *Johnny Carson Show, The Phil Silvers Show (Sergeant Bilko),* and *The Ernie Kovacs Show.* Usually I would rewrite the copywriters' copy, and they would complain to Golden. But Golden would look at my jobs and say, "Hey, George, why don't you just write it on your own, and let's keep these people out of it." That's how incredibly supportive he was.

If not for Golden, would CBS have been such a design giant?

If not for Golden and Frank Stanton—Stanton was his client. Everybody with talent in the world wanted to work there.

Is it true that you designed the official CBS typeface?

Golden wanted me to redraw Didot Bodoni. He didn't want people to think we just used an existing typeface, he wanted it to be CBS's own. There's nothing more beautiful than Didot Bodoni. I blew it up in stats, redrew it a little bit, and gave it a little more style (what I thought was more style). I did six letters to show Bill where I was going: *A, B, C, D, E, F.* And Golden loved it and told me to do the final pen-and-ink lettering myself. I did one letter a week. They were fairly easy. It was the numbers that were hard! But they turned out beautifully.

Was there a particular piece of advertising or promotion that you would call a watershed? Something that revealed the unique approach that would become your signature?

One in particular was done when *The $64,000 Question* [CBS's most popular quiz show, which was eventually investigated by Congress for impropriety] was on the air. A contestant, a priest, was deciding whether he might or might not go for the $64,000 question, and we needed a special ad to promote the show. Everybody had gone that particular night, but Kurt Weihs and I, as usual, were still working. A programming guy ran in and said, "We've got to do an ad for the *New York Times* tomorrow." I did an ad that showed the priest's picture and underneath I wrote, "Will he go for the $64,000?" I didn't use a logo. I didn't put in the time the show would air. Nothing. I gave it to the production guy, who of course asked, "Where's the logo? It's got to have a goddamn logo." I said, "We're running it as is." The next morning the shit hit the fan.

You committed the sin of omission?

Golden asked how I could do such a thing! I said, "Bill, it's a terrific ad. You don't need a logo, and you don't need a time. The whole world knows. It's got balls." He said, "Jesus Christ, you're terrific, but you can't do that!" At that point I felt that I'd let him down; I shouldn't have done it. Twenty minutes later he comes into my office to say that now everybody loves it because Stanton and Paley are getting calls of praise from the shakers and movers in town.

How would you position that ad in relation to your subsequent work. What makes your ads, then and now, different from others?

I like to do things that change people's minds.

What does that mean exactly? Is it the power of persuasion or the craft of salesmanship?

It's the power of a hungry mind and a hungry eye. Back then, I was hungering to work on selling bread or cars or an airline. I was hungering to get my face into changing the culture, my way.

So, you left CBS and joined the hard-core advertising industry. Did you, in fact, get to engage with different parts of the culture?

I was asked to be a head art director for the American Airlines account at the Lennen & Newell agency at three times the money I was making at CBS. So I started doing ads like you've never seen before. I had a great beginning. I belted out fresh, exciting ads like an assembly line. I had ads covering all the walls and all over the ceiling. Since American Airlines had new destination times to L.A., I did an ad with a Brooklyn Dodgers hat on a guy's head with his eyes looking west, and above it the headline read "Thinking of going to L.A.?" This was when the Dodgers were threatening to move from Brooklyn to L.A. It was a killer ad. The day it ran in the *Times* a million New Yorkers smiled. And with that ad under my hat (by the way I posed as the Dodger in the ad), I thought I was gonna kill them at the agency! So I kept doing ads. One was better than the other, all touching on aspects of the culture. But, somehow, the client didn't like them. Why? The head of the account was a good ol' boy by the name of Bill Smith, whose brother was C. R. Smith, who ran the airline. That's why Lennen & Newell had the account. I think the little brother didn't much like that the Dodger ad made so much noise.

Did you have to accept his caprice?

A month later, I said that I wanted to see the client. And Bill Smith said no. So I threatened to quit. The next day his secretary said that Mr. Smith would like to see me. I went up to a gigantic room, and on the floor was every ad I did—two hundred ads laid out. And Smith said, "Lois, I understand you are moaning and groaning about. . . ." And he started walking toward me, walking on the ads! As he came, I tiptoed very carefully around the ads, making sure not to step on any of them. I walked all the way to his desk and turned his gigantic desk over. As luck would have it, there was an inkwell on it and it splashed on the pristine white wall. I turned around and began to walk out, and Smith chased me and said in a Texas drawl, "Lois! Goddamn it, don't leave this agency, boy. I'm gonna make you a king 'cause I'm a kingmaker!" It was so charmingly crazy, he convinced me into staying for six more days. Then I came to my senses and left.

From there you went to Sudler and Hennessey (S&H), the agency where Herb Lubalin was creative director. What did you work on there?

All their consumer stuff. I looked at the book on Lubalin a couple of months ago [*Herb Lubalin: Art Director, Graphic Designer, and Typographer* (American Showcase)], and by mistake it includes a bunch of jobs that I did.

What was the difference between your approach and Lubalin's design?

He tended to do beautiful type, typographic concepts, and he made type talk. His thinking was absolutely exciting and unique. I, on the other hand, wanted to rip your throat out. I always tried to get a big idea into all my work.

I understand that you were very protective of your work, even belligerent when you experienced interference. How did this manifest?

I had trouble with Nat Hennessey, a partner and account executive. I'd give jobs to the bull pen (there were a dozen or so in the bull pen), and I was talking to someone when I saw Hennessey talking to somebody about my job. I went over and said, "Nat, what did you just tell him?" And he answered, "I want to change something around." My response was, "Get the fuck out of here before I punch your face."

I presume that you couldn't tolerate that kind of situation for too long.

No. Around that time Lubalin and I decided to leave and start an agency with Lou Dorfsman, called Lubalin, Dorfsman, Lois (I wanted to be the last name, like Bernbach was at Doyle Dane). Herb was hot to trot. Even though he was king shit at S&H, he was very unhappy. It was Lou who just couldn't squeeze the trigger.

You did, however, leave S&H for the hottest agency in America, Doyle Dane Bernbach, the launch pad of the creative revolution.

That's when life really got interesting.

But your first account did not sound like something that would spawn a creative revolution.

My first assignment was the Kerid account. It was a new earwax remover. The account guy had no information whatsoever. So what else is new? But it was easy enough to understand that when you put the stuff in your ear, the wax comes out. So I took a photograph of an ear with pencils and paper clips and stuff sticking out of it, a dynamic symbol of the strange and dangerous objects people used to clean out ear wax. I did that ad and a bunch of others, all hot stuff. I knocked them out and slapped them all over my walls, boom, boom, boom. No writer or anything, in one furious day. The next morning, Bernbach came to welcome me, and he sees the stuff and he asks, "Who are you working with?" I said, "I'm not working with anybody. I don't have a writer." He said, "I'll be your writer." I said, "Great." I found out afterward he hadn't been a writer for anybody in fifteen years.

You did work that stimulated people's minds but also ruffled people's feathers. Why was this ear ad, for example, so controversial?

A few weeks after the Kerid campaign went into production, I was given a great new office with windows, next to Bob Gage [the chief art director] and Helmut Krone [art director on the famous Volkswagen "Think Small" campaign]. I liked Krone, but he was kind of a crazy Kraut and nasty. He went around the agency criticizing the ear ad—rounded up a whole bunch of pussy writers and took them to Bernbach to protest against the terrible advertising coming out of Doyle Dane Bernbach from the young barbarian who just moved in next door.

Were you angry?

I was angry, but not mad enough to go in to Helmut and say, "I'll punch your head off." Also, I respected the guy's work. I took it as a guy who was jealous of a different kind of talent and didn't understand it. One of the complaints against me was that I was one of *those* designers; I was a "Herb Lubalin–Lou Dorfsman graphic-schmaphic designer." I was told by two people present at the protest meeting that Bernbach's reaction to Helmut was "I'll decide what's good for the agency. What you don't understand is, George Lois is going to be a combination of Bob Gage and Paul Rand." Now that's what I regard as the ultimate compliment.

You are a designer and typographer, but the message and how to present that message have always been your first concerns. Moreover, it seems that for you, design isn't just about composition, it's about format. Most advertising is about the glorious full page. Have you tried formats that are more effective?

Lou Dorfsman had given the CBS radio account to Doyle Dane and requested that I do a full-page ad in the *Times* to announce that CBS was introducing news "every hour on the hour." It was about the eighth station in town to do so and was so behind the times that doing an ad bragging about it would have been a lousy strategy for CBS. So, I wanted to do twenty-four small space ads, two-column ads (which worked out to about a page), and I wanted to run them throughout the paper: "1 A.M.," "2 A.M.," "3 A.M.," "4 A.M." I did twenty-four of them, each with the logo and "every hour on the hour." We would own the paper that day. It was an exciting visual way to make people remember it, and at the same time not crow over it and say, "Look what we finally did." Of course, the copywriter said I couldn't do that because "At Doyle Dane we don't do small space ads." Talk about anal. I did it anyway and it was terrific. But I got some noses out of joint.

The terms "creative revolution" and "Big Idea" suggest the shift in advertising in the sixties from formulaic pitch to creative thinking. Will you talk about this revolution?

Well, it was pretty dramatic. Bill Bernbach was the man who had an understanding of how copy and great graphic imagery work in harmony—how one and one becomes three. He gets all the credit in the world for that. Bernbach recognized the fact that the writer and art director had to work together as a team. But, of course, it had to be two terrific talents or it didn't work. Bernbach smelled it when, as a writer, he would watch Rand work. Starting with Paul, Bill recognized what he considered the genius and magic of the graphic art director. God knows, he was almost mystical about it. When I worked at Doyle Dane, we'd always go to Bernbach's office to show him our stuff. And I'd go up there to preen! Because I always knew I had something that he would love. I'd go up there with the writer, we'd show the work to him, and he'd go, "Jesus, oh, wow, George, how did you do it?" The writer didn't count. It was almost like Bill can write and this other guy can write, but the writer didn't do the magic, the art director did.

What impact did that have on you?

Bernbach was smart enough to look at a guy like me and say that this Greek kid is someone different and something else is going on here. It's rougher, it's rawer, it's street. He loved to look at my type and say, "You don't break lines the way other people do." In fact, I still break my copy lines by thoughts and phrases. So he saw me as a different kind of cat.

At what point did you finally take the plunge and open your own agency, Papert Koenig Lois?

Julian Koenig and I were at Doyle Dane, and Fred Papert was at Sudler and Hennessey. I liked him because he was a very good writer. He did a lot of things good. He did some good headlines too. A little tame, but his copy! I loved his body copy. So he starts Papert & Free (two husband/wife teams). They were hot, they had a couple of big accounts. But after a couple, three, four years, they had trouble and split. Freddie came over to me when I was at Doyle Dane and said, "George, listen. I want you to go into business with me." I said, "Freddie, why the hell would I want to leave the best job in advertising to go with you?" He came to me twice, and one day I said, "This is interesting. I'd love to start the second creative agency in the world."

Weren't you courted by Ogilvy & Mather as well?

They tried to hire me to be the head art director. I said, "You limeys got to be kidding. How could I possibly? Look at your ads. Don't get me wrong, a lot of them are terrific; but there's not one thing in your book, Mr. Ogilvy, that I agree with." He had all these rules. You had to have a square halftone; the logo had to be in the right-hand corner; you couldn't drop the type out of the photograph. Ogilvy had rules for dos and don'ts as long as your arm. So, basically, trust me, there was only one creative ad agency in the world, and that was Doyle Dane Bernbach.

So you formed the "second creative agency in the world."

Yes. I said, "Freddie, if we bring Julian Koenig with us, I think maybe I'll do it." He said, "Who's Julian Koenig?" I said, "He's a writer." He said, "What do you want a writer for?" And I said, "Because he's a much better writer than you. You do the account hustling and the ass-kissing."

What happened when you began?

We got a call from the Renault-Peugeot distributorship. They had a $300,000 account, which was enough to pay our rent. A couple of weeks later, the *Ladies' Home Journal* called us up and gave us their account to do their circulation ads.

The *Ladies' Home Journal* ads were very precocious at the time.

Ladies' Home Journal came to us, and within two days I had called up Dr. Benjamin Spock and got a picture of him when he was a baby. Under it we said, "What kind of a baby was Dr. Spock?" Then another ad was a story about baby veal, and I had a head of a cow, a sweet young cow saying, "Please don't read this month's *Ladies' Home Journal.*"

Your offices were in the Seagram Building, and it was there that you developed ads for Seagram's brand, Wolfschmidt vodka. I'd say that this was the kind of advertising—witty, irreverent, and a little bit racy—that typifies the Big Idea method and style. Would you say that this put you on the map?

Yes, but the story is that Sam Bronfman Sr., the head honcho for Seagram, thought his son Edgar was a boob, and never gave him any responsibility. Finally, he gave him their vodka because Mr. Sam didn't really regard vodka as a serious or prestigious product. Smirnoff was the leading brand. My idea was to position Wolfschmidt as a "tasteless" vodka. Since it left no aftertaste, you could drink it at lunch and not be found out. When I did those ads with the talking fruits and vegetables, everybody talked about them. Sales exploded and young Bronfman's old man said, "Gee, the kid's a genius."

Another client was Xerox. It became such a generic name that it is part of our collective language, but it did not start out that way. What was your contribution to the company's image?

Ogilvy originally had it but had to give it up because of some strange perceived conflict. Then Doyle Dane got the account, but their Polaroid client thought there could be a conflict with xerography some day. A week later we won the account. Joe Wilson [the Xerox CEO] had thought about changing the name from Haloid Xerox to Haloid, but I convinced him that Xerox could be a memorable brand name. And I showed him a storyboard for a TV spot. He said, "Television? What are you talking about? There are only five thousand people we want to reach in America." He meant the purchasing agents for companies. But I told him that we have a chance now to make Xerox famous fast. I asked him, "If we can make you famous fast, can you make a lot of Xerox machines?" He said, "All we want." So I showed him the storyboard: A little girl goes to her father's office, and he says, "Would you make two copies of this, please," and she toddles off to this funky music over to the Xerox 914. (You've got to understand, in those days making photocopies was unheard of. The first time I saw it, I almost had an orgasm.) She presses some buttons, lays her doll on the glass plate; then skips back and hands the copy to her father, who says, "Which one is the original?"

Sounds like a good concept to me.

After I finished the presentation, Wilson fired me!

Were you too aggressive?

He thought we were nuts to spend his budget on television. He wanted us to run trade ads, for chrissakes. So, the next morning, as I was telling Freddie and Julian that I was fired, I get a phone call from Joe Wilson. He said, "I changed my mind. Produce the commercial." So we ran the commercial, and he called again and said, "Oh my God, my salesmen are so excited; everybody thought Xerox was an antifreeze, now it's a famous brand." Two days later we get a cease and desist from the FCC.

This story just keeps getting more byzantine. Why did you get a cease and desist?

A. B. Dick, a leading office printing company—and, I always thought, a company aptly named—complained that a little girl couldn't possibly make a copy that easily. So I said, "I'll call you back." An hour later, I called the FCC and told them that I was going to reshoot the commercial so that they could witness the copies being made! They sent down two guys in gray suits, and I shot exactly the same spot, except instead of shooting a little girl, I shot a chimpanzee. A chimp comes up to the same father, who says, "Sam, would you make a copy of this?" The chimp makes the copies (easier than the little girl did), toddles back, swings on a rope, gives him the copies. The father says, "Terrific, Sam, but which one is the original?" We ran the little girl commercial at the beginning of the evening news show and we ran the chimp at the end—and all hell broke loose. I mean, stories, articles—everybody went nuts. It went from a $350,000 account to a $9 million account in two months. Xerox really became famous, and almost literally overnight.

I know this sounds like a naive question, but how does that happen? What is it about us consumers that makes us so susceptible to advertising?

What is an even crazier question than that is, How do you know that you've got the Big Idea that will change world?

Okay, I'll bite. How do you do it?

You try to epitomize the uniqueness of the product by doing it in a way that's incredibly memorable. The first rule is theater: Attract attention by doing something absolutely fresh and dramatic.

But does it have to be researched and market tested to make sure that the public will understand it?

Of course not. For Braniff airlines I came up with the "When you've got it, flaunt it" idea. I said to Harding Lawrence [the CEO], "If you're going to research this, forget it; it's going to be a dog." He said, "Well, we've got to research it." So they researched it, and I think 84 percent of the people who saw the ads and flew Braniff said they would never fly it again. That's how much the test groups hated the campaign. But Lawrence had balls, and he gave me his okay. I did spots with Salvador Dalí telling Whitey Ford how to throw a curveball, and Sonny Liston eyeballing Andy Warhol as he explained the significance of soup cans, and Mickey Spillane, of all people, explaining the power of words to the great poet Marianne Moore. Braniff's business went up 80 percent. You can't research an idea like that. The only ideas that truly research well are mediocre, "acceptable" ideas. Great ideas are always suspect in research.

To get those incongruous characters together anywhere, whether it's a plane, a car, or a park bench, is a wonderful idea. But explain to a layman like me what you wanted to convey.

I was basically saying, "Why fly a dull-ass airline like American when you can fly an airline where some hot shit might happen?" In research, everybody said, "That's terrible, that's ridiculous, that's silly." But when you sit at home and watch it, it's entertaining, it's exciting, and you say, "Gee, next time I go to Dallas, put me on Braniff." You just know that people are going to go for it. It's like reeling in fish.

Do you understand psychology, or is this just intuitive on your part?

It's probably intuitive. I'm not sure about understanding human psychology. But I can think of everything I've ever done in my life and I know exactly why I did it, and I can write a book talking about each campaign. For example, OTB [New York's Off-Track Betting] had a terrific first year in 1973. Mayor Lindsay asked me, "What do you think of OTB?" I said it was a winner, but the advertising was running out of money. I thought OTB could be doubling its handle if its advertising could convince everybody who was ashamed to be seen in a betting parlor to go. You don't have to be genius to know there's an image problem. So I developed the concept of the New York Bets: "You're too heavy for the Mets? You're too light for the Jets? You're too short for the Nets? You're just right for the N.Y. Bets!" I approached Broadway stars to be in full-page *Times* ads wearing N.Y. Bets T-shirts. I got Carol Channing, Rodney Dangerfield. Then, before you know it, I had every entertainer who was coming to New York begging me to appear in ads: Jackie Gleason, Bob Hope, Frank Sinatra. We did about two dozen ads, and all of a sudden OTB doubled its take. For me it was a no-brainer.

I recall that the Greek tourist board came to you to save what was becoming a tourist industry disaster following a comment by President Reagan that Americans should not fly to Greece after an air hijacking.

There was a terrorist incident over Athens. A plane was going from Athens to Rome and was hijacked. So President Reagan came to life and announced that no American should go to the dangerous Athens airport. I'm sure he said it because Papandreou was the premier of Greece, and Reagan hated him because he was a socialist. Travel to Greece virtually stopped. The Greek government came to me, begging me to come up with some magic that could save their tourist season. I got thirty-nine celebrities to make testimonials, like Lloyd Bridges who said, "My great-great-great-great grandfather came to this country from England on the *Mayflower,* and now, finally, I'm going home . . . to Greece!" Joe Namath said, "My father came to this country from Hungary in 1906, and now finally I'm going home . . . to Greece!" I was saying that everyone's home is Greece because Greece is the home of democracy, the home of Western civilization.

I shot them one day in L.A. and got them on the air. What the spots actually said was "Fuck you, Reagan; I'm going to Greece." And they also said that before you die, you've got to visit the cradle of civilization.

So you were responsible for rocking the cradle.

It was PR at its most aggressive and convincing. I got the head of the Greek tourist organization, a young guy, to do all the morning news shows and all the shows at night, saying "Greece is fighting back and we ain't takin' this shit anymore," and the planes filled up within four days! You couldn't get a flight to Greece. I knew it was going to happen. Maybe not that fast, but I knew it was going to happen.

Why is there so much bad advertising?

I don't think so-called creative people understand cause and effect.

In the industry, there's so much meat-and-potatoes advertising that gets a product name out there, and because it's so insidious, it stays in your brain and you accept the brand.

The only way it's insidious is if they're spending $20–$40–$50–$60–$80 million. But there are hundreds of brands that spend over $40 million, and nobody in American has any awareness of the advertising. I don't do campaigns where you spend zillions of dollars. I do campaigns where they spend not much money, and I don't have much time to make it famous, and I make it work, pronto.

I know how you convince a client that your ad is good. How do you prove it to yourself?

I take civilians into a room and show them one of my commercials and ask, "What happened? What did you see?" If they don't explain the concept, if they show me that they don't "get it," the commercial sucks.

I'll watch something entertaining and never know what they're selling.

A lot of it is entertaining, and you don't know what they're talking about, and you don't remember the brand name, and you don't buy the product. Now, if they have $100 million and they keep running it, sooner or later it might get under your skin. Nike wouldn't be the brand it is if it didn't spend a shitload of money with Michael Jordan imagery, from day one. There's a lot of advertising that has to be seen twenty to thirty times to be semi-understood. The way I judge my stuff is, you've got to see it one time, you've got to get it, and it's got to grab you by the throat.

Let's talk MTV. Here's this hip new network, now one of the most successful in the world. When you were asked early on to do its promotion campaign, was it a culture that you could appreciate?

I thought rock 'n' roll was garbage. I didn't like any of it. I'm a Cole Porter, Giuseppe Verdi man. But I don't have to love a product to sell the hell out of it. Some young guys came to see me. Their leader was Bob Pittman, who was twenty-seven. They had three accounts, the Movie Channel, Nickelodeon, and a total unknown named MTV. They were going to pick two agencies and somehow split the work up. They asked me to pick two of the three. The Movie Channel was worth $6 million, Nickelodeon was $3 million, and MTV was a quarter-million. I said, "I've absolutely got to have MTV. If that's the only one I can take, I'll take that. I abhor rock 'n' roll, but I think it's a big programming idea that young people would eat up." They admitted that cable operators wouldn't touch it, the advertising business thought it was a joke, and the music business thought it was ridiculous. "No one will give us the time of day," Pittman said, "so what makes you think you can do it?"

What was your idea?

I said, "Do all you young punks remember, 'I want my Maypo?'" [a famous mid-sixties advertising campaign that Lois created for a kid's hot cereal]. They all had vivid memories of it. I said, "Now you are all twenty-five to twenty-six, and we're going to say to the world, 'I want my MTV.'" I explained the commercial, to take the *M* logo and always show it with crazy variations (one had a tongue sticking out). A lawyer in the room said I couldn't do that because every time I did they would have to reregister the logo. I told the lawyer to kiss my ass. I said, "I want to create a style that is funkier than anything else on the air." And then, I showed them the commercial where at the end a voice says, "If you don't get MTV where you live, you pick up the phone and dial your local cable operator and say—" Then I cut to Mick Jagger, and he bellows, "I want my MTV!"

And the result?

We bought four spots on a Thursday night and waited to see what would happen on Friday. The cable operator in San Francisco called Pittman and said, "Get that commercial off the air! I'm getting thousands of phone calls. I had to shut the line. Oh, by the way, I'll take it!" We blitzed through America that way, and six months later MTV hit the cover of *Time* magazine as the greatest pop-cultural revolution in the last quarter of a century. It became wildly successful, but we probably destroyed world culture.

How much of your output is just you, and how much is you in collaboration?

The idea, almost always, has got to come from me—the truly Big Idea. I'm never satisfied with somebody else's idea because I always feel that I didn't push my own head. Once I feel I have all the input I need, I totally concentrate and nail the idea. If I have trouble coming up with what I consider to be a thrilling concept, the reason is that I didn't really understand all the input. But when I nail the idea and I'm bursting with it, I love to work things out with a great writer. Boy, is that great fun.

Where We Were
Where We're Going

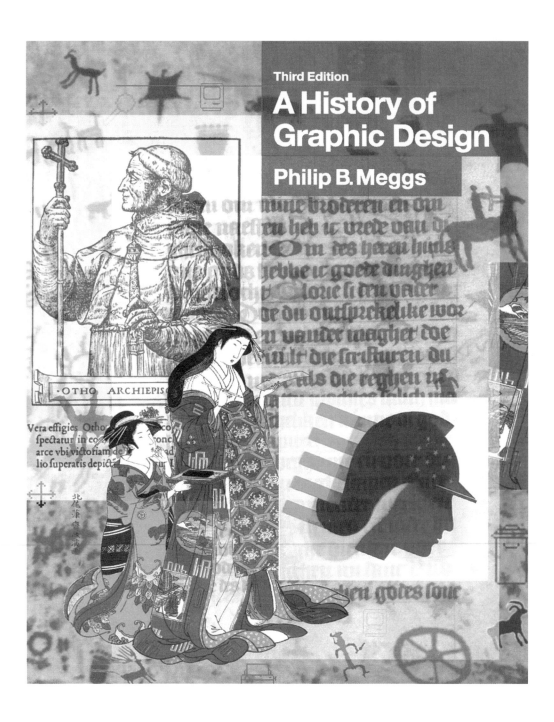

Third Edition

A History of
Graphic Design

Philip B. Meggs

Philip Meggs on Graphic Design History

Philip Meggs began his design career handsetting metal type in 1958. After study at the University of South Carolina and Virginia Commonwealth University, he served as senior designer at Reynolds Metals and art director of A. H. Robins Pharmaceuticals before joining Virginia Commonwealth University's communication arts and design department in 1968, where he is currently school of the arts research professor. Meggs is author or coauthor of a dozen books including *A History of Graphic Design,* first published in 1983, which has been translated into Chinese, Korean, Japanese, and Spanish. The third edition of *A History of Graphic Design* is published by John Wiley & Sons.

It seems there was no codified graphic design history twenty years ago. When did it really begin?

The belief that design history and criticism are new areas of inquiry is not correct. Design criticism and history have been around since the early 1500s; each era documents what is important and/or controversial. People are repelled by the shock of the new; much of my design history is simply recording what appalled the establishment, from Baskerville to the Bauhaus.

As author of the first, and only, design history textbook, you opened the doors of a relatively unknown legacy. What did you, as the pioneer of this field, use for guidelines or a standard in deciding what was historically important?

My goal, as a design educator teaching design history beginning in the early 1970s, was to construct the legacy of contemporary designers working in the United States. I believed this could help designers understand their work, comprehend how and where the semantic and syntactic vocabulary of graphic design developed, and aid our field in its struggle for professional status. Design education is advanced when young designers learn what is possible by understanding the philosophy and concepts that shaped graphic design.

History happened the way it happened; it's the historian's job to figure out what was significant. One of the most useful methodologies is to study events from two historical points of view—synchrony and diachrony. This can help avoid many problems. Synchrony is simultaneous occurrence, while diachrony is an investigation of events as they occur and change over time. When I was researching French graphic design inspired by cubism between the world wars, the large number of posters and ads by a score of excellent designers was at first overwhelming. However, tracking the evolution of forms and imagery leads to a 1923 poster for the Woodcutter furniture store, designed by A. M.

Cassandre. Further research reveals that Cassandre was, in fact, the seminal designer who revitalized French graphic design after World War I; he emerges as a significant designer who must be included in a design survey.

Because there is so much eclecticism and plagiarism in design, anyone researching graphic design history must be very careful in attempting to identify significant work. When people suggest designers and works they believe should be added to *A History of Graphic Design,* I ask them to please write a concise paragraph stating why these are unique and influential contributions.

Of course, sometimes visual ideas evolve from the dialogue between designers over time and space, forcing the historian, for lack of space, to choose a work to represent a complex set of related works.

How had the history of the field previously been recorded? What sources were definitive enough that you took them at face value or used them as primary sources?

Actually, I found that an abundance of material existed, but it was in piecemeal form. Printing magazines and books from the early nineteenth through the early twentieth century stashed about in the Library of Congress always included design issues, and even reproduced and reported on work dating from the incunabula and Renaissance. Unfortunately, there is a lot of contradictory and inaccurate data around, and so I always try to corroborate information from at least two sources. It's so embarrassing when you learn that you depended on an unreliable source.

Your book, *A History of Graphic Design,* is not "the" history of graphic design. What other ways of recording history are there?

I insisted that this book be called *A History of Graphic Design* instead of *The History of Graphic Design.* This was to acknowledge that the book was not the encyclopedia of graphic design, but a concise overview for contemporary designers and design students.

The contract called for a three-hundred-page book with six hundred illustrations. I delivered a thousand-page manuscript, plus over a thousand illustrations with captions, only after deleting whole countries and hundreds of illustrations. At that time, my decisions were based on the direct lineal relationship between our contemporary spot in time and space and the works that influenced it. Greek and Roman alphabets were included, but my research on Indian Sanskrit was dropped because it did not have this relationship. Inclusions and exclusions were determined by a "roots" assessment.

There are numerous possible approaches to an investigation of the evolution of graphic design. These include the following: an exploration of the relationship between design and its audience, analysis of the evolution of formal or visual attributes, and study of the social and economic impact of design activities. Some of my critics complained that I studied design and designers instead of social and economic issues. I believe design is a culturally valuable activity. The intent of *A History of Graphic Design* is to identify and document innovation in semantic and syntactic aspects of visual communications. Designs from each period discussed were assessed in an attempt to distinguish works and their creators that influenced the ongoing evolution of the discipline. This information provides a conceptual overview useful for further study and practice.

Why hasn't graphic design history been afforded the same serious attention as other arts?

Academics and fine artists have been marginalizing graphic design for a long time; many of my detractors are merely followers of that ignoble and naive tradition! In the past, this related to social class. Nineteenth-century working-class teenagers with art talent went into what was then called industrial arts, while the well-to-do trained in Europe to become portrait painters to the wealthy.

Critics have accused you of perpetuating a canon—an official cast of characters and events—that is essentially modernist or traditionalist and ignores the quirks and nuances of graphic design. Have you limited your coverage in any way?

The only person I am aware of who has "accused me of perpetuating a canon"—your phrase, not hers—is Martha Scotford, a prominent design educator and historian at North Carolina State who wrote a rather brilliant assessment of the limited treatment of women by various design historians. Her research is important work, putting design historians on notice that gender issues should be considered.

I believe Scotford would agree with me that certain designers such as El Lissitzky and William Morris have had a catalytic influence and should be venerated for their accomplishments. "Canonized" is too strong of a word; very few designers deserve sainthood.

As far as my ignoring the quirks and nuances of graphic design, we're talking about a one-volume history contractually limited by the publisher to five hundred pages, period. This provides a basic conceptual overview of the field, a first step in an exploration of design history. A large bibliography is included for anyone who wants to explore a given period in depth.

It seems naive to criticize a history book, surveying five thousand years, for "coverage of the mainstream, waiting to see how the 'new waves' pan out." Actually, when the first edition came out I was blasted by Bill Bonnell in an *AIGA Journal* book review for overemphasizing April Greiman, whose work was quite controversial in 1981 when the first-edition manuscript went to the publisher, but she is now respected as a major designer of her generation. Other reviewers questioned the wisdom of a history book including contemporary material. I haven't waited to see how the new waves panned out—whoever said that must not have read the book.

Is history objective or subjective? And how do you address this issue in your own work?

History can be objective or subjective. Much of my work has been written from the vantage point of an educator trying to determine what has significance for the reader/viewer, who is typically a designer or design student. After reading a number of period accounts about World War I posters and studying hundreds of original posters in the Library of Congress collection, my question was, Which selection of images will best convey the range of communicative and formal concepts used by World War I poster designers? Knowing this is my mind-set, I think you can understand why I am so bemused if someone accuses me of trying to create a canon. Perhaps the awards-oriented mind-set of contemporary design, fueled by scores of competitions each year, feeds this frenzy.

Anyone who tries to write history should be allowed a margin of subjectivity to explore her or his passions, but not to the point of distorting the record. I don't much like to look at William Morris's work, but to leave him out would have been untenable. In the third edition I had to grapple with the arrival of Web-site design. I did a search for graphic design sites, and the search engine identified over a million sites. The new edition has three Web sites. Are these designers canonized over the designers of the other 5 billion Web pages out there? No, they were selected based on the points about Web-site design I wished to make.

Is criticism a part of this process? As a historian, do you make value judgments about the quality or efficacy of work that ultimately affects the writing of history?

Critical evaluation is the root source of any historical account. One searches for significance, and value judgments are often made from the station point of the writer, who is stuck in time and place with a fixed vantage point. If you research deeply, though, you can find out what people from earlier eras valued and the motivating force behind their work.

Who, in your opinion, are the underrated historical figures? And conversely, who are the overrated ones?

I think most designers are underrated, and I can't think of a single one who is actually overrated. Approaches and sensibilities pass in and out of fashion; postmodern designers dumped on the Bauhaus and modernism all through the 1980s. Perhaps Herbert Bayer's reputation is like IBM stock, it goes up and down in a process of being alternatively overvalued and undervalued as design sensibilities change.

Writing a general textbook, and having two opportunities to revise it, what did you feel was lacking from the first to the third edition? And how did you rectify that?

Each edition of this book is unfinished because for all three editions I was forced to send the manuscript to the publisher after exceeding the word and image count specified in the contract and having to request an extension of the manuscript deadline.

I suspended work on the first edition because I was mentally exhausted from working sixteen-hour days, seven days a week, and I was economically broke from spending thousands of dollars on photography and reproduction permissions. Plus, I had missed the deadline. I left out whole sections on stuff like Japanese prints and Persian manuscripts because I adopted the criteria—since I did not have enough pages for everything—of presenting the lineal historical relationship to contemporary design practice in this country.

The reception to the first edition was generally positive. How do you feel about that initial work in retrospect?

The dialogue created by the first edition educated me about certain omissions and helped me fine-tune my methodology. The world has changed dramatically in the intervening two decades. America is becoming the first truly multicultural nation, and technology has reinvented graphic design once again. My challenge in the third edition was how to better reflect multiculturalism while retaining the documentation of our European and North American design traditions, even though the publisher would not let me have any additional pages. The chapter "The Alphabet" becomes "Alphabets," with non–Greco-

Roman alphabets added; "Medieval Manuscripts" is changed to "Manuscript Books," with an Islamic section; "Art Nouveau" becomes "Ukiyo-e and Art Nouveau" because Japanese prints are more fully covered. Glaring omissions from the second edition had to be rectified, such as postwar Dutch design.

Also, I had to deal with technological revolutions occurring by the month. The second edition was produced just before PageMaker or QuarkXPress was advanced enough for a project of this scope. It was one of the very last typeset and pasted-up books. For the third edition, the publisher allowed me color reproductions throughout, and so I had to acquire five hundred color images—in eighteen months.

Graphic design history is very complex, and it is made even more difficult by the large number of gifted designers and sheer volume of work. This makes the selection process very difficult.

Can you address in one book the myriad forms of historical perspective? For example, can you, and would you, inject Marxist, feminist, and postmodernist viewpoints into your narrative?

Social, political, and economic history are embedded in the history of graphic design as content. One can use graphics to learn about social and political history. We need to study design as part of social history, but we also need to study it as an independent force in society.

I believe in graphic design's cultural significance as an autonomous entity, worthy of independent study and evaluation. Design, along with the order and aesthetic it brings to a community, is not merely decoration or style; it is a necessity for a healthy society. The breakdown of this order within a society's communications and environmental systems has serious consequences. Those who disparage the aesthetic impulse in design as they seek to accommodate their marketing goals, or to advance narrow social or political agendas, actually attack the very fabric of the human community.

The task I set for myself in this particular book was to sketch out the general history of graphic design as it has shaped our profession today. Had I laid other agendas on top of this mission, such as advancing my political, environmental, or social views, this would have distorted the primary goal. In addition, this would have gobbled up valuable pages, when I already had more to say than pages to say it in.

Let me take your specific examples one at a time. Marxism. Viewpoints from classical Marxism—people's defining attribute is their creativity, especially in the ability to exert labor to meet needs; and that Homo sapiens are "social-species" beings who should direct their labor toward the needs of their community as a whole—are significant in the history of ideas. While working on the second edition of *A History of Graphic Design,* I struggled in an effort to inject philosophic ideas from Marxism and capitalism, structuralism and deconstructivist criticism, and so forth, into the book. This became unwieldy, and I was unable to successfully weld together the two opposing approaches, especially in view of the limited number of words available in each chapter. We do need a body of literature relating graphic design to major philosophic concepts, but this is too complex to embed in an introductory historical overview.

Feminism. I am a strong advocate of equal rights and equal opportunity. During my thirteen years as chairman of Virginia Commonwealth University's communication arts and design department, at one point we were over 40 percent female, and we hired two African-American faculty members.

Historically, there were very few women designers, but since the 1960s social revolution, large numbers of women have entered the profession with a predictable result: many such as April Greiman, Zuzana Licko, Paula Scher, and Carol Twombly have made significant creative contributions as designers and are finding their way into the history books. I believe there were quite a number of female designers before the 1960s revolution who simply weren't identified. Anonymity has been a serious problem for the study of graphic design history, whether male or female. Right now I am trying to get information on two mid-nineteenth-century British sisters who were graphic designers, but I can't even locate obituaries.

Postmodernism. This term is so overused—architecture, art history, feminism, literary criticism, even theology—every discipline seems to have its own definition. The third edition has a chapter titled "Postmodern Design" that combines the major thrusts in graphic design that have been branded as postmodern.

How should design history be taught in the classroom? Is it a collection of persons, places, movements, and dates? Or is there a more vital lesson to be taught?

I've always believed the purpose of teaching design history is to strengthen studio education and professional practice. It should be taught through critical evaluation: how the work functioned in its culture; syntactic and semantic attributes should be explained; the impact of technology on design; and the relationships to religion, politics, business, and industry need to be articulated.

When I started teaching my design history course, it was offered for third-year students. The faculty requested that it be moved to the first semester of the sophomore year because students were actively applying methodologies, concepts, spatial arrangements, and message-forming approaches to their work. Faculty wanted this process to begin when students started their first graphic design and typography courses. It wasn't a matter of mimicking earlier designers or the look and feel of their work, but understanding what was possible, and strategies for accomplishing it.

Do you feel that the field as a whole has acquired and benefited from more historical knowledge since you began? Or is history really a marginal area of study in a field that is changing so quickly and where doing work—getting jobs—is the primary concern?

In 1978, I gave a lecture at a seminar for government designers in Washington. Afterward, a designer in his mid-thirties came up to me and said, "People keep telling me my work is real Swiss. What do they mean?"

His work was very good. He was copying the surface of a whole approach to design without a clue about who created the spatial concepts, typographic approach, symbolic forms, and objective photography that formed the basis for his work. Nor did he understand the philosophy and social conditions in Germany and Switzerland that gave rise to the designers who invented the visual language he was using.

Knowing design history can help designers get beyond style and surface, and understand their work on a deeper level. It can provide reference points in the rapid flux of contemporary culture. Since 1970, the graphic design community overall has become smarter, better educated, and more capable. This is partly due to the design history movement, stronger education programs, and the development of graduate education.

Finally, how do you, as a historian, feel the design field has changed, and how will this affect the next revision of your book?

Technology, the global economy, and the information age have conspired to explode graphic design into a series of interrelated but quite diverse areas of activity—print design, image and identity, environmental design, kinetic and broadcast graphics, Web-site design, book art, electronic games, advertising, and information graphics.

Things are changing so fast that only fools predict the future. When I started the third edition of my book, the World Wide Web and Internet were not yet factors, then all of a sudden they were the major events of the decade. I was forced to ponder, How do you write history that is just breaking?

Menace and Jeopardy

INTRODUCTION

PLAY FIND CONTENTS

Rick Prelinger on History as Commodity

Rick Prelinger began collecting advertising, educational, industrial, and amateur films in 1982. Since then, he has been exploring North American social and cultural histories as expressed in ephemeral culture. He has published *Our Secret Century,* a series of twelve CD-ROMs on hidden or misunderstood social issues, and is working on a film on the history of the twentieth century as seen through changes in the landscape. He is currently directing *Danger Lurks!* a dramatic feature film on risk in America, constructed completely from archival material. He lives and works in New York City.

How is history a commodity?

History has become the raw material used in producing television shows, books, exhibits, theme parks, movies, mass spectacles, museums, and more. As raw material, it's quite often generic: something to be fabricated, reengineered, shaped, reshaped, mixed, or softened. Historical images, artifacts, and documents are sold, licensed, or rented directly to the public or to aggregators who make secondary or tertiary products to sell, broadcast, or stage.

Also, the business of producing historical material directed toward the public has grown greatly in the last few years. Any Sunday arts and leisure section, travel section, or TV listing will confirm this. As life spans lengthen, popular interests become ever more specialized and social consensus becomes more difficult to achieve. Many people will retreat from the anxieties of the present into the contemplation of history. This trend creates many business opportunities.

Is there anything fundamentally wrong with this kind of escapism?

Not inherently. People should be able to contemplate history as and when they desire. But a problem arises when historically conscious people shrink from intervention in present-day affairs and leave pressing issues of the day to those who have learned little from the past.

What can society learn from industrial, advertising, and educational films?

Two things, in general. First, these films reveal the look of the past with greater detail and elegance than do most other media. They provide what the anthropologist Clifford Geertz calls "thick description" of cultures, landscapes, historical periods, and activities that are no longer with us. They are one of the most profound instances of film as evidence.

Second, they reveal past persuasions. Since so many of them were produced to influence opinions, sell products, and educate, they constitute a wonderful record of society's system of creating and sustaining consensus. At the same time that they show how things looked and moved, they also show how our elders were supposed to think, behave, and buy. We live in a society where persuasions of many kinds intervene in our lives on a daily basis, and I have found that the mechanism of past persuasions can often illuminate the workings of media, advertising, and mass psychology today.

Are these lessons something that we can act upon or do we sit passively by?

I believe in historical intervention. To me, this means digging into the historical record and reinjecting historical images, ideas, text, and artifacts into contemporary culture. Strategies of historical intervention may differ, but the goal is to help bring about social change. Such intervention can sometimes resemble culture jamming, where results aren't always predictable, but I feel strongly that the presence of historical consciousness makes radical innovation much more likely to thrive.

So, looking back to history for specific lessons or examples is part of the picture, but the major part is infusing the present and the future with content and ideas from the past. And it's the activity itself—the intervention and reinjection—that makes the familiar present a little less predictable.

How do you separate nostalgia from the historical importance of the artifacts?

You cannot. Nostalgia is deeply entwined with history. Of course, nostalgia has been seized upon by commercial interests who seek to market a vision of a rosy, simpler, consensus-driven past—a vision that's naive and retrogressive. On the other hand, the phenomenon we call nostalgia may incorporate other desires as well, and not all of these desires need to be discouraged. When people look at an old film and wish they could catch a ride on the next transport back into its world, they're of course yearning for an escape from a complicated society, but they're also trying to negotiate their own way out of a situation they find intolerable, to move in a more traditional direction. Now, this can be good or bad, depending on who stands to gain and lose, but I like to think that there's a utopian side to this escape. Many of the changes that we most need to make in this society actually constitute steps backward: putting the brakes on globalization, strengthening local communities, living more sustainable lives, putting the sport-utility vehicles out to pasture. Many other steps backward we don't need to make: I want nothing to do with nostalgic visions that are built on oppression and exclusion.

So, to bring this rant full circle, I think that nostalgia is a powerful vehicle for getting people to think about history. Many times I show films that reek with kitsch, and with a few carefully chosen words of context, shift the discussion in quite another direction. If people ooh and aah about fifties populuxe design, start to talk about how all of this great stuff actually served as a fig leaf for the military/industrial complex. If *Boogie Nights* awakens desires in our young to live a seventies lifestyle, point out how it depicts a culture of latchkey children left behind after our defeat in Vietnam.

Designers look at your films as a source for retro pastiche. Is this the correct way to look at and use these relics?

Most archivists believe we have a responsibility to provide access to our materials. I actually think we're responsible for much more than that—for actively reinjecting the content hidden in our collections back into the culture. Now, I earn income from supplying imagery to all kinds of people and projects, and have very little control over who does and doesn't get images from me. No doubt I've helped make a lot of retro stuff happen. But in my own work, I'm not interested in retro pastiche. I'm trying to set a different kind of example. This is made possible by my relative privilege as owner of an archive.

How can artists use this material to create new messages?

Just about any use of this material constitutes a new message. Most of the novelty comes out of the context into which the message is turned loose. The issue is whether the culture itself makes everything seem old and wilted after a short time. What looks or sounds new for more than a few minutes, anyway?—at least, until its revival.

Historically, why has this material gone largely unnoticed?

The United States is a very media-rich country. Too much is happening all the time for everything to be noticed. That being said, the other reason why ephemeral films were largely unnoticed is that even though they were ubiquitous, they were difficult for people to put their hands on, and it took the intervention of middlemen like me to make them available to the creative industries.

Are films like these being done today? Have contemporary filmmakers learned anything from the past?

Hundreds of thousands of corporate videos, educational videos, and infomercials are being made every year. It's a big business. Production is much more dispersed; it's not like the old days when several dozen companies were responsible for a huge percentage of production. They look pretty different from the old industrial films of yore. Their production values are lower, and they look outdated after just a few years. Today's corporate and institutional videos do share one thing with many old industrial films, however: they consciously resemble mainstream entertainment genres (musicals, talk shows, adventure movies, et cetera). They do this for the same reason that a dog owner puts a pill inside a glob of peanut butter: to send the message using stealth technology.

With such easy access to this material in the commercial arena, does one run the risk of trivializing history?

"Sticks and stones may break my bones, but images can never hurt me. . . ." People have been trivializing history for thousands of years. As long as history is about contention and conflict, there will always be people who seek to mute its force. It's just that making media is faster, cheaper, and easier now, and there are lots more people making it. That doesn't mean that our successors will lack a sense of history. I don't think that history is extinct today, either. The apparent lack of interest in historical complexity today is just that: perception rather than reality. People are still fighting wars over history, both complex and trivial, and this will continue to occur no matter how many hula hoops or *Hindenburg*s we see in prime time.

Are you a snob when it comes to the pop-cultist who steals from the cultural tombs versus the serious researcher who is attempting to understand the past?

Nothing in the archives is sacred. We can learn from lowly cultists and high priests alike. They're each tremendously affected by one another's activities, even though they may speak different languages. And both affect the culture in very profound, albeit different, ways. Both, however, have been very selective about what kinds of historical content they focus on, and each community tends to shut out a great deal of dissonant input. I want both groups in the archives, and I wouldn't mind if they tried to engage each other more fully.

My only prejudice is that the pop-cultists quite often seem to come in with bigger budgets and shorter attention spans. This kind of baggage can sometimes be frustrating.

Who owns the intellectual property rights to ephemeral films?

No one owns the rights to about 60 percent of them, because they're in the public domain. Most commercially sponsored films were never copyrighted, or their copyrights were never renewed. The ones still under copyright are mostly recent (post-1963) works or educational films owned by large media corporations. It's a ripe field for all to play in, though you may have to pay someone like me for access to their images.

Can art be made from these found objects?

Like many other artistic questions, that will be up to the artists.

Stack
SOLOTYPE HAS IT!

Postcard Light
GAME OVER

Postcard Dark
POWER PLAY

Overlapping the shadows
doubles the price.

Richfield
THE HOUSE UP HILL

Figgins Shaded
NO ABSINTHE

Sacramento
STOP AHEAD FOR FALL SAVINGS

Forum One
ADVENTURE TOUR PLAN

Forum Two
MARKET REPOR

Regina
QUEST FOR THE KNOWN

Stereo
STEREO ART

Fat Shaded
RIGHT OF WAY ALWAYS

Thorne Shaded
DIMENSIONA

Stack
VERTIGO AWARE

Premier Shaded
PHOTOGRAPHIC ESSAY P

Elongated Roman Shaded
THE ABC BOOK FOR ADULTS

Block Dimension
THIRD DIMENSION

Bullion Shadow
GOT TO BE TOUGH

Telegram Open
MORAL GAMES AND OBJEC

Riccardo
FRED AND ETHYL

Kickapoo
KICKAPOO INDIAN

Gill Shadow
STATION MASTER

Orplid
TWENTY-SIX MAGIC

Sans Serif Shaded
TREASON AND PLOT

Uncle Bill
SMOOTH SHAVIN

Dan Solo on Antique Type

Dan Solo, a former radio announcer and printer's devil, is the proprietor of Solo Type in Oakland, California, and the author of many books on and catalogues of antique wood and metal type. His is one of the largest collections in America. Here he talks about his passions, type history, and the effects of the computer.

How did you become so obsessed with type?

I was a boy printer. I always loved printing. I'm still a boy printer, really. When I was six or seven, my grandfather gave me a cast-iron toy printing press from his childhood; it came with a little case of type. There wasn't enough to set a coherent sentence, but I played with it until I was about nine years old. Then I had a tonsillectomy that went wrong, and I was bedridden for the better part of a year. It was the best thing that ever happened to me. We had a neighbor who was a pressman; he'd bring over his own jobs that went wrong and others that he corrected and showed me why something was a good job or not. There's nothing more valuable that you can teach a person in any trade. If you know what good work looks like, you're able to do it.

You must have grown out of that small press pretty quickly.

I saved up enough money to buy a handpress that was offered in one of those ads in the back of *Popular Science* that said "Print Your Own Cards and Stationery."

Comparable to desktop publishing today?

Yes, I guess. So I had a working press, but what I really needed was type! Well, type was always on the costly side. There was a local type company that actually made type in Oakland, and I went to them, but I couldn't get much for the money I had. The kindly guy who ran the place suggested that I call on job printers to see if they had type for sale. And this was the turning point. I found a place that had six cases of type stacked in the back of a dusty old shop. I paid $12 for all these gorgeous Victorian antiques with a lot of curlicues on them.

Why did he part with them?

They were fifty years out-of-date. And the only thing I could do with them was print stationery for friends. I knocked on doors around the neighborhood to get orders.

Did you study the aesthetics of type? Did you read D. B. Updike or Frederic Goudy?

Not until I was about nineteen. And by that time I had quite a collection of antique types.

At the time, I happened to meet somebody who was a type collector with a terrific print shop. He showed me all the things he was printing with antique type—cards for friends, et cetera—with lots of rule work with curved lines. That was a turning point for me in becoming a typographer because I realized that I really hadn't done anything ambitious with type.

You became a typographer. What is the difference between a printer and a typesetter and a typographer?

The typesetter knows how to operate the equipment, and the typographer is not concerned with the equipment, he is concerned with the aesthetics. Moreover, typographers are all interested in the history of printing type.

All typographers?

There comes a point at which, if you become a typographer, you'll become a scholar. The two go hand in hand. It can't be otherwise. I doubt that there are any really good typographers who are not scholars by nature. They may not be knowledgeable about anything else, but they all know a great deal about why things are designed the way they are. The thing we see today, now that the computer has absolutely killed the old typographic industry, is that typography is in the hands of graphic designers. Before, they were ordering the type and telling the typographer what they wanted. Now they do it themselves.

Does this suggest a decline in typographic standards?

Like I said before, if you know what good work looks like, you'll do good work. But you get young people out of school (and I just hate to say it this way, because I sound like such an old curmudgeon), and they have never done design or typography any other way than by computer. Their entire thinking is structured by what the computer will do so easily.

It's bad in typography because many of them believe that if the computer spaced it, it must be right. A typographer can't live with that. Typically, the typographers I know that use a computer will print the job out three times—the first two times they're marking it for changes of spacing.

I've been collecting articles from trade publications from the 1920s and '30s, like the *American Printer,* which contain angry debates about the degradation of certain standards. In fact, a number of the antique types that you now sell were frequently criticized.

Theodore Low De Vinne, who had a book printing operation at the turn of the century [and was a prolific writer on typographic standards] was vehemently against antique display types; he called them monstrosities.

In 1800, there were three kinds of type: roman, italic, and black letter. Then, fat faces came along, and after that, 3-D shaded effects and outline letters with shading. Around 1816, Caslon, in an effort to be different, took the serifs off and made a sans serif type that was ultimately rejected. Nobody wanted it. It was a monstrosity. I guess monstrosities depend on the time when they are designed.

But novelties did become popular, if only for the duration of their novelty.

Over the years, people looked for novelty, and they came up with the Tuscan thing, the bifurcated stems of letters and so forth. In 1839, something happened that changed everything, and I think it is the most underrated aspect of what happened in Victorian times. If you look in the literature of typefounding, you find a lot of talk about how punches were cut, the steel punch and the matrix and so on, but you find practically nothing about electrotyped matrices. That's where you will cut something in metal, one original pattern letter or model, and an electrotype, and then cast more type from it.

Which is how a lot of those novelty faces were produced.

There were ten times as many types produced that way than were done by punches after that period. If you want to know how fast something happens: in 1842, the New York typefounder George Bruce prevailed upon the Patent Office to arrange a new category of patent that it called a design patent specifically because he wanted to patent designs of printing types; they were being stolen all over the world. Customarily, after that, typefaces with sufficient novelty were patented—and the patents now provide a great source of information about typefounding in those times.

Like today, the technology had a great impact on type design.

It was possible to very easily engrave shaded types and inline types. You could take an existing type and hollow it to make an outline type, and make a new set of mats from one piece of each letter. It is my contention that you really can't name any current category of type design that wasn't present in Victorian times.

What caused people like De Vinne, Updike, and others to rail against this stuff?

By 1890 it was outrageous. Sample page upon page of ruffles and flourishes.

Who designed in those days? Job printers or typographers?

There were not typographers to speak of. They didn't exist in those days. It was quite customary for the art supervisor of a large department store to get the copy together, to show the size, and then write "Garamond" on the job sheet so that the printer could see what he wanted. The printer would select the sizes, arrangement, spacing, leading, et cetera.

Incidentally, with all this ad hocism, when did uniform standards come into the picture?

In 1888, the Type Founders Association of the United States decided that we should have a uniform system of type measurement. Until then, each foundry had its own standard. And nobody wanted to change because it would be too expensive to change all the molds.

Finally, though, in 1888, they decided to institute the American point system, which was ultimately adopted in Great Britain. There's a lot of argument over who invented it. I don't think it matters.

How did that affect the quality of printed material?

It made it possible for a printer to have types from various foundries in one shop, whereas before, the printer might have wanted to stick with just one foundry so that the types would work with one another. But it also affected the way type was used.

The foundries advertised heavily: "Turn in your old type for metal." Well, that came just at a time when things were being simplified in decorative types. The first simplification was, however, not the sort of thing that Updike loved. It was art nouveau—some beautiful type, like Auriol and Eckmann.

And another thing, typefounders are always a few years behind what's going on because it can take a while to get these faces designed and cut. But an interesting thing happened at that time. A lot of the art nouveau types have a pen-lettered look, a ragged edge. And the reason for that is that in the 1880s photoengraving became practical. Suddenly, we had a lot of handlettering produced as type. It became a deliberate style. So, in order to compete with that, without having the expense of engravings and an artist, the printer would buy these handlettered-looking types. In later years, when someone like me came along to be a collector, most of the decorative types had been dumped.

Decorative types were used for what purpose?

Job printing. There was a sort of Victorian rule about the decorative types: Never start the next line with a type that was used in the line above. That doesn't mean you can't use the type twice, just not twice in a row. They believed that the variety attracted people.

Did customers specifically ask for this?

No. Printers felt that it was something they could sell. The printers were designers of a sort. A customer was lucky if the printer was also a *good* designer.

I used to know a very elderly man in San Francisco who had started a typography business in the twenties and claimed to have been the first person in San Francisco to call himself a typographer—as a separate business from job printing.

Let's talk about how you have preserved this treasure trove of metal and wood material.

Decades ago I bought a machine called a Phototypositor. And while I never think of myself as adroit at business—I'm a mechanic, really—I did a very smart thing. I designed and had built, at great cost, the equipment to make the fonts for the typositor. Then I started making fonts commercially. I gave that part of the business up when I realized that I didn't want to make fonts, I wanted to do typography. Nevertheless, I kept the machine, and once I saw how to make the transition from metal and wood to phototype, it opened wonderful doors. So now I have this unlimited supply of brand-new type.

Has the interest in antique faces, like those in your collection, increased?

It has changed. When I first entered the business, we had come out of the dullsville fifties. Too much Futura for my taste. And Helvetica. The typositor came around and you could get anything, and I had huge standing orders from many typographers who would take any new revival I had. Now my Dover books do very well. But I don't know where we are because the computer has changed things. There are many faces that it would be nice to have on the computer that are not. Type styles come and go. I can't predict the future.

eye

Rick Poynor on Design Journalism

Rick Poynor is the founder of *Eye* magazine and edited twenty-five issues from 1990 to 1997. He has written on art and design for *Blueprint, I.D., Frieze,* and the *AIGA Journal of Graphic Design,* and is author of *Typography Now: The Next Wave; The Graphic Edge; Typography Now 2: Implosion;* and *Design without Boundaries: Visual Communication in Transition.* As an editor and writer, he has chronicled a significant period of design experimentation and has set a new standard for the current practice of design journalism.

Why did you launch *Eye* magazine?

Looking at Britain's design magazines in the 1980s, I saw a number of superficial monthlies but nothing in the established genre of the international graphic design review. One could see them in other countries: *Print, Communication Arts,* and *Graphis.* Looking to Japan, there were *Idea* and *Creation.* But this approach hadn't been tried with any success in Britain since *Typographica* ceased publishing in 1967.

How did you set out to distinguish *Eye* from other graphic design magazines?

Apart from studying all of them very closely to see what they did well or badly, my approach was to say, Let's create a graphic design magazine that is as good as the best art magazine we know, and takes very seriously the standards of mainstream journalism. "Critical journalism" has become the term I use to describe what I was trying to do with *Eye.*

What exactly do you mean by the term?

The key difference between a piece of critical journalism and a piece of ordinary journalism is that the writer, instead of just doing a job of reporting—intelligently perhaps, but telling the story and stopping there—supplies an additional level of personal input and analysis, a feeling for the broader context.

How can the concept of critical journalism be applied to graphic design writing? With some exceptions, design writing has traditionally been a showcase—essentially, publicity. We call it "trade journalism" because it is dedicated to supporting the trade.

You start with writers who aren't constantly bowled over by things that are new to them yet are not new to their readers. This is the mistake a lot of design journalism makes. It doesn't realize how sophisticated its readership is. That's why over and over again you encounter designers who call trade magazines "comics" because they know more than the writers who put them together.

Is it difficult to find critical journalists?

Yes. For the last seven years I've struggled to find people with the conviction to say it like they see it. But there are some practical problems here. The writers with the necessary degree of experience are probably designers themselves. They're putting themselves at risk, trying to sustain a working life in the design community while writing about colleagues and friends.

Meanwhile, professional writers cannot make ends meet writing about graphic design for design magazines. One has to be a general journalist or take on more "commercial" writing assignments, such as doing capability brochures for the very designers one might be asked to report on. This leaves the critical field to others, like academics.

Yet I have found that people coming from the academic direction are also very careful of what they'll say in print. You might think, "Ah, the Academy, with its searing insightfulness," but in fact, when it comes to graphic design, academic commentary is often hedged with caution and compromise.

Founded in 1990, *Eye* had, and retains, a postmodern leaning—much of your coverage was on design emanating from Cranbrook, CalArts, Studio Dumbar. Was this a response to the times, a personal preference, or both?

Both. In the mid-1980s, I collaborated on a multilayered publishing project about Brian Eno that explored new processes in contemporary music and a visual response to them by the artist Russell Mills—equally experimental within the context of illustration. In 1989, I wrote a monograph on the British architect Nigel Coates, who was exploring an approach called "narrative architecture." With *Eye*—and with my book *Typography Now: The Next Wave*—I gravitated toward the areas of graphic design in which new thinking was happening. Of course, talking about this from a 1997 perspective, developments that were once regarded as wild are now thoroughly mainstream. But those developments were what drew me to this kind of graphic design in the 1980s when critical supporters were comparatively rare.

From the start you defined *Eye* as inclusive of a particular wing of design and exclusive of others.

At the most basic level, my policy was to cover material that other magazines either weren't covering, certainly not in Britain, or weren't covering in sufficient depth. I was never interested in showing mainstream, middle-of-the-road, possibly award-winning and professionally celebrated projects; they were fine on their own terms, but we'd already seen them a hundred times before.

Since we were publishing only four issues a year, we had our pick of the world's stories. We had every reason to be ultraselective. Recently, I did a content analysis, and it confirmed that only in the last two and a half years did we start to feature very much British graphic design at all. In the magazine's early days I felt the interesting experimentation was happening elsewhere. When we ran the Cranbrook story in the third issue, in 1991, hard on the heels of the book *Cranbrook Design: The New Discourse,* that was the first time Cranbrook had received any serious analysis in Britain, so far as I know. And I went to an American writer, Ellen Lupton, because there simply wasn't anyone in Britain at that point who would have been capable of writing the kind of article she produced.

Are you avoiding naming names of designers you refused to cover in *Eye*?

You want a list? There are hundreds. We wouldn't publish Trickett & Webb or the Partners or staunch contemporary modernists like CDT and Roundel, and others who were at the very heart of the British design profession. Even though they were producing immaculate work, it didn't represent new thinking. It wasn't contributing anything that we hadn't seen many times before.

Is it fair to say that you began covering the designers *Emigre* uncovered, and in putting them in your context—a beautiful context as far as magazine design goes—you were pulling them out of the "underground" and giving them mainstream status?

There are some designers who were published in *Emigre* first. But we always had a broader sense of the design landscape and a deeper sense of design history. From the start we ran the "Reputations" interviews, where our writers talked to a senior generation of designers whom I identified as having a progressive intention and observations to make that still seemed relevant today. And I can't imagine *Emigre* running a profile of Henryk Tomaszewski, or an interview with Roman Cieslewicz or Pierre Bernard. They would probably have been seen as belonging to an earlier generation of designers and design thinking.

Some, perhaps many, designers have the idea that design magazines rule the professional roost, that the editors make selections based on particular biases, which in turn determine the present and future of the field. How were *Eye*'s subjects chosen?

There wasn't some big panel of advisers that I would straw-poll. In the end, subjects were chosen because, as *Eye*'s editor and as someone who was obsessively immersed in this work, I felt they were significant. I wanted to know more about them, and I believed our readers did, too. We ran the first serious analysis of ReVerb's work. We ran a profile of Irma Boom, a Dutch book and publication designer whose uncompromising approach had caused controversy in the Netherlands. In 1994, I wrote a piece on Tomato because they were a phenomenon that needed to be addressed and I'd read nothing that engaged with their ideas about process, which were clearly central to their working practice. More recently, we looked at people like the British designers David Crow and David James, the French experimental type designer Pierre di Sciullo, and Cornel Windlin, a Swiss designer who worked with Neville Brody in London for a while and is now back in Zurich. These are people in their early to mid-thirties who weren't part of the earlier wave of highly publicized late-1980s experimentalists, but have come through since and are exploring new directions.

***Eye* reflected a seemingly strategic desire to expand the range of design journalism. You included surveys of Fluxus, *RAW,* Peter Greenaway; critiques of mass-market style and babe imagery in men's magazines; discussions of the feminist "underground matriarchy"; high and low design; the role of the designer in society. Did you believe there was an audience for a culture magazine based on graphic design, or were you simply indulging your own idiosyncrasies?**

Here, too, I was pursuing my own interests. I leave it to others to decide whether these had some larger application. I saw *Eye* as a visual culture magazine aimed primarily, though not exclusively, at designers, rather than as a "graphic design" magazine in the traditional professional sense. I find professional definitions of what design is to be rather limiting sometimes, and at their most unimaginative, a kind of self-policing. I hoped publishing some of the less obvious material would encourage young designers to challenge these restrictions. As time went on, the general sense of cultural meltdown, the constant talk about the blurring of boundaries across all cultural forms, seemed to confirm that this was a productive approach to take in the 1990s.

I remember a rather controversial profile of P. Scott Makela written by Michael Rock. It was a respectful look at a "significant" figure that was cut with strong criticism. What was your motivation in running this piece?

The work engaged me. I felt it was speaking in a new and contemporary voice. I liked its digital aggression. And because I had that response, I wanted to hear more about it. But, as you say, the way it turned out, it was a critical piece. I could have found a hundred design groupies to write about Makela in breathless tones. But that wasn't what was needed here. I've said this many times, and I've said it to some of the designers involved, though some still don't get it: We are paying them the courtesy of taking their ideas and work seriously. If designers really want a mature design discourse, they will have to be prepared to risk the critical process and take the rough with the smooth. Makela took it very well and I respect that.

You yourself have written two critical profiles that have earned you the ire of your subjects—Neville Brody and David Carson.

The impulse for doing the piece on Brody came from his *Fuse* project in the 1990s and what seemed to me, at a certain point, to be an assault on language—"language" being a word he uses throughout the interview in a rather ambiguous way so that you think he's talking about verbal language when in fact he's talking about visual language and taking it for granted that you'll realize this. The visual has supplanted the verbal. This tendency is something that occurred to me over time through looking at his work, meeting him, and writing about him. It was the fifth piece I had done on him.

Did you have any hesitation about writing it? The piece certainly questioned Brody's motives, if not his ability. It says to the design world, Here's your hero, and he's not without some blemishes and inconsistencies.

If this example really is so remarkable within our little patch of the world, it can only be because we don't have, in any quantity, writing that reflects a mature discourse.

Is graphic design really meaty enough for the good writers to write about? Does our field offer enough challenges to sustain their interest?

Yes. But really good writers will probably want to write about it for a broader audience. I am surprised sometimes that even some of the more academic writers, whom you would expect to take a broader view, seem to see the ultimate purpose of criticism as the creation of better designers. "Better" in a 1990s sense: more responsible, more socially informed, more questioning of their own design practice. That's one function, but a very inward-looking view of the cultural meanings of design. Art and film writing, for instance, is not aimed exclusively at the shaping of artists and filmmakers. Professionals form just one section of a much wider readership. In graphic design, we have a literature that, even with its more expanded recent concerns, exists to serve the profession. So, inevitably, that's going to be too narrow for ambitious writers.

Does this mean we are left with a second-rate literature?

Not necessarily in the long run. But as we all agree, these are early days. America is off to a reasonable start. In twenty years' time, when people routinely use sophisticated digital tools to communicate by word and image, then many more of us will have a stake in talking and thinking about these issues. It's already happening, and the audience for a sophisticated commentary on "visual culture"—I much prefer this more inclusive term to "graphic design"—can only broaden as our technological engagement with design develops. I believe this subject matter will become an everyday concern of journalism and critical discussion in the way that television and advertising are now. But it won't necessarily be called graphic design.

All this said, why did you retire from *Eye*?

Because I'd edited it for seven years and twenty-four issues. Because I felt that I'd said what I have to say through the medium of editing a magazine. I think *Eye* arrived, by a mixture of luck and judgment, at exactly the right moment. The technology at that stage was still relatively new. There was a sense that everything was up for grabs, that it was a time for new ideas, and that the kind of critical approaches that interested me were called for. It's seven years later. A lot of the things that were remarkable in 1990 are commonplace now and even rather boring to design insiders. I've had, as I said, a commitment to the experimental, but I think we've reached a point where, certainly on paper, there is nowhere left to go other than back from the stylistic edge and into a deeper engagement with questions of content. The so-called radicalism of so much 1990s experimentalism has turned out to be a hollow boast. Its ultimate fate was to become part of advertising and the commercial machine, and that's the way some designers seem to want it. This is a phenomenon that calls out for more critical attention than it has received, but the commodification of style leaves me cold. Those weren't the possibilities that I saw in this work and wanted to pursue. So, in a wider sense, too, I feel that the storm is over.

With experimental work becoming mainstream, and little new and exciting on the horizon—the calm after the storm, so to speak—is graphic design still of primary interest?

I'm still interested in graphic design, but I'm particularly interested right now in points of confluence between design, art, and photography. My concerns have always been to some degree historical, and I've just completed a lengthy research project in this area. I plan to go further in this direction. I'm still interested in recent experimental work, but I want to revisit some of it from a more critical perspective, partly because it's become a new and, on occasion, rather self-regarding "establishment" in its own right. All these endless conferences at which the same old "stars" say the same old things are uncomfortably close in tone to the very thing the new guard claimed to be replacing. It's a club. It strikes me, too, that a watered-down, nontheoretical awareness of postmodernism has made it very easy for some designers not to face up to the implications of what they are doing. I'm interested in some old-fashioned but enduring issues such as questions of value and the ethical underpinnings of personal choice, and it would be revealing to put some of the new design to more rigorous forms of test. I've been very struck, reading the historical literature of graphic design, how much clearer some designers were thirty or more years ago about the significant issues. We like to believe we are more sophisticated, but I'm not so sure. People always see and experience changes more sharply when they are new. Once they have become naturalized it can be hard to perceive them at all, let alone to understand the ways in which they may be problematic.

The stylistic principles of Neurath's ⬚ remain the basis of international pictograms today: *reduction* and *consistency.* Many Isotype signs are flat shapes with little or no interior detail, as in ⬚, ⬚, and ⬚. These flat silhouettes suggest a rationalized theater of shadows, in which signs appear to be the natural imprints of material objects—Plato's cave renovated into an empiricist ⬚ laboratory. When depth is expressed in ⬚, isometric drawings ⬚ are used instead of traditional perspective. Parallel lines do not converge, and dimension is fixed from foreground ⬚ to background.

Consistency governs the stylistic uniformity of a symbol set. The D.O.T. system, for example, is a world of coordinated objects, including ⬚, ⬚, ⬚, ⬚, and ⬚. The sign system designed for the Munich Olympics in 1972 was the semiotic climax of international pictures: a geometric body alphabet ⬚ is deployed on a consistent grid: ⬚, ⬚, ⬚, ⬚, ⬚, ⬚, and ⬚.

The reduction and consistency of international pictures heighten their alphabetic quality. Neurath's ⬚ and ⬚ were a critique of writing that resembled writing, a utopian effort to transcend the limitations of letters by exploiting the visual characteristics of typography. **★★★★** Neurath's preferred typeface was **Futura**, designed by Paul Renner around 1926-27. Paralleling the machine aesthetic in architecture and industrial design, **Futura** is stripped of references to handicraft and calligraphy. Neurath conceived of ⬚ as clean, logical, free of redundancy: writing as a machine ⬚ for living in.

The current figure ⬚ might be called **Helvetica Man**, his style coordinating with the favorite typeface of post-war institutional design culture. A more inclusive pictographic land-

116

**Ellen Lupton** on Curating Design

Ellen Lupton is adjunct curator of contemporary design at the Cooper Hewitt, National Design Museum (Smithsonian Institution) in New York City and the curator of *Mixing Messages.* From 1985 to 1992, Lupton was curator of the Herb Lubalin Study Center for Design and Typography at Cooper Union. Before turning thirty, she had emerged as a pioneer historian and critic of graphic design. With J. Abbott Miller, she founded Design/Writing/Research, a design firm devoted to the unique marriage of scholarship and practice. She has written scores of significant critiques of the field, some collected in the anthology entitled *Design/Writing/Research,* published by Lupton and Miller's own imprint, Kiosk Books, and distrbuted by Princeton Architectural Press. With Miller, she is cochair of design at the Maryland Institute of Art.

How would you describe your mission as the curator of contemporary design?

My goal is to do exhibitions that expand the design community's own knowledge and understanding of itself and that also speak to the general public about the role and value of design in their lives.

Working in a national museum you have these two publics, at least: the specialist public, whether it's the practicing designer or design historian, and the general public. You have to be able to expand both groups' understanding of design. In my case, it's contemporary design, by which I mean twentieth century.

As I understand it, yours is a unique position at the Cooper-Hewitt.

Curators at this museum are all linked to collections; so they do research and collecting around a particular medium, and each of those media spans centuries of history. Dianne Pilgrim, director of the Cooper-Hewitt, decided that she wanted a curator who would not be bound to a particular collection but could look at design from many points of view.

I'm a curator in the intellectual sense but not in the sense of one who cares for objects. And that suits my sensibility. I'm not a person who collects in my personal life. I am more interested in studying and interpreting than in building a collection. Although I like to work with collectors, collecting is a certain kind of genius that I don't have.

In your role, however, don't you search out and uncover as well? You don't work just with existing collections?

I tend to approach it from the point of view of an intellectual question first. That leads me toward looking *for* certain objects, as opposed to a lust for objects that leads to intellectual inquiry.

When I do an exhibition, I always do the writing first, whereas most curators find the objects first. I like to know the story I'm trying to tell. So for me, the exhibition is just another medium, like teaching, lecturing, designing, and writing.

Has having access to the Cooper-Hewitt's space and collections changed the way you tell your stories? Has it influenced the kinds of stories you want to tell?

Well, being around real things is different from looking at reproductions in books. Whether it's the museum's collections or Elaine Lustig Cohen's collection (of avant-garde letterheads) or Merrill Berman's collection (of Russian avant-garde posters), having access to the actual objects cannot be compared to book research alone.

What does the real thing offer that reproductions or secondary sources do not?

It gives me a sense that things have been made. There's a tendency in graphic design to reduce everything to image, and that certainly is something encouraged by all the publishing in graphic design—including the books that you and I do. Graphic design scholarship doesn't usually tell you how things are made. Everything is flat. But a poster, letterhead, envelope, or book—these are objects. They're not just flat surfaces. When you actually see the object, you get a sense of how it was bound, how it was constructed, how it's printed, how the thing is put together. That comes directly from the thing, not from a photograph of the thing.

Before we discuss the stories you are currently telling, I want to return to your first job as curator of the Lubalin Design Center and the exhibitions you did there. But as a way of getting into that, how did you get involved in graphic design?

I went to Cooper Union in New York and studied graphic design and other things. Cooper Union has a generalist program, and so I didn't have to major in anything.

Why Cooper Union?

I grew up in Baltimore. In 1981, I applied to a bunch of art schools. Cooper Union was free, and it was in New York. Like a lot of eighteen-year-olds, I didn't really know anything about graphic design or anything about art at all. At Cooper Union I took courses in graphic design and painting and sculpture—the latter with Hans Haacke. Graphic design was always a baseline because it brought together visual activity and writing. In courses with Hans Haacke, an artist who deals with media and type in his work, it was just natural to bring together graphic design with a more critical activity.

Did Haacke, who is known for his polemical art, stimulate your interest in political issues?

Yes. But my student work was not especially political. I was more interested in design as a medium and doing more theoretical explorations.

Actually, the really influential person at Cooper was George Sadek, who had a literary approach to graphic design that was grounded in the tradition of the book, and yet with this perverse dada side to it. He came out of the European modernist aesthetic, but it wasn't purely rational. It always had an element of Duchampian upset to it. It related to what was going on in the fine arts, with the kind of neoconceptual tradition of people like Hans Haacke. For me, that all came together in graphic design as a legitimate language. It wasn't just a means to an end or a way to get a job, but a whole way of thinking.

Was there a dichotomy between theoretical and commercial work?

It wasn't much of a dichotomy because George treated graphic design as a serious formal and intellectual undertaking. He was not especially interested in it as a commercial language. There was some conflict with that at the school, at the level of the trustees. But George really dominated how design was taught. He had a humanistic view of design as an aesthetic discipline that could entertain intellectual ideas, that it was not simply a means to an end.

How did that manifest itself in your student work?

I did projects dealing with Derrida (the French poststructuralist philosopher) and typography. This was before the Macintosh; so I would cut out pages from books and slit the letters apart and do these little books that were attempting to explore in a visual way ideas from poststructuralism, which was all very much in the air in the art world at that time. I did one project where I made international symbols for psychoanalytic ideas, which ultimately became my first exhibition as curator at the Lubalin Design Center. I was exploring ideas from philosophy and psychoanalysis, trying to see how they related to design issues. My experimental projects were the basis for my thinking now.

Were you aware of what was going on in theory at Cranbrook or Rhode Island School of Design or elsewhere?

I was more aware of Dan Friedman and Willi Kunz—what was called the New Typography at that moment. To a lesser degree Cranbrook. I had seen Cranbrook's issue of *Visible Language,* "French Currents of the Letter," and it triggered something in me about how you could put spaces between type and develop a fundamental idea about communications.

That's an interesting leap, to go from the philosophical underpinnings in the art world to putting spaces between letters. How did that click?

As a student I was really interested in poststructuralism. I was into Saussure and Derrida and Roland Barthes and Foucault because they presented fundamental ideas about the nature of representation. It constituted the hardware of my mind. My twin sister was a student at Hopkins at the time, and then a graduate student at Yale; she was engaged in all that stuff at a professional academic level. So we would have intense discussions about it, and she would feed me these texts. I kept looking at it in terms of what it said about vision, what it said about visual form, and the idea of representation helping to construct the way we perceive reality. I was interested in a simple idea, that things aren't just as they appear.

At that same time, I resisted what I considered an overintellectualization of an essentially intuitive practice. But this was also the time that Tom Ockerse, on the academic side, and Massimo Vignelli, on the commercial side, were introducing the idea of semiotics to graphic design.

But that was a different approach. That was more of an attempt to use semiotics as a scientific vocabulary for describing the communications process. What was coming out of the French tradition, referring back to Saussure and the kind of founding of structural linguistics, was not about rationalizing the communications process; it was more the critique of how things were. So, whereas Massimo was talking about using semiotics as a way to get to the essence of communication and clean things up, someone like Roland

Barthes was looking at the kind of bottomless pit of communication, that behind every sign was yet another one, and you were never going to get to the bottom of things.

Were other students interested in this?

In the graphic design program there was only one other person, Abbott Miller. But there were lots of people in fine arts who were interested in that kind of material, who were engaged in it, interested in film theory and poststructuralism as it related to art at that time, specifically to a kind of media-based art. I think at Cranbrook, that's the avenue that it came through, too, people working in photography and the fine arts getting together with graphic designers. This was a period when photographers were no longer trying to capture the perfect moment in time, but were seeing their work as being more narrative and having a more literary basis; somehow language and writing and image had to come together.

With this underpinning, did you know what your next step would be in terms of a career?

The moment I graduated was the moment that the Lubalin Design Center was founded and was getting ready to open to the public. George Sadek asked me if I wanted to work there. My original job title was girl Friday—that was literally what was typed on my contract. By the end of my first year, he had changed my title to curator. I had the opportunity to create some projects that were completely my own and handle other projects that came in from above.

What were some of these original projects?

Well, one of the first ones was this exhibition called *Global Signage: Semiotics and the Language of International Pictures,* which was an attempt to look at the form-language of those ubiquitous airport signs, and trace their history and philosophical movement from the twenties. It was my first opportunity to really look at theory and practice in graphic design together.

Did you feel that design students or professionals were sophisticated enough to understand this theoretical approach? Or were you actually doing it for yourself?

I wanted to make things accessible, but there was definitely a high level of indulgence in what I was doing. I wanted to make public exhibitions, but I often didn't make a big effort to get people to come and see them. One reason it was always important for me to publish something for every exhibition was so that I had some document I could send around to people. That is what created a reputation for the center.

The exhibits were certainly arcane, but unique in contrast to the typical vanity shows at the AIGA and Art Directors Club.

Yes, the stuff was esoteric. It was directed at a design audience, and at quite a sophisticated one. I've always prided myself on writing clearly and being fairly accessible. But these were dense little projects. The big change in my work in the last few years is having to create things for a much, much wider audience. But in a way, the Lubalin Design Center was graduate school for me. I was creating these very narrow, little thesis projects.

I remember a number of exhibits coming from the Lubalin Center on a wide range of engaging subjects. I can't remember comparable exhibitions on contemporary practice or history in either design schools or museums. *The Bauhaus and Design Theory* was one of the freshest approaches to that historical moment I had seen.

Abbott Miller and I did it in 1991. It brought ideas from design history into the present. It looked at the kind of theory of design developed at the Bauhaus and then talked about design in the last fifteen to twenty years as a response and aftermath to that. To me this is an exciting way to deal with design theory. I did that in the signage show too, looking at these intense avant-garde notions and then their dissemination into airports.

Was the Bauhaus show a pivotal moment in terms of wedding criticism to your research?

Yes, in the sense that it didn't deal with history or theory as being separate from contemporary design. It brought them together. It made it more relevant. It made it less narrow. And, also, it was the first time we did a book that actually got published, instead of a pamphlet. So it was a coming-of-age, a maturing of the whole process.

Over the course of time, you were developing a vision in terms of what the Lubalin Center should be in relation to graphic design professionally and graphic design education. What would you say that vision was?

Because of its size and because of its academic nature, the center was not really in a position to speak to the general public. It was a narrow mission, and yet ambitious in its own way. I was going toward confronting contemporary issues, and trying to find ways that criticism and theory had relevance to the immediate practice of graphic design. One project that I was going to do was on the vernacular and this idea of "high and low" in graphic design, which had really shaped a lot of the dialogue in the community for that period.

Shaped it intuitively or by design?

Very deliberately. For example, Tibor Kalman and M&Co., work going on at Cranbrook, and Charles Anderson: many quite divergent ideologies all grappling with the difference between a professional and a nonprofessional language. Barbara Glauber ended up doing that show. I had gotten NEA funding to do it, and it was on the books for the following year, but I couldn't continue to work on it. She did a beautiful job in her own way.

What you did at the Lubalin Design Center was certainly embraced by students and professionals alike. But there has always been a tension between theory and practice—theory being primarily a student concern; practice being, well, the meat-and-potatoes of commercial endeavor. Can you talk about that in terms of your own approach?

Theory often has to function not as a how-to guide or a basis for making decisions in design, but more as a tool for understanding design's cultural role or its aesthetic issues. It's more of an analytical device.

That's going back to talking about semiotics, and Massimo Vignelli versus Roland Barthes. You know, Vignelli has developed a true methodology of design that includes criteria for making decisions. That's one way that theory can function as a tool for making decisions, a framework in which you operate. But theory can also function to open up the object of design or the practice of design, and it's not so much about the internal day-to-day practice of choosing typefaces or designing the margins in a book, but more about seeing how the margins in a book relate to other things in the world. It's a more humanistic approach. It's more about design as a cultural activity.

Is it the responsibility of the designer to develop and then understand theoretical ideas? Or must it come from the outside—the design critic or the design teacher?

In other fields, theory and criticism are often generated by people who are engaged in practice. Maybe then they become more interested in criticism than in practice, but they do it from the vantage point of knowing how to do it. That's true in architecture and in fine arts: it's not always the professional scholar who generates the most interesting criticism, but it often comes from within. Which doesn't mean that those same people are always the best designers or artists or architects. They come to it from this basis of being within the language of what they are talking about.

In the book of essays on design that you wrote with Abbott Miller, *Design/Writing/Research,* you design, report, and critique the field from the inside looking out. As adjunct curator of contemporary design at the National Design Museum, you must look out and in. You are responsible for telling stories, indeed informing the public about a wide range of design endeavor that may be foreign to them. Your first exhibition at the Cooper-Hewitt, *Mechanical Bride*s, in 1994, was about the way industrial and advertising designers targeted the women's market between 1930 and 1960. It veered away from graphic design and addressed industrial design in ways that must have been foreign to the general public. How did you make a show that appealed to both the specialized and general audience?

Mechanical Brides took industrial design as its subject. These are objects from twentieth-century mass culture that have been associated with women's work, and for me the challenge was how to talk about the kind of social history and feminist history of these objects without just a bunch of text panels about statistics: how many hours women spend in the kitchen and stuff like that.

We tried to do it by linking these objects to a world of images so that advertising, film stills, documentary photographs, and oral history became the voice of the object. That was, for the most part, a very visual way of telling the story about these industrial appliances and how their evolution as forms and technologies could be charted and interpreted through this world of images—with very few words.

What was the key to telling this story?

I wanted people to see their own lives presented in the museum, as opposed to seeing something rarefied, obscure, and precious. I wanted to have people look at very familiar objects in a new way. I think people enjoy that.

Would you call it a confrontational or polemical show? Some critics, I'm thinking specifically of Herbert Muschamp in the *New York Times,* rebuked it for being too "feminist."

No, it wasn't confrontational. It was very pleasure-oriented. It was never saying to women who had spent their lives at home that they'd been wasting their time. It wasn't negative. It was almost nostalgic in a way. There's a pleasure in looking at these things from the past, and we tried to incorporate that pleasure into the experience of the show.

But there was also the critical viewpoint that you brought to it. You presented a new version of a history that was not the popular view of history. Cultural studies have only recently addressed these issues. And you were presenting it both to a younger generation and a generation who lived through the experience. How do you reconcile the two?

Well, by drawing on feminist history and feminist sociology that talks about the realities of job segregation, for example, around technologies. The field of telephone operating continues to be 90 percent women today. Before 1974, it was 100 percent women. So, we were talking about some of those realities and trying to show that there's a myth that technology freed up women from certain kinds of labor. The sociological research on women and technology shows that that's not the case. As these appliances changed the nature of certain kinds of housework, other kinds of housework came in to take out the space that had been made. It was really women moving into the workforce that made the amount of time they spent doing housekeeping go down, and housekeeping standards went down. It wasn't the machines that triggered that. It was how women were spending their time, what the economic value of their time had become.

What inspired this show in the first place?

The show built on an exhibition I had just finished with Abbott Miller called *The Bathroom, the Kitchen, and the Aesthetics of Waste*. It was a history of domestic technology in relation to consumption. An undercurrent of that project had been feminism and this research on women and technology. I wanted to carry that forward and use some of those ideas to really focus on women and media.

What inspired you to do research in this area?

Abbott and I were both involved at CUNY [City University of New York] at the time in the art history program, where we were both in a course on American art in the thirties, which got us excited about industrial design. I started doing research on food and packaging in the kitchen—which in our house I control. He started working on design as it related to the bathroom—and that's what he controls in our house.

We realized that they were front and back of the same story. The kitchen is the entry point for consumption and goods into the house, and the bathroom is the exit point. We had this portrait of the domestic structure from these two sides that usually get forgotten. Henry Dreyfuss once said that modernism entered the American home through the back door of the kitchen, the bathroom, and the laundry room and then rode into the living room on the back of the vacuum cleaner, and that these technologies of consumption and bodily care were what gave modernism its voice in the American home.

What assumptions did you have before you started researching this show? And what changed after you finished?

The thesis was that there was a link between bodily consumption and economic consumption. And I love going into a show with a simple metaphor, a kind of structure, and then you uncover it and see how it plays out.

When you begin a project, you're doing research in a void, and you're looking at everything. Then you start to see a pattern, and hopefully there's an Aha! moment when you have an idea, and then the rest of your research is directed around that idea.

What was your "Aha!" moment with Mechanical Brides?

The telephone. I had never even considered that the telephone would be one of the objects in this show. Instead, the show was going to be of laundry and office equipment, typewriters and office furniture, Dictaphones and whatever in the office; and then in the home, washing machines and irons and electric dryers and all that kind of stuff. And while I was doing the research, in magazines like *Fortune, Good Housekeeping, Ladies' Home Journal, Life,* and so forth, images of the phone kept coming up. They were images that communicated between, quite literally, the world of gender-segregated office work and jobs that defined women's place in the office and then in the home. In the home section, the telephone emerged in the fifties as a commodity directed at women as an element of home decoration. There is a history of women and telephones. Women do, indeed, talk on the phone a lot, and that's been borne out in sociological studies of who uses the phone.

There was a kind of amazing moment of seeing that, well, here is an object that literally communicates between these two worlds. It's an object that more than anything in the show we think of as neutral, having no sex, and yet it has this resonance in popular culture and in the reality of use—women have had a special relationship to this instrument.

The phone has symbolized so many things in addition to mass communications: status, progress, et cetera. What else did you uncover?

At the turn of the century, a whole pornographic literature developed around sort of erotic postcards showing women talking on the phone—the origins of the call girl, the sort of freelance prostitute. *Butterfield 8* is a great example. Elizabeth Taylor played the call girl in the film, and the graph of her virtue is mapped onto the moment that she cancels her answering service and becomes a pure woman—and is then killed in a car crash, and has to pay for her sins anyway.

Phones were not always a consumer product, though. It wasn't so long ago that phones were rented from the phone company. Colors cost extra per month.

Before the breakup of Ma Bell, AT&T didn't consider the phone to be a consumer product. There was a sea change in the fifties of realizing that it could be commodified, that it could be invested with personality and style—the way the toaster had been, and other objects that originated as being simply neutral. So you have the Princess phone; the wall-mounted kitchen phone—that's this kind of telephonic kitchen cabinet, doesn't take up space on your counter; phones in decorator colors; extensions for different parts of the house, often marketed to make women feel safe at home. They would have a phone in more places and therefore be kind of watched over by this technology.

That's something that really hadn't been talked about before. And yet it is evident from the marketing materials and advertising that women were being very directly addressed as the consumers of this new and proliferating phone network in the house.

What was the most satisfying outcome of the exhibition in terms of what you brought to the consciousness of your audience?

It's clear that the exhibition really hit a chord. This was narrow in focus in its way; but it was reaching people who weren't interested just in design but in the culture of these objects.

Was it indeed a design show?

It was definitely design from a sociological point of view, as opposed to design from the point of view of aesthetics or technology or invention or the designer. It focused on objects insofar as it dealt with aesthetic issues, like the use of color and form in the telephone, or streamlining in the washing machine. I tried to see the cultural implications of that, as opposed to looking at that as an end in itself.

Did you go into this project to prove that women had been manipulated by a male-dominated media?

I went into it with a lot of assumptions. There were a lot of things that got refined. By the end, it was feeling more positive than negative. I began by having strong negative feelings about the material and thought that it would be a more negative show. Coming out the other end, I felt more open.

You mean you uncovered new evidence about the role of women at this time? Or did you have some other revelation?

I realized that the story also included a sense of the pleasure and fun that a lot of women associate with that work. In the fifties, new machines and better-designed houses actually improved their lives—that was not just a conspiracy. There was a review of the show in *Design Issues* by Susan Sellers, which is very nice. But she makes some critical comments, like, "The curator never makes a convincing case for a conspiracy against women." I never made that case because I don't think there was strictly a conspiracy, and design did not by itself create the division of labor. It participated in it, it visualized it, it enforced it, it made it more bearable, it mythologized it to some degree. But I think designers have this illusion that what they create is a more powerful force in society, and that by changing the shape of objects they're going to change huge patterns. I tried to express that in the exhibition. We didn't want anyone coming to the exhibition to feel like their whole life was being attacked.

Let's talk about the media you work in. You do a book to supplement the exhibition. What are the major differences other than form?

The book is a stand-alone document, not a catalogue of the exhibition. There are lots of images in the *Mechanical Brides* book that aren't in the exhibition because that's how the scale works out. They communicate something differently. I wanted to reflect the spirit of magazines and advertising in the quality of the book, which has a collage aesthetic, and it's very readerly, with lots of pullout quotes and time lines and stuff that you can read in a couple of different ways.

Do you see the show and the book appealing to two different audiences?

The book should always be a way to say more than you could say in the exhibition. Here you have more words and fewer pictures. The balance has shifted, and it gives you a chance to do things in greater depth and use footnotes; so you're providing really interested readers with access to more information and what your sources are, which is something that you can't do in an exhibition. It's definitely a scholarly book in that sense. It's not written in a journalistic way, where it's just a story being told and you kind of have to take it on faith. It's a documented book. But the way it's presented visually is very fun and free, it does not look like an academic book.

One of the characteristics that separates you from most curators I know of is that the exhibitions and the books and other printed matter are designed by you. That's quite a juggling act.

Well, on the one hand, it means that I have to work really hard because I have to do all of these things at the same time. On the other hand, there is an incredible freedom and empowerment knowing that you can do something yourself, more or less. I think the empowerment and freedom ultimately make me move faster and lighter.

Do you have a design philosophy? I would say there's a Lupton (and Miller) graphic style going back to the Cooper Union days that emerges in your catalogues and books.

I am a scholar for whom design is both my subject and my medium. I am interested in how strategies of designing can be used to amplify and interpret a subject. And that subject need not be design.

What interests me is the ability to use design as an interpretive medium, which means having a very intense relationship between the design and the text. There are other people doing work like that; Bruce Mau's work is an example of a very similar approach, different visually, where there is an interest in the entire document and not simply in what it looks like, but there is a real engagement in the structure of the text.

I can't see anything in three dimensions. It's hard enough seeing in two dimensions. How does that work for you? Does one discipline feed the other?

I don't see myself as a three-dimensional exhibition designer, either, and on really ambitious projects I work with three-dimensional designers. For *Mixing Messages* I worked with two architects. I wouldn't dream of trying to design that installation.

You designed the displays for the *Avant-Garde Letterhead* exhibition (at the Strathmore Gallery, AIGA Design Center, spring 1996), and it was a very skillful design that wed the geometry and color of the letterheads themselves to a three-dimensional environment.

That was a lot simpler. The AIGA gallery is an easy space to manage. The exhibition involved a small number of objects all the same size, very different from trying to deal with the Carnegie mansion—the building that houses the Cooper-Hewitt—with four hundred or five hundred pieces of graphic design in it, ranging in size from six-foot posters to business cards.

This takes us to *Mixing Messages,* the first museum exhibition devoted to graphic design since the Walker Art Center's exhibit *Graphic Design in America* (1989). How does this show differ?

This a survey of graphic design in the United States for the last fifteen years. It's been an important fifteen years. It's also been the period that I have been aware of graphic design. It's when a lot of people came of age as graphic designers, a kind of third generation, perhaps, of graphic designers. It's been an extremely productive time, when a number of different things have been going on simultaneously. There is not one monolithic institution of design in this period.

I wanted to do an exhibition about what's going on right now. *Mechanical Brides* was historical; *Avant-Garde Letterhead* was historical. I wanted to do something that looks at contemporary graphic design, which the museum has never done. As the National Design Museum, that's something that we should be doing.

Why has it been, with the exception of the Walker show (which traveled to only one other museum, as well as the IBM Gallery in New York and the Design Center in London), that no other American museums have addressed graphic design in terms other than as collections of vintage posters or rare books?

I don't think very many museum curators realize that graphic design is even a field, that something connects a letterhead to a poster to a logo to a book to a magazine. These seem like totally disparate types of objects, each with its own tradition and convention, and it's a very mixed bag of things. Not many museums recognize that graphic design is a discourse.

Even though they use it every day with publications, advertising, exhibition labels, et cetera?

It's a service that they use. Moreover, contemporary graphic design is not collectible yet, it doesn't have the kind of value of, say, the avant-garde poster or something from the past. It doesn't have that patina. So it doesn't fit into the agenda of most museums, whereas architecture has such a respected place in our society, and it's much easier for museums to think of exhibiting contemporary architecture.

I actually think it would be much more exciting to see contemporary graphic design. It's much more exhibitable. Architecture shows are really difficult because you're showing either photographs or architectural drawings, which are really hard to understand, or models, which are great but very expensive, and you usually can't show very many of them.

With graphic design, you're actually looking at the thing. And it's wonderful to look at.

Aside from the fact that graphic design is wonderful to look at, how do you make the links? How do you tell the story of graphic design so that the public understands what you already understand so well?

Putting all of these hundreds of things together in a fairly small space will help communicate that this is a unified practice. Seeing the medium of typography as a code, as a structure that links all these things together—that in itself will really help communicate to people that this is a connected universe. Not a coherent one, necessarily. Certainly not a holistic or singular one that is dominated by any one person or style or philosophy. But there are things that might fit together as a medium. Typography is the crucial link. So, a whole section of the show is devoted to typography and to trying to make the public conscious of this form that is second-nature to us all.

I suspect you could do an entire exhibit on typography and that would encompass virtually everything you want to address in this show.

Typography is the grammar, the currency, the set of technological and formal possibilities that kind of draws design together. The ability to turn manuscripts into type is one of the basic skills of graphic design; the very democratization of that skill is one of the things affecting design now, and it makes it possible to produce more casual publishing enterprises and so forth.

What are the other components of the show?

Another section deals with identity. Graphic design is used to create visual personalities to bind people, or companies, or products together into families that have a visual character. We're looking at everything from global corporate identities, like the FedEx logo, down to Women's Action Coalition and things that are happening more at the level of the street, where graphic design is used to broadcast the identity of a group.

You are aware that the Walker Art Center's *Design in America* exhibition came under harsh scrutiny for ignoring some important designers and celebrating others. The discretion of the curator is key to a strong show, and so I'm interested in your curatorial process. What determined your decisions? What made you select, for example, FedEx or Women's Action Coalition as paradigms? Where did you draw your critical line?

In the contemporary period, there aren't the great corporate identity programs that there were in the sixties and seventies. It was very important to me to include some examples of really large-scale corporate identity done by big firms who had really invested in the research. And, oddly enough, some of the great ones failed, like the Time Warner logo. (We're going to be showing the one that Steff Geissbuhler did for Time Warner). But it's not a success story like Mobil was in the sixties.

What about identities like Reebok or Nike?

We're doing Nike from an advertising point of view, and will show some of Wieden and Kennedy's work. But I'm not going to do a whole history of the swoosh logo.

Typography, identity . . . what else is an important realm of design?

Another section deals with publishing. That's where we're looking at design as a medium. Publishing is to make information public and to build a public through the sharing of information. And that section deals with books, book covers, magazines, and electronic media.

The introductory section of the show is called "Design on the Street." The Great Hall of the museum is a kind of streetscape—the street as a microcosm of what graphic design is, a medium that gets mobilized by many different parts of society, from major corporations to activists and local music groups and theaters. It's a way for us to show posters that's legitimate. You know, most museums, when they do design at all, they show posters. And there's a real reason for that. Posters are great to look at. They have wonderful exhibition value, and they're really fun. I have found places to put them where it's legitimate, one medium among others, as opposed to having a poster section where you're looking at the poster as an art.

You mentioned that with _Mechanical Brides_ you were looking at the objects as opposed to the creators. Is it the same here? Is the creator less significant than the objects themselves?

This show is more oriented toward the creator. This is not a sociological view of design. While it's not organized around people, we made our best effort to find out who did everything, and to interview designers about why they do what they do.

And how do these responses appear in this show?

A lot of the interviews will be on the Web site. I've talked to lots of people and transcribed these interviews, including people who are no longer alive, like Muriel Cooper and Dan Friedman.

This is not a show about designers per se, but certain designers appear in several parts of the show because they are relevant to different aspects of design. There is no Paula Scher or April Greiman section, but their work comes up where it's appropriate. It is important that the show say that all the things that we look at every day were designed by people.

We make choices when we are writing or curating and ultimately presenting our findings to the world. What guides your choice of who is an important designer? Is there a difference between an important design and an important designer?

Lots of things go into the decision. I'm really trying to strike a balance between recognizing the achievements of the design community and people who we all understand are influential, and trying not to have all decisions dictated by that. I want to be open to looking at other things that aren't necessarily on the map yet.

Have you applied a standard for how to define or determine who it is that is part of this canon? Is there anything else that figures into that, either aesthetically, philosophically, or politically?

Is it visually exciting? If you're putting together an exhibition, you want things to be powerful to look at. That's very subjective, obviously, and the exhibit definitely reflects my taste and what I think is important. I definitely show a bias toward modernism, but I think it's a very open-ended view of modernism. So, for example, I'm resisting, because I don't like it, work whose appeal is derived entirely from nostalgia. But that does not mean that work in this show is not drawing on history.

How do you make this distinction?

The work of Drenttel Doyle Partners I think has zero nostalgia, and yet is based in a kind of tradition of the book and typography as a literary medium. Much of the work of a designer like Charles Anderson is highly nostalgic, but a lot of what he's doing with clip art and funky old typefaces is done in a very fresh and inventive way. The visual power of it is not derived wholly from a kind of re-creation of the past. Because it's not the past. A lot of the work in this show is bound to history. Much of what I think is important in contemporary type design is rooted in history—in a way that recognizes the continuation of the word and a sense of design being a literacy, and therefore something that is shared and is always dealing with some kind of common ground. One can intervene on that common ground in ways that are strong and clear and direct and new, or one can do it in ways that are very weak and saccharine and commercialized.

Let's return to your open-ended view of modernism. Given the fifteen-year span of your exhibition, this is not the modernism of Paul Rand or Rudolph de Harak. Is it the "radical modernism" of Dan Friedman?

There are ideas from the early-twentieth-century avant-garde, from the moment modernism emerges, that are very much about diversity of language. Dada, futurism, surrealism, even constructivism, were not singular. Interest in collage and the found object and the found phrase, and taking the existing elements of the technology such as letterpress and doing something new with it by using its structure—that way of thinking is endlessly productive. The current period is one of diversity and mix, and that's why we're calling it *Mixing Messages*.

Where does contemporary modernism and fifties modernism diverge?

The identity movement of the fifties and sixties that was extremely systematic and about uniformity and perfect forms and the perfect system, the seamless system that would accommodate every possible situation, is not one that makes sense in contemporary culture and is not one that ultimately succeeded or was validated in the marketplace or anywhere else. But that doesn't mean that, therefore, other ideas from modernism are to be thrown away or discarded. The idea of design having a potential to be critical is something from modernism—of design being about not just meeting expectations, but exceeding them. That design can be more than just making do, just being decorative, just being good enough, just filling the brief, but that design can be more visionary—that's something that comes out of the avant-garde. Then there is the notion of the designer as artist and thinker and social actor, and not simply a service provider.

What in this show represents that in the clearest way?

Dan Friedman's designs for the series of books with Jeffrey Deitch are examples of using design in a very active and visionary way, when the designer becomes an editor and where design becomes a form of research in the way that I've been talking about in my own work. A lot of the experimental work done at Cranbrook in the late eighties uses design as an experimental medium, and that's had an impact on design in the real world as well.

These are more art- than consumer-based projects; what about more mainstream work?

Paula Scher's work for the Public Theater, which we're doing a lot with in this show; it's just amazing to see that on the streets of New York. Paul Davis's work was amazing, too. So in a sense, Scher's challenge was to come up with something different, and she did that by making type the center.

What do you want your mainstream audience to learn from this exhibit?

Since the opening of the show I have been talking with journalists from the general "cultural press," who are interested in design but not immersed in it like you and I. They see graphic design as a service of selling—designers promote products and create corporate images. I want the exhibition to show this kind of audience—the educated general public—that graphic design has its own independent vitality. Every poster on the street is an ephemeral work of art. The mix of messages on the street parallels the mix of people walking by, their lives briefly crossing. In the field of font design, which has bubbled up into public consciousness over the past decade, letterforms have assumed powerful personas, from the weird to the elegant—the characters of the alphabet have their own story to tell.

After almost two years of preparing *Mixing Messages,* what ideas have you drawn from studying all this material?

I've devoted a whole gallery to the field of publishing, where designers have crucial roles to play in constructing content. The design of a book, magazine, or CD-ROM shapes the user's experience and understanding of the product itself. Whereas advertising is a text about a product that resides elsewhere, the design of a magazine *is* the product. A magazine relies on design to set a stance toward its audience and its subject matter. In the field of publishing, designers are emerging as authors. On both large and small scales, from elaborate CD-ROM products to independent fanzines, publishing is a place where designers have a chance to articulate their own vision. This development is exciting to me personally, and this is where I see the future of design.

After devoting your energies to such a massive survey, is there more to pique your intellectual curiosity? Is there more to explore in graphic design?

I'm more excited than ever with graphic design. While *Mixing Messages* is a broad survey designed to introduce the public to graphic design, the next thing I want to do, building on that foundation, is more detailed and narrow. This may be an exhibition or a book. But I'd like to continue what Abbott Miller and I did in *Design/Writing/Research* and focus on various relationships between graphic design and other design disciplines, such as typography in architecture. This survey gives me the license to become more focused. Frankly, after all this, I've earned the right.

What ideas have you drawn from studying all this material?

One is that graphic design isn't one thing. It is both a discourse among people interested in some very refined questions about form and function and an extremely and utterly pervasive cultural phenomenon. It is both of those things. What I would hope for the public to come away with is an understanding of design being a discipline that embraces issues, but also to see design as being everywhere. I really think it is both everywhere and nowhere, that it's at once a very specific dialogue with quite refined points to it and an activity and culture that lots and lots of people have access to and that is becoming more and more open.

Now that you are cochair of the graphic design department of the Maryland Institute of Art, do you plan on changing the core of design education?

We want graphic designers to be culturally literate—that is, aware of their place in society and aware of the history and possibilities of their own field. Typography continues to be the heart of graphic design. It is what connects print media to multimedia and beyond. We seek to build on typography as a body of knowledge and as a means of expressive communication.

Do you feel that what you've done as practitioner, writer, editor, and curator will influence your teaching? If so, in what manner?

When I was younger, I felt that design students should learn the history of graphic design because it was "good for them"—history would make them critical and socially aware; it would make them better citizens. Now, I still believe that, but I also believe they need history because it will make them better designers. Students who don't know what has gone on before or what is happening now are simply not equipped to practice in a competent, creative, and culturally literate way.

As a teacher, do you encourage your students to follow style and fashion, or is there a larger goal for the young designer?

Students need to be able to understand and engage content. Style is important, too—they need to be able to read the content behind the great styles and recognize the unique style of good content.

Do you believe that the roots of your design education—postmodern theoretical models—is still valid today?

The idea that knowledge is culturally relative and that design exists as a language of relationships at work within a broader social realm remains crucial to my understanding of graphic design. I'm not ready to turn away from these fundamental insights, although many of my peers seem to have found more comforting answers in religion, mysticism, and the worship of the self.

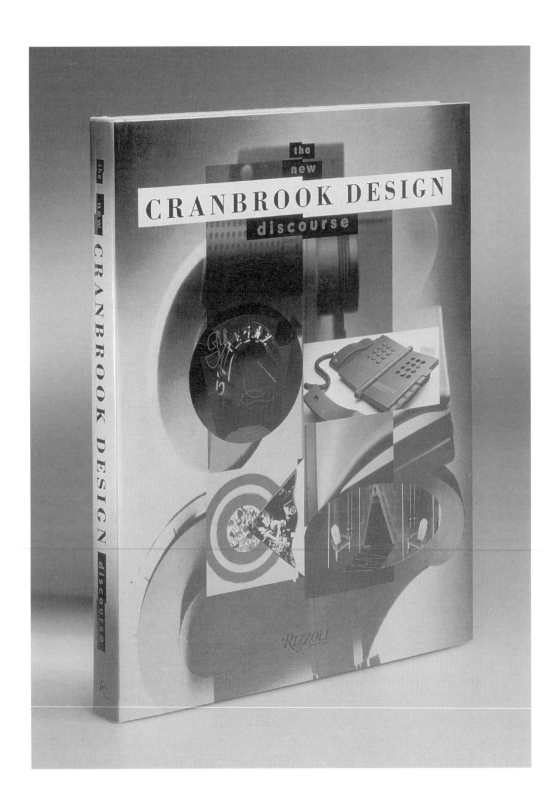

Katherine McCoy on Design Education

Katherine McCoy is a professor of communications design at the Institute of Design at Illinois Institute of Technology (IIT). For twenty-three years she was cochair (with husband and industrial designer Michael McCoy) of the graduate design department of Cranbrook Academy of Art, where she administered an influential program that challenged the presumptions of modernist design. She consults in graphic design and design marketing for international corporate and cultural clients that have included the International Design Center Nagoya, Tobu Department Store, Philips Electronics, Unisys, the Detroit Institute of Arts, and Cranbrook Educational Community. Her work in design criticism has included coproducing the television documentary "Future Wave: Japan Design," and co-authoring and designing the book *Cranbrook Design: The New Discourse,* published by Rizzoli International.

How has your professional life changed since leaving Cranbrook?

The twenty-three years at Cranbrook had made it so thoroughly familiar that I was very ready for change. And I do enjoy change. Perhaps that was one of the main reasons for leaving. Although the Cranbrook structure of autonomous departments allows great flexibility, we had pretty nearly explored the possibilities of change for us within that setting. I miss the collegiality of many of the Cranbook faculty and staff, but as magical as the Cranbrook architectural setting is, I do not miss the place. Probably the fact that I grew up five minutes from Cranbrook is pertinent. Our final departure from Cranbrook was on Independence Day in my fiftieth year.

How does the IIT experience differ?

At IIT's Institute of Design I have the benefit of so many resources from my colleagues in communications design and the rest of the faculty. The program is a mixed soup of influences, theories, and methods, combining design with cultural anthropology, sociology, computer science, and strategic planning in an approach we call human-centered design. I am always discovering great articles and handouts used by my fellow faculty for their IIT classes, a virtual banquet of ideas to feast on. In our end-of-semester faculty wrap-ups, each of us summarizes courses taught and shares class materials. We all agree we would like to take each other's courses if we could only find the time. And I am thoroughly enjoying the shift to an urban university, the city of Chicago, and a different set of theoretical design concerns.

How has your teaching changed?

For the more structured communications theory courses at IIT, I have put together a body of lectures, slides, handouts, and projects that formalize a lot of the studio experimentation we were doing at Cranbrook. In addition to each fall's teaching at IIT, my husband and partner Mike and I are embarking on High Ground, a seminar center based at our Colorado studio. During the seven months each year that we spend in Colorado, we plan to offer several workshops annually in graphic design and industrial design for professional designers who might not have the opportunity to pursue graduate school yet are interested in adding to their design resources. We envision workshops lasting ten days, with one or two guest faculty joining us for short intense projects with small groups of design participants. Our studio seems to be a natural gathering point; last July, twelve designers, architects, and design critics joined us in Colorado for three days of nonstop discussions on each person's view of the emerging issues facing design. We taped these, and an edited version will be published as an issue of the *Journal of the American Center for Design*. In the coming months I will be putting together our HighGroundDesign Web site that will draw on my interests in editing/writing, design, and teaching.

How do you feel about theory-based design education now? If you had to do Cranbrook all over again, would you change anything?

That could be as presumptuous as changing the course of the Mississippi. I probably couldn't have, even if I had tried. My role was to attract and choose the right students, to set the stage with some guiding structure and lots of resources, to insist on integrity and rigor, and then to stand back out of the stampede! Actually, IIT's program is even more theoretical than Cranbrook's, like jumping out of the frying pan into the fire. Because of IIT's emphasis on understanding our users and audiences, the theories we were investigating at Cranbrook are very applicable—literary criticism, semiotics, and poststructuralism explore how audiences construct meaning out of messages and the process of interpretation. So I have included a lot of these in the courses on communications theories I have been teaching. I am very excited about these courses and have been looking more deeply into rhetoric and narrative as well. It is so important for designers to have these resources to structure their design processes, both as synthetic methods and tools to explain the successful dynamics in design work we intuitively know is strong. They also help us communicate our design concepts to clients.

Cranbrook was a hothouse for a great many ideas, especially midway through your own tenure, with the introduction of "theory" and the adoption of ideas from French linguistic theory. Do you feel that this was an important evolutionary step in the practice of design that made a formative impact on current practice? Or was it a flash in the pan?

French literary theory (also referred to as poststructuralism, deconstruction, and criticism) is an important resource for communications designers, as are many other theories including semiotics (which preceded it), which design schools are just beginning to utilize to structure the communications design process. Graphic design is still a young discipline and has had very little theory until recently. The Big Idea approach of the New York School of the sixties is about all that we had, and that stressed personal intuition and cleverness rather than a codified method. But that raises a curious point. I have to say, current work in the magazines and most competitions do not hold my attention these days. Instead, I find I am looking at the best of advertising design from the past forty years more and more, especially as examples of these language theories I have been teaching. Although Doyle Dane Bernbach's VW ads were conceived intuitively—I am guessing their creative department had little knowledge of semiotics, poststructuralism, or rhetoric—these ads are eloquent demonstrations of communication theories. Or rather, I should say that these theories explain what is so successful about that classic work.

Cranbrook was an open situation, now you are teaching in a more conventional—I suspect syllabus-driven—program. Is there an advantage to the way you are teaching now as opposed to the less proscribed hothouse method of your past?

I am a terrible pluralist, unable to choose between opposites. I want to do it all, have my cake and eat it, too. I refuse to see that design (or life) must be all this way or all that way. (Why do so many in design feel that to validate their vision, they must discredit all others?) It is a broad discipline with many varieties of practice; shouldn't it also have a vigorous breadth of theories and methods, philosophies, practice, and personalities? I find IIT's more academic environment of courses and classes a stimulating complement to the unstructured studios at Cranbrook (although IIT's courses have only skeletal outlines and rely on the special vision of each faculty member to supply the content, allowing a lot of opportunity for exploration). But as different as the two schools are, I think of them as connected on a continuum. At Cranbrook, we inserted theory into studio experimentation. At IIT, projects are referred to as demos, opportunities to demonstrate the application of the academic courses' theories and methods. Aren't these two sides of a coin? A mature discipline has a range of approaches and specializations; it is appropriate that there should be a range of design schools so that students can carefully choose the design education most suited to their own interests, abilities, and goals.

How do you see design education changing?

We will see the duration of a design education extended, with perhaps five years the norm expected for informed practice, especially true in light of the wide range of theory and skills required in interactive digital media, a far more conceptually and technically complex field than traditional print graphic design. Graduate study has become a widely accepted route to career progress, and I would not be surprised to see undergraduate predesign liberal arts and sciences programs develop for students planning on graduate study at the outset of college. IIT's Institute of Design recently established the country's first Ph.D. program, and we look forward to other schools joining in the codification of a body of design knowledge—then graphic design will finally become a true profession.

I perceive a kind of retrenchment. Veteran designers are fine-tuning their skills and craft. The era of busting boundaries is over. The so-called new wave is much more codified. Are your students more or less apt to lock into the fashions and trends that marked the past decade?

Right now graphic design is in a tremendously fertile and exciting period, nothing less than a revolution brought about by new technologies. But this is not the graphic design we see in most of the magazines and competitions. The motion, sound, and interactivity of multimedia open up vast new challenges for designers. Those veteran designers that lament the plateauing of design must have their eyes closed! IIT is very involved in interaction design and the theoretical underpinnings necessary to make meaningful and useful experiences for our audiences in virtual information/communication spaces. Interactivity in design is waiting for a grammar to be written in the way film was seventy years ago when Sergei Eisenstein wrote the book on film theory. This involves a wide range of exploration, from information systems to expressive electronic environments. I find the ideas of interactivity very useful for generating more compelling conventional print design—after all, the typical newsmagazine is fairly nonlinear and interactive, and these ideas have a lot more room for exploration. I am also very interested in the continuities between electronic and print media. Many communications programs use several media, and each medium offers unique opportunities to translate different aspects of a message.

How do the experiments that took place at Cranbrook influence this?

Many of the past experiments at Cranbrook are finding a natural extension into the realm of electronic space, and the current work in Cranbrook studios is energetically exploring forms for these new media.

What do you see as your new role as teacher and mentor?

My current enthusiasms come under the heading of audience-oriented design. These include rhetoric and narrative as means for delivering rich and compelling messages. Storytelling is especially important in connecting threads in virtual message spaces. I am fascinated by the interaction between information and persuasion, and the role each plays in delivering resonant communications. I am anxious to explore eccentric design languages tailored appropriately for subcultures and specific interpretive communities, drawing on IIT research methods from cultural anthropology. I am continuing to formulate project assignments as laboratory experiments in which to explore current issues. A gratifying thing about IIT students is that they tend to follow directions. Those ornery Cranbrook students hardly ever would follow a project brief! Because the Cranbrook digressions often brought terrific results, I rarely tried to reign them in. But now it is a pleasure to choose an area of investigation for a class and have the students pursue it rigorously.

Would you, looking back, describe the best and worst achievements of your time as an educator?

An educator's measure of success must ultimately be her graduates. I find enormous gratification in my students' career progress and achievements. But maybe that is too much like parents living through their children? So, to round out things, it is important to also engage in some writing and lecturing and, of course, designing.

Johanna Drucker on Design Theory

Johanna Drucker was associate professor in the art history department at Yale University, where she taught contemporary art theory. She is currently chairing a graduate program at SUNY/Purchase devoted to the theory of art and design. Her publications include *The Alphabetic Labyrinth* (Thames and Hudson, 1995) and *The Visible Word* (University of Chicago Press, 1994). She is also well known for her typographically experimental artists' books.

Why is theory useful in the teaching and practice of art and design?

It is a metalanguage. It lets you see that there are ways to talk about things at a level that articulates the ways in which meaning is produced, not just *what* meaning is produced. Here is a simple example. In a nontheoretical reading, you understand that the meaning of the stop sign is an imperative command that you, as a socialized human, obey. In a theoretical reading, you would describe the relation between "material codes of production" (the shape of the sign, color, conventions, placement, size, et cetera) and the "production of meaning in a social system." Having distinguished these two things— material codes and production of meaning—you could begin a critical analysis of the variety of relations between these two aspects of any sign in different historical or cultural circumstances.

Let me take a reactionary approach. Theory also establishes a vocabulary that tends to be exclusionary; it is a foreign, even nonsensical, language.

Those things are true, but you have to realize that the language of theory is not the same as the content of theory. When people first learn theory, they get confused as to whether they're learning a language or a set of ideas. Within the academy, the use of esoteric theoretical language is rewarded with prestigious positions at prestigious institutions. I think it's best to speak theory in the vernacular—to just use ordinary language to talk about things that theory gives you access to.

Why retain any terms from the language of theory, then?

There are certain terms that come out of theory-speak, such as "subject" and "subjectivity," that are useful. Nothing else serves as a good shorthand for those concepts. You could talk about them, but it would require more explanation. I remember the first time I read a book by Derrida, I just wanted to throw it across the room. I thought, Why is this guy bothering to do this? And then you make your way through it.

It is like reading a novel in a foreign language. It takes months to get through a book that would ordinarily take a week.

But after a couple of years, you can read those novels in a week. And the same thing happens with theory language. You get good at it. But I think the challenge at this stage is to translate theory for a wider audience.

Can you give an example?

If you're trying to raise the consciousness of young women, for instance, you might talk about things like beauty contests or the sex industry. You could ask: What is excluded by the fact that beauty is so highly valued in our culture? And likewise, questioning the sex industry: Who's really making money off it, and how does that system work? Why is it that sex-industry jobs are the one type of work available to women in our culture where they can make quick, easy money? What does that say about this culture?

Does graphic design require a theoretical foundation?

On one level, absolutely not. I don't think theory is ever going to make somebody better at creating a printed page, a Web page, an object, or anything else. Now, I know there are a lot of people who disagree with me, who think theory is a useful creative tool. I don't believe that. People who work from a theoretical perspective, whether it's in design or the visual arts, often do very stilted, self-conscious work that ultimately is only an illustration of the theoretical position.

But should there be something working in design in addition to pure talent or intuition?

I don't think that design needs theory, but I think designers need theory. Everybody should have a course in Ideology 101, beginning in kindergarten, then in sixth grade, then again in high school, and as a freshman in college—because I think we are so blind to ways in which we absorb the culture around us. We need to be given the tools for thinking through our relationship to the power structure—something for all those people who went to see *Forrest Gump,* didn't know that it was a modern version of Leni Riefenstahl's *Triumph of the Will,* and thought, "Wow, what a great movie."

On the other hand, what can the visual arts or design offer to theory, and how can there be theory that's specific to the visual world, that isn't merely borrowed from theories in other, nonvisual fields?

There are many aspects to visual experience that have no parallels within the linguistic sphere, for example, focus. How does focus work? What is the degree of resolution in relationship to focus in a visual work? How does it communicate to us, and how does it help to produce meaning in a particular image and a particular circumstance? Questions like these could be explored in theoretical terms that would grant the visual realm its own specificity. Language is the tool we use to analyze it, but there is no linguistic analogue. We would not be borrowing a concept such as discourse versus narrative, first person versus second person—any of those models.

What do you propose?

You'd probably go to cognitive science, perhaps the work of J. J. Gibson, *Visual Perception and the World,* or to Rudolf Arnheim's Gestalt psychology or to writers like William Mitchell and W. J .T. Mitchell—even to the history of style. If you were talking about advertisements, you'd address body language, body posture, body style, not to mention hairstyle and grooming.

Despite theory, designers continually run up against what marketers believe is necessary to identify and attract consumers—market research, which is more practical than theoretical. And this is where I have a problem with theory being applied to design. At some point it seems totally removed from the object and ignores an important part of the significance of that object, which is its appeal.

Some things theory can't explain at all. It can be a useful prescriptive tool for analyzing structures, relations, the historical specificity of situations. But there is an analogy to those mass-produced china dolls with faces painted on in about half a second. Those faces are a little cockeyed here, a little bit crooked there. It's a grimace, it's a smile—and yet, when you describe the dolls in theoretical, structural terms, they are all the same thing. If you're standing there as a little child picking one out, you want to pick out one that has the expression that you like. I don't think there is any theoretical model sufficiently sophisticated to explain why you'd pick that specific one.

Why do you think that some designers want to embrace these critical models?

Part of it is the inevitable colonization of every area of inquiry by theory, once theory upped the ante of academic and critical discussion—if you can't "do theory" in your particular domain, then that domain is not going to have the same clout as those employing theory. There's been an increasing trend toward giving the history and theory of design a place within the academy. And why shouldn't this be done? Design is as interesting and legitimate a historical discourse as any, and the amount of information we get through the culture industry and commercial sources is much greater than what we get through fine art sources.

Can theory be pushed too far?

Sometimes its application to commercial products gets very parodic. I had a terrific student who wanted to do an analysis of cereal boxes in terms of psychoanalytical structures of desire. The spoon represented the phallus and the milk was the mother. . . . Come on—it's a cereal box! What else would you show, a knife and fork? I couldn't go for it because it wouldn't tell you anything about the cereal box that you don't already know, and if theory doesn't tell you something you don't already know, then why do you need it?

Can theory tell us anything about graphic design that we don't already know?

Theory is useful for analyzing historical and cultural codes, but also for tackling new design challenges. You may be familiar with a particular phenomenon, say, Hollywood cinema, but not be able to articulate the way it works as a narrative system. When you gain an insight into the formulas of such a system, you realize they mutate in relation to different expectations about morality, and that's what I call a "theory moment." You are able to identify the working of the codes (unfaithful wife must lose family versus unfaithful wife is allowed a second chance). Or you learn the distinction between discourse (which is the structural organization of a text, such as the distinction between an author and narrator) and narrative (the actual story). When you watch an episode of the television series *My So-Called Life,* you realize that the author of the show is giving you one side of the story while the young woman narrating the episode in first person is telling you another. These simple distinctions are powerful in talking about the structure of news, fiction, documentaries, and any other instance in which we tend to align whoever is speaking with what is being said.

But how does this work with graphic design?

These distinctions become increasingly important as designers tackle the difficult task of figuring out the presentation of complex information and databases. The structure of presentation or display, like the layout of a traditional print media newspaper or reference book, already encodes levels of hierarchy and importance into the work at the level of discourse (the material structure of the piece). But in a mobile, fluid, information environment, such hierarchies may be unsuitable or distorting, since the information may have a different value in any of a number of presentations. Structure and information (discourse and reference) are not the same: a company's employees are not the same as a company's operational structure. Imagine a phone book for an organization that is organized spatially according to rank and position rather than alphabetically, but which could be rearranged to display decision-making trees relevant to specific tasks or projects within the organization—and you have an idea of the ways structure and information begin to relate. The implications for understanding the way that structure is a part of information will become even more crucial as designers work in database navigation and organization, where relations between discourse (apparent structure) and reference (intended meaning) will be mutable. As structure and information interpenetrate, the designer's task requires more rigorous theoretical skills.

Can theory have an adverse effect on graphic design?

I think too much theory can make you too sophisticated for your market. You can start to produce graphic design that's interesting only to other designers. I saw that happen while teaching in an architecture department. Theory-doused architects designed some interesting things, but they had nothing to do with living. They might be compelling ideas, but when it really came down to it, I didn't want to live in an uncomfortable environment in order to have my consciousness raised about how family structures are merely functions of the bourgeois mythology of the nation-state!

One of the current design tropes is multilayer design, which often verges on illegibility. Is this a visual manifestation of theory?

Somebody asked me this question in another interview and I was puzzled by it, and so I asked Sheila Levrant de Bretteville, the head of Yale University's undergraduate design department, what she thinks. Does it have to do with a phenomenon of the illegible as a cultural notion, or what was this about? She said that, in her experience, students will do that kind of design when they're working with somebody else's text. When it's their own text, they won't make it illegible; they actually want it to be easy to read. The illegibility trope seems to signal, There's so much stuff already out in the world that we're not really trying to get you to read this; we're just trying to get you to look at it long enough to see whatever logo is on it. This is an admission that most text produced at this point is just noise.

How would you analyze it?

As frustration on the part of the individual: Will anybody pay attention to anything I have to say? And then: Well, why should they? The culture we live in promotes a notion of the celebrity as the privileged object of attention, and people often think that if they're not being perceived at a celebrity level, then they're not being perceived at all. Since when has existence been about being perceived? It's supposed to be about experience.

Who or what do you think exemplifies this noise factor?

David Carson's work seems like visual noise and style for its own sake, part of this celebrity phenomenon. You do something that's at the radical extreme of what people think is acceptable to produce yourself as a celebrity. Reasonableness, middle-of-the-road positions, and moderate analysis are never going to sell.

Will there be anything for critical theorists to dissect in years hence?

Graphic design is absolutely ripe for symptomatic analysis. You have to look at two aspects. First, what is the internal discourse of design, and what are the narratives that it tells itself about what it's doing? And also, what is the external discourse within which it functions so that it represents certain things? Discourse is like the individual. It tells itself certain stories, and it believes them, and they are true. But if you step outside of it, you think, How in the world are they telling themselves that? And why?

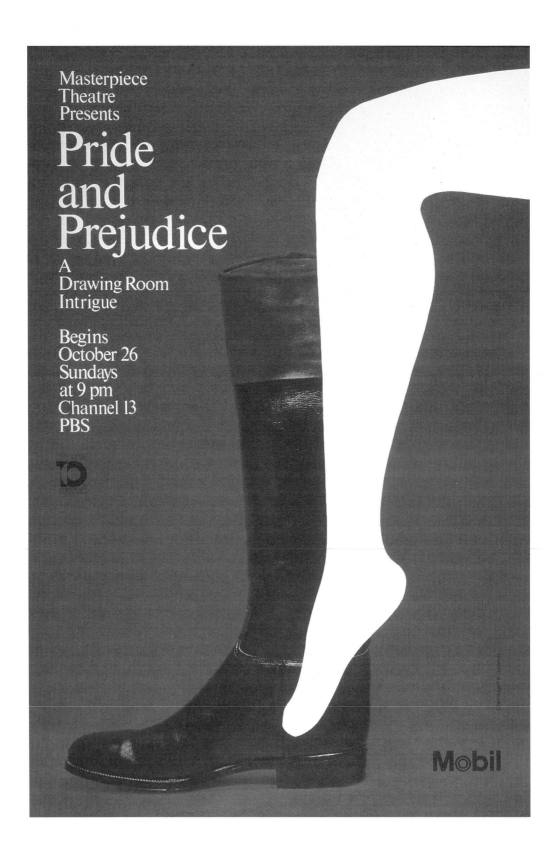

Masterpiece
Theatre
Presents

Pride
and
Prejudice

A
Drawing Room
Intrigue

Begins
October 26
Sundays
at 9 pm
Channel 13
PBS

Mobil

Ivan Chermayeff on Modernism Past and Present

After attending Harvard University and the Illinois Institute of Technology, Ivan Chermayeff received a B.F.A. from Yale. With Thomas Geismar and Robert Brownjohn he founded Brownjohn Chermayeff Geismar, an early exponent of "late modern" American graphic design. In 1960, the firm became Chermayeff & Geismar and designed identities for scores of American corporations, including the groundbreaking abstract mark for the Chase Manhattan Bank. He has also developed the design schemes for many exhibitions including the immigration museum on Ellis Island. Chermayeff's fine art has been collected in a monograph, *Ivan Chermayeff Collages,* and his books for children include *First Words* and *First Shapes.* His work is in the collection of the Museum of Modern Art, New York.

Why did you become a graphic designer?

I was brought up in an environment in which all the arts were very present: architecture, painting, sculpture, and creative writing. My father was a modern architect, and other modern designers were his friends. They were the people who influenced me. However, I quickly came to the conclusion that in architecture there is too much waiting and limited success. You have to get involved with many other people—boards of directors, committees—and an awful lot doesn't come to fruition. The best part of architecture seems be in the first hour or two, and from then on, it is trying to keep the project alive.

With graphic design, I accomplish 95 percent of what I do, and there is a lot of it. It may have a short life because it is conceived, printed, and thrown away, but there is a great deal of variety—and a great deal of success. That, psychologically, is a much better existence, as far as I am concerned. Also, you are constantly learning from your clients—it is a free education to be a designer; instead of paying tuition, you are actually being paid to learn.

Your father was a modern, and you took the teachings of modernism into yourself. What did modernism mean to you when you were starting out, and what does it mean today?

It meant more at the time because the process of thinking about modern design in relation to other professions such as architecture, landscaping, photography, or any of the arts that grew out of the modern tradition of Europe—instilled with logic and cleanliness and removal of chaos and making order out of things—was really more prevalent than it is today. Everything is permissible now, including all kinds of stuff that I consider highly questionable. In the beginning it was hard to get anybody to do modern design. If you were allowed to, it was usually because the clients who understood it wanted to be part of the cutting edge. But back then it was just harder to find clients. Now it is easy to find clients and they will accept anything, and there are more people competing with you. So, modernism is not quite what it was, but it is still a tradition that I am certainly a part of.

Is design a force that can help shape the world as a better place?

Yes, but I don't think it is as important as a lot of other activities. It is not surgery, for example, but it is vitally important to the shaping of our cities and our environment and in helping people understand all kinds of causes and needs. You could say it is a helping force, not an initiating force.

How does the utopian view of design as curative for social ills mesh with the realities of the commercial world?

I don't know what utopian views of design really are. I don't think that it means very much if it isn't understood and acted upon. Design is about solving the problem; if nobody is listening, you have not solved it. And if that is the case, it means you are above or below your audience and your purpose; therefore, it is a bad design. When we talk about design, we are talking about good design, it meshes when it is thought through within the realities of the world that we are in, whatever that may be. It is not just about commerce, it is about the society that we live in. There is a big difference between design in the Third World, for example, and design in sophisticated nations within Europe or the United States or in Japan.

As a designer, you focus on graphics but base your practice on a wide range of design. Can graphic design alone be a social force?

No, I don't think graphic design alone can be very much of anything, yet it is not devoid of being part of society, which is different somehow from being a social force. But design is not just graphics in any case. Exhibitions, which I spend a lot of time on, can reach a lot of people. Chermayeff & Geismar is designing an exhibition now in Singapore, on the history of Singapore, that in five weeks is going to be seen by at least 500,000 people. Because it is reaching an awful lot of people, it has force and it is graphic design and language and all of these things brought together, which make exhibits a form of communicating. I prefer to think of it as communications design. It is hard to distinguish between graphic design and other forms of design now. There are a lot of gray areas.

How do you relate to that part of the so-called postmodern thought that is a reaction against modernism as trite and archaic?

I don't relate to that postmodern thought at all. I think postmodernism, as we know it, is dead. It came, rose, went, and did not mean anything. In architecture it is completely past. Nothing ever goes away entirely, but the reaction against modernism was, I think, not a reaction to modernism as being trite and archaic so much as its being limiting, cold, and undecorative. Modernism changes in any case, and it always has, since the minds that have been involved in it have evolved.

Do you see a resurgence of modern thinking in design, other than a nostalgic conceit, that is?

I don't think it has gone away, and there is still a lot to be said for it. The question makes "modern" sound as though it is style—it is not; it is process. Thinking in terms of problem solving is never going to go away; that is what modern thinking in design is all about. That cannot go away, and trying to make it go away by a sort of revisionist looking back and picking up the styles of the past, whatever the trend of the minute may be—art nouveau or cubist—is also of the past. That kind of style-playing was never very interesting in the first place. It is looking backward and not looking forward.

Graphic design requires reaching to its highest levels. Right now there are an awful lot of people who do what they are doing with computers, layering different images. It does not matter if it is a pair of shoes, a car, or AIDS, it is always the same solution; it just happens to have different language attached to it. Getting away from the techniques that are available and getting back to thinking in ideas takes awhile, and I do not think that we are going back to where design is fully understood at all levels very quickly. But I have no doubt that it will happen. What form that will take exactly, I haven't the ability to see that far ahead because we are looking at ten or fifteen years.

After so many years, how do you continue to be fresh in your work?

In order to be fresh you have to understand what it is you are working on and be very critical. Only through self-criticism can you be open to new approaches and new attitudes. I think that is the most important thing you can do—not to follow, but to lead and think everything through that you are doing as best you can without inhibitions and without falling back on your old tricks. It is a different thing for every person, too; there is no single way to do it.

The Imaginary Life of Claude Monet

Milton Glaser on Professionalism, Education, Celebrity, and Criticism

Milton Glaser attended the High School of Music and Art and Cooper Union in New York City, and won a Fulbright scholarship to study at the Academy of Fine Arts in Bologna, Italy. In 1955 he founded Push Pin Studios with Seymour Chwast, Edward Sorel, and Reynold Ruffins and remained its coprincipal until the mid-1970s, when he started Milton Glaser Inc. He is a graphic designer, illustrator, typographer, art director, and educator. He helped found *New York* magazine and served as its "Underground Gourmet" restaurant critic. Over his long career he has developed exhibitions, public environments, packaging, retail stores, and restaurants. His classes and workshops at the School of Visual Arts are a magnet for students who want to expand the boundaries of the design profession. His books include *Milton Glaser Graphic Design, The Milton Glaser Poster Book, I Manifesti di*, and *Milton Glaser/Piero della Francesca*.

How has the design field changed since you entered it over forty years ago?

The most important change is the acceptance of the fact that design is an absolutely essential part of the process of business and, consequently, that it is too important to leave in the hands of designers.

Do you mean that designers have reverted back to service personnel?

How to communicate is determined within organizations significantly more than it was when I entered the field. The design process has now been integrated into a client's control system so that instead of going outside for people who had more understanding about how to communicate effectively, they now make their determinations from a marketing point of view and then, more often than not, go outside to implement those ideas.

I don't quite understand. Hasn't this always been true? Clients made determinations and then hired designers to solve their problems. The only difference, it seems to me, is that when you entered in the mid-fifties, the profession was smaller.

Smaller and more amateurish.

Do you mean that the client now has a greater preconception of what is wanted?

Much. The briefings are very different now. The determinations of what's appropriate are very often those of a marketing department, as opposed to the somewhat casual and random solutions that occurred when people didn't know better.

So, are you saying that before design became as sophisticated as it is today, the designer had more license to play and experiment?

In a way. An intense professionalization has occurred, and a hardening of the authority between the client and designer. In the old days, clients would go to somebody like Paul Rand with the hope that he would invent the form that would communicate what they were not imaginative enough to communicate. Today, they go to a designer and say, "These are our objectives, this is the vernacular we hope to use, these are the key elements to be expressed," and so on.

Do you think this newfound literacy is a result of there being too much professional design?

Well, part of it comes from the professionalization of the practice and the fact that there are more people who are more experienced at doing this than ever before. A consequence of this professionalization is that accidents don't happen as much, and there is more conformity based on previous success. Accidents are often the opportunity that people have for expressing ideas and personal vision.

But doesn't this contribute to an underground that subverts convention or, at the very least, finds alternative ways of expression through design?

Sure. But it's very important when you talk about design to realize that it is so highly segmented today in terms of objectives and activities that there's no general definition that applies to the whole field. Those who are outside the commercial system—who don't have a practice that helps people sell goods, and who use design as a kind of theoretical enterprise (much in the way that painting traditionally explored the possibility for communication and ideas)—are on a different track. Design can certainly be subversive when its subtext is to undermine the assumptions of a political or social system, not to mention an artistic one. Frankly, I am nervous about all ideologies, whether it's the ideology of business or the ideology of bolshevism. I get nervous in the presence of absolute certainty.

You have admitted that your impetus for becoming a designer was, among other reasons, to bust the Swiss canon that was dominant in the fifties. Wasn't that ideologically subversive?

Every emerging generation has to find something to fight against—to energize themselves. You have to struggle against a resistant canon in order to move toward something that's your own. I understood that the idea of modernism and the Swiss school formed a great theory, but I also understood that I couldn't adapt to it or do it as well as the practitioners who had already mastered it; so I knew that I had to go elsewhere. And very often, when you go elsewhere, what you end up doing is challenging the larger idea. A single way of doing things seemed too doctrinaire, too limiting, when there was so much beauty, so much excitement, so much potential in what the world had already offered. So, curiously, Push Pin Studios' posthistorical efforts were to find out what it was in history that was as interesting as modernism.

Was that a conscious decision?

Part of it was a sense that modernism was used up. As the Chinese say, "Everything at its fullness is already in decline." We were looking at stuff that we had seen for many years, and it wasn't going anywhere; it was not improving on the original model. It seemed to have limited people enormously in terms of their options. It's not that you couldn't do beautiful work within the tradition—and people still do—it was just that in terms of its expressive potential, it seemed to me it had reached its fullness.

Please contrast what you set out to do back then with the rebellion that has occurred in design over the past decade.

It's different in one respect: my great models for what to do were largely historical. For example, I felt that art nouveau was a profound movement that had an extraordinary reservoir of ideas contained within it, which I could still use. I looked at Charles Rennie Mackintosh, for example, and realized how compelling his ideas were and how he helped set the stage for the Bauhaus. In other words, why use the Bauhaus as your only model, as the modernists did, when you can see the arts and crafts movement, and Mackintosh, John Ruskin, William Morris, Frank Lloyd Wright, the Viennese Secession, as well as the Bauhaus as a continuing series of linked ideas?

I presume that you do not believe that the current generation understands the historical continuum?

It seems to me that the new intent is not to follow the historical models and understand that this continuity is the essential idea that pervades human history and enriches it, but rather to say, "There's nothing there," and to try to invent something from scratch.

I want to understand what you mean by ignoring history. For example, David Carson, through _Beach Culture_ and _Ray Gun,_ is indicative of one aspect of the experimental phase of contemporary work. He appears to be pushing the envelope, rather than simply ignoring history. Do you think this work lacks a historical framework or understanding?

No, I wouldn't say that. In trying to broaden the role of typography, these experiments are ultimately beneficial—although a knowledge of dada and Russian constructivist typography would enrich the inquiry. To some extent it represents the same kind of response to a rigid system that serves to energize people by searching for alternatives. On the other hand, it seems to me that if you are going to be a revolutionary, it's best to be an informed one.

Is historical ignorance really detrimental? Don't we make our own historical context?

When I was going to school, abstract expressionism was in its ascendancy, and most of the students began painting like abstract expressionists. One of the great attractive qualities of avant-garde work is that you put yourself in a position where you can't be easily criticized because one can always say that the critics don't understand the new value system. One of the great attractions of doing abstract expressionism for a lot of ordinary kids was that they could not be judged.

And the consequences of that?

The consequences were very sad because once abstract expressionism had passed, the adherents were thrown back on their resources, and those who were not trained had nowhere to go. I think that analogy may hold up today: the attractiveness of working in the manner of today's expressionistic nihilism is that it looks cool and explores new territory. The bad part is that its surface qualities can easily be mastered without discipline or understanding. It celebrates the decorative and the expressive at the expense of other things.

What are those other things?

Structure, clarity of intent, form, history—all the things one traditionally needed to make judgments. Design is about making judgments. The question is, How do you train people to be able to judge what is good, what is bad, what is meaningful, what is fraudulent, if they don't have the understanding of what those ideas have meant historically?

How did you learn?

Hard to say exactly—certainly partially by studying history, living in Italy, learning how to draw academically, staying curious. I also was fortunate in that my practice has been a broad one. But it hasn't been about "effects," and it wasn't primarily about how things looked when you subjected them to the astonishing capacity of a computer and so on.

How do you feel teaching has changed since you began?

Many design teachers don't seem to understand the degree to which the nature of the audience is really the preeminent influence on design. The focus in art school is often on me me me and "my" expression and "my" vision and "my" career and "my" name-it, linked to the delusion that if you reveal your soul, people will be willing to spend money for it.

How do you teach?

Well, I try to be very specific and propose that every problem starts with the same questions: Who am I talking to? Who are these people? What do they know? What are their prejudices? What are their expectations? et cetera. The three cardinal factors of design are the following: Who is the audience? What do you want to say to them? How do you say it effectively? If you don't follow this sequence, you're always going to make some terrible mistake.

Then, where does the personal expression fit?

It fits in the cracks—because the drive to express things personally is so profound that no matter how objective the rules, good people want to make it their own! But given the two choices, making it your own and not communicating versus communicating and not making it your own, there seems to be very little question about which is the more appropriate role for a designer.

Have your students changed considerably over the past ten or fifteen years?

I generally get people who choose to study with me, which suggests that there is something in my work that they already value. So it's a little difficult for me to say that my students are different. They are different in the sense that most of them literally can't work without a computer.

Are you tolerant?

They can work any way they want, as long as they are thinking straight. Personally, I find it regrettable that people no longer have the skill to address even a simple problem without the computer. There is no way of preventing its use at this point, since even the most rudimentary drawing skill seems to have vanished. Drawing skills are not about becoming an illustrator. The most fundamental way of understanding the visual world is through the act of drawing. When you are about to draw something, you become attentive to its appearance (and sometimes humble before it) for the first time. I know of no better way of preparing yourself for a career in the visual arts. That said, I can't imagine why it has virtually disappeared in the education of young designers except for the fact that it requires consistent devotion and practice. As you know, the Italian word for design and drawing is the same, *disegno*—as usual, the Italians know something about the subject.

Do you think that reliance on the computer has somehow impaired the thought process?

Nobody clearly understands how the use of the computer changes the nature of the way you think. I believe that it does. One way it does that most profoundly is that it gets you much more interested in "effects" than in content.

Given that design schools have so much to teach in a short time, how does one avoid the quick and easy answers?

The question is, What should people be teaching at school, and what is the basis for visual understanding? My conviction is that if you don't have the bedrock of understanding, you will become a victim of style.

The paradox is that this field feeds on style. And clients are coming to the designer looking for style. It's a vicious circle.

In personal terms, the question becomes, Should you follow each passing style to stay hip and on the cutting edge, even when you recognize that the style of the moment is transitory and trivial? I suppose this question is no different from how you choose to dress at a particular moment in time. One of the social roles of fashion is to define generational difference. I assume the same rule applies to the world of design. I would be embarrassed to imitate the work that is fashionable now for the same reason that I will not wear my old bell-bottoms when the style returns. The most style-conscious designers inevitably find themselves in a dilemma when the style that made them famous is no longer of the moment and begins to recede. The larger question might be, How can you retain your interest in doing what you're doing for a lifetime? How do you stay in this field without becoming a service provider?

So, how do you do that?

That's the struggle that every old professional has had to deal with. I've had a long career. And the pull has always been the same: How do you stay relevant in this field if the assumptions change?

Well, can you answer the question?

I tried to broaden my understanding so that I could do more than one thing, as well as develop new ways of working that didn't resemble the work I became noted for in the sixties and seventies. The moldy smell of a previous decade can destroy you.

Let me ask you, then, about Starbucks, the immensely successful national chain of American coffeehouses. Consistent with its retro-based corporate identity, the company hired you and Victor Moscoso, among others, for your historical or nostalgic style. So, do you reject the offer because it makes you into an oldie but goodie, or do you accept it because it's a good-paying job?

That's a good question. When Starbucks gave me the job, I had to consciously try to replicate an old style of mine. It was hard for me to do it. I couldn't do it very well in every case. But in this case, doing a self-parody seemed okay. I've been doing very different work in recent years, and people who know anything about my work could recognize the distinction between something I might do today and a work of self-parody.

Well, the cognoscenti would know. But on the other hand, Starbucks is this huge new phenomenon, building its identity on a certain kind of retro sensibility, and is appealing to an audience that does not know you and that your work is self-parody.

For this time it doesn't matter. I didn't think that would have much meaning to either the cognoscenti or the people in the street. I don't approach any of these jobs indifferently, but my work has gone in another direction. I think the poster I did for the "Art Is" campaign for the fiftieth anniversary of the School of Visual Arts is much more representative of what I'm doing currently, and I don't think there is any relationship to my identification as a sixties icon.

People know Milton Glaser, the sixties and seventies image-maker. How do you sell clients on who you are today?

I have a funny and varied collection of clients. I have an entirely different reputation as an editorial designer, for instance, with my business with Walter Bernard (WBMG), I have a lot of experience designing magazines, which is not linked to my personality in the sixties at all because, in a sense, my hand is not involved at all, only my brain is.

Is it correct to say that you can be more anonymous as a magazine designer?

I think so. An ongoing professional problem is that exposure produces boredom. If your career is based on celebrity, you have to be careful.

Speaking of celebrity, you certainly had it with Push Pin Studios. Why did you leave?

I left Push Pin because it had become too celebrated, people knew too much about it, and there was too much expectation built into that identification. I wanted to try to do something else that had no relationship to history.

You confided a few years ago that your business was leveling out. Did you have a sense that the time was over?

Certainly the time that I was hot was over. Actually, some years ago at the AIGA "Dangerous Ideas" conference in San Antonio, when I looked out over the audience, mostly people between thirty and forty, I realized that I had become marginal to the field.

But what does marginal mean? You create beautiful work, you understand the forms, you're intelligent about the profession. . . .

The field has moved in other places. For instance, the field became obsessed about business practices; the focus of the field seemed to be entirely about insurance, contracts, documentation, maintaining business control, dah-da-dah-da. That was never at the center of my interests. I am not speaking critically about this change; it has real reasons to occur. The fact is, I never ran a business in my own mind, I just put people together to help me do things.

Like an atelier?

Yes, an atelier. It was very important for me to have that model. The idea of business as such was something I dreaded. When we started Push Pin, it was a bunch of guys getting together and doing good things. And I must say, for a long time that really was the spirit of the place; the first ten or fifteen years we were running it like a bunch of art students trying to change history.

What is valuable in current design?

The very things that you think are terrible are very often linked to what is valuable. The enlargement of possibilities that exists in terms of extending expressive possibilities in typography through the use of the computer is one current example. The fact that the computer offers ways of seeing that are different and challenging is the best part of what has happened. At the same time, these powerful technologies have the capacity to be enormously valuable or enormously damaging. I suppose what worries me is that I can't see the underlying value system that informs the work around us.

In what sense?

I don't understand the way the system works now, between the critics, the magazines, the juries, the professional organizations, and so on.

The design magazines have become more critical; they're not just showcases. There has been more debate.

Well, I don't think it's so much debate as there's been argument, which is a little different. I'm not sure whether they're about professional practice as much as they are about egocentricity or self-promotion. There are a handful of critics who are now dominating the discourse and they are linked by an amazingly similar ideology.

What implications does that have for the field?

It narrows the field of vision. I think that there are more issues in design than expressive typography, for instance. For some reason, the big hot issue in design has become typographical manipulation as well as the question of whether it's readable or not—not exactly the most informed issues that criticism might deal with.

For years there was the call for a critical voice. Now that we've got it, is there a way of doing it better?

More generosity on everybody's part. There's nothing wrong with a critical dimension in our field, but it has taken a peculiar and polarizing direction that doesn't serve the profession very well. I think the role of design is so all-enveloping that it's hard to separate its characteristics critically. Is design a job that gives many people basic employment providing a utilitarian product? Is it a craft requiring measurably objective skills that should be maintained? Is it an art that can serve as a potent means of self-expression? Is it a profession whose members can influence the health and well-being of the general public? Is it a discipline that involves a philosophical inquiry into the nature of truth, beauty, and reality? Is it an instrument for social change or manipulation? If the answer is "all of the above," then I guess I'm looking for a broader critical voice that makes the significant differences between these issues clear. I haven't heard that voice yet.

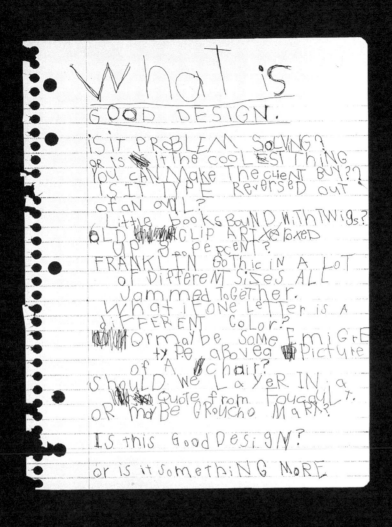

What is GOOD DESIGN.

is it PROBLEM Solving?
or is it the cooLEST Thing
You caN Make The client Buy??
IS IT TYPE Reversed out
of an ovaL?
Little booksBouND withTwigs?
OLD CLIP ARTxeroxed
up 300 PercENT?
FRANKLIN GoThic iN A LoT
of Different Sizes ALL
Jammed ToGether.
WhatifoNe Letter is A
Different coLor?
or maybe Some EmiGrE
type abovea picture
of A chair?
Should We LayeR IN a
Quote from FoucaULt.
OR maBe GRoucho MaRX?

IS this GooD DesigN?

or is itSomeThiNG MoRE

CALL FOR ENTRIES
THE FIFTEENTH ANNUAL AMERICAN CENTER FOR DESIGN
ONE HUNDRED SHOW

ALEXANDER ISLEY, JILLY SIMONS, ERIK SPIEKERMANN, JUDGES
MICHAEL BIERUT, CHAIR

ENTRY DEADLINE: MAY 1, 1992

DESIGN: MICHAEL BIERUT / PENTAGRAM
LETTERING: ELIZABETH ANN KRISZ BIERUT / TRANSFIGURATION SCHOOL

Michael Bierut on Design Criticism

Michael Bierut is a partner at Pentagram, New York. Born in Cleveland, Ohio, in 1957, Bierut studied graphic design at the University of Cincinnati's College of Design, Architecture, Art, and Planning, and graduated in 1980. Prior to joining Pentagram in 1990, he worked for ten years at Vignelli Associates, ultimately as vice president of graphic design. In 1991, he and his partner Paula Scher chaired the AIGA national conference in Chicago. He was president of the New York chapter of the American Institute of Graphic Arts (AIGA) from 1988 to 1990 and is currently a member of the AIGA's national board. He has also been director of the American Center for Design. In addition, he has designed identity and environmental graphics for a new children's museum in St. Paul, Minnesota; coordinates all promotional material for the Brooklyn Academy of Music; and serves as graphic design consultant to Mohawk Paper Mills, where he is responsible for corporate identity, packaging, and advertising and edits *ReThinking Design*, a journal of critical perspectives. He is also the coeditor of *Looking Closer*.

You worked at Vignelli Associates for ten years. What did you learn?

Probably the most interesting thing I learned is that a lot of the things about design that tend to get designers really interested aren't all that important.

Are you talking about the decorative aspects of design or what?

More or less. See, Massimo would arrive at things from an ideological point of view. For instance, he always has had this thing about there being only five good typefaces: Garamond 3, Futura, Century, Helvetica, and Bodoni. I agreed with this, not so much as a moral issue, but for the practical reason that normal people like my mom could only distinguish between five typefaces and that the time that designers would spend splitting hairs between Garamond and Bembo and Sabon was a waste. Likewise, all the attention that designers give to clever layouts and putting the page numbers in a cool place, when normal people just want to read the words and look at the pictures. Massimo taught me to focus on the big ideas, and I thought that big ideas were what connected with the greatest number of people.

Was this method a revelation for you, or was it accommodation to the will of your employer?

It was a revelation. Maybe unconsciously the whole thing was like the Stockholm Syndrome, where hostages identify with their captors. But I honestly don't think it was.

Did Vignelli view good design as a moral imperative?

Massimo's point of view is that cluttered or self-conscious design bespeaks some sort of moral failing. But I never felt that. I always believed that if you have the time to show you were awake while you were designing, then, why not?

Why has Vignelli become the spokesman for the old guard and the target of reaction in the debate between the old guard and the new?

To Massimo's credit, he's always felt it's incumbent on him to engage with this stuff. You have Massimo on the one hand, who takes a lot of the heat from the younger generation, but then you have armies of designers of his generation whose way of dealing with it is just to grumble and pull the shades down. Massimo is always in the front row, saying, "How can you do this crap?" To me, if more designers actually just stated their position and got dialogues going, it would be more interesting. It's dreary when there's just a single, stupid conversation about "You can't read that, it's ugly" versus "How can you keep doing that boring stuff?" It goes nowhere.

At the end of your tenure at Vignelli Associates, what was going on in design that interested you?

When I first came to New York in 1980, there was this thrilling ascendancy of avant-garde design as represented by the Basel school. Dan Friedman was working at Pentagram and Anspach Grossman Portugal. April Greiman was really just beginning. There were firms like Doublespace and Carbone Smolan doing things that I thought were cool-looking.

But by the middle of the decade, I was surprised to see that the avant-garde stuff had been absorbed by the mainstream. What you had were many firms, fueled by the real estate and retail and financial businesses, who were all just pouring out nice-looking brochures that had gradations and spaced-out type—all the stuff that looked astonishing on *Wet* magazine seven years before, all of a sudden being used to sell mortgages for Manhattan banks.

You absorbed Vignelli's ideas, but you also found your own path somewhere in the zeitgeist. At what point did you begin to have a more singular vision?

Well, it began to happen slowly. But first, Paula Scher, whom I had become friendly with, became a real pipeline to the outside world for me. Paula is a perfect example of the anti-Vignelli approach in the purest way. I remember Massimo and I going to a presentation where she spoke. I just loved her work. It was exactly what made me go into graphic design in the first place. We came out, and I said, "Man, Paula is great." And Massimo said, "All that novelty stuff and those Victorian typefaces, that's not the way to do it." And I said, "Massimo, if you design two hundred album covers a year, you have to become eclectic. You can't just do all the classical ones in Garamond and all the rock ones in Futura." And Massimo, of course, said, "That would be fantastic!" Paula's kind of virtuosity really spoke to me deep down inside.

I have an image of you with your veins popping out, panting to just jump out of your skin and do some of this stuff too.

I can do some virtuoso stuff sometimes, but there were a lot of things that I couldn't do. I couldn't just effortlessly do a modernist-looking thing at nine o'clock, a historicist-looking thing at ten o'clock, or something else at twelve o'clock. It bespeaks, I suppose, a kind of ideological bankruptcy to be able to slip in and out of all those clothes. But it's certainly something that I had been toying around with for almost all my life. I remember seeing things I loved, like the stuff that Katherine McCoy was doing at Cranbrook, and I'd try to do some of that. I just was bad at it.

Were you accepting of all these approaches equally, or were you beginning to establish hierarchies?

I'm one of these people who has this craven, meaningless point of view where you say "There's good graphic design, there's bad graphic design." And I think good graphic design can look lots and lots of different ways. In 1988, there was good Charles Spencer Anderson and there was bad imitation Charles Spencer Anderson. There was good Cranbrook and there was not-so-good Cranbrook. Just like now, there is good Tomato and there is bad Tomato. And the good stuff always seems to come out of someone's conviction and proceed directly from passion.

Tell me about that layered look. You said you were incapable of dealing with problems in that manner. Why? What was inherent in the layering process, was it an ideological or aesthetic objection?

I just don't think that way. When I have a design problem to solve, the solution I come up with is usually pretty simple. I haven't come to grips with it as an ideological position. But I would say that I like my graphic design to be accessible, understandable in some way to the greatest number of people, all of whom can put their own personal interpretation on it. Layering in a bunch of coded references for the edification of other trained designers always seemed a little mean to me; mean to the people who weren't trained as members of the design elite. Plus, like I said, I'm really not good at it.

Okay, ten years have gone by. You're approached by Pentagram to become a partner. What goes through your mind?

Through the years I'd been approached by other people of Massimo's generation who thought I would just want to trade Massimo for someone else for fun. That never interested me. And the other thing that didn't interest me was going out on my own.

I always thought if I could just run into a partner that I liked a lot, that would do it for me. I never thought that those partners already existed, and that they were Woody Pirtle and Alan Fletcher, David Hillman and Kit Hinrichs.

You were also out there movin' and shakin' in the design world. You were president of the AIGA/New York, a habitué of design conferences and mixers.

I love graphic design. I've been a glutton for this sort of stuff. So, being the guy that always showed up for every single event, you eventually get to run the slide projector at the AIGA. I volunteered for some AIGA committees, then eventually got on the board, then eventually was one of those few people who were smart enough to be able to be the president and dumb enough to serve.

What was your goal as AIGA/New York president?

To make the AIGA like the "big tent" that the Republicans always talk about. I was the guy who said yes to anything. I was president when the Walker Art Center's *Graphic Design in America* was at the IBM Gallery here in New York, and there was a lot of contention about who was included and who wasn't. I set up a program to have professional designers—a few who were critical of the exhibit—act as docents.

Since you brought up the Walker show, did you take a critical position?

First, I loved it because it was rooms filled with graphic design. If you go beyond that level, it just seemed inconsistent to me. I could never figure out what part of graphic design history it was supposed to be. It wasn't so much that there was no Milton Glaser in it—I think it's a perfectly valid view to take of one kind of graphic design history, to show the rise and permutations of modernism, for example. But if it's about modernism, why wasn't Rudy de Harak in the show? I think the problem with it was that it was just derived from a Rolodex that wasn't quite as full as it should have been. I just don't think it was based on a broad enough knowledge base to do the right kind of thing. It should have been either narrower or broader.

In your position as a design glutton, would you presume to be the curator of such a show? If you were picking a thread, and the mandate was to create something that had some controversy, something that addressed either issues or problems of graphic design, what would it be?

What has always fascinated me is watching how style is used and abused. I know that interests you too. But I think you could actually do real case histories. The funniest little part of the *Mixing Messages* show is where Ellen Lupton shows the typeface Neuland next to all those African-American book-cover things—the oddity is this typeface designed by Rudolf Koch in Germany in the thirties all of a sudden becoming the signifier for "There's African-American literature in here."

It's pretty easy these days to sample, appropriate, and steal.

Now we have relatively total freedom, and it means that people who have conviction and people who just have enough time on their hands to click the mouse a few more times can achieve very similar results. It used to be that mediocre work looked bland and boring. Now it looks complicated and boring. But I think you still have the same challenge, to sort out what's really interesting, what's really original, and what's not. And also, I think it just fuels the style cycle much more quickly. Cycles that took years now take months, and things that took months now take weeks.

In your own work, how do you avoid falling into those traps? Is it a conscious effort? Is it an instinctive effort? Is it an effort at all?

The last time I really came to grips with this question was when I did the ACD 100 show poster.

The one where your daughter did the artwork?

Yes, exactly. They asked me to judge the show and I thought, "Fine." I had been cast somehow as a critic of the previous show, sort of unintentionally. At that point I had an ideological bias toward eclecticism. I was very ideological about things not following one ideology, which is inherently oxymoronic.

You were rather critical of the one-dimensional stance of the show. Very Cranbrook inspired, as I remember.

I was quoted as saying that the work had a certain bias. I actually counted how many things were associated with Cranbrook, and said, "I wasn't just sensing it; there actually are a lot of things from Cranbrook in this book," and Lorraine Wild, the chair of the show, thought I was accusing her of throwing it toward her buddies. I really hurt her feelings—which I didn't mean to do.

So, I was asked to chair the show after that, and it was in my essay that I said, "This last show had been driven by either conscious or subconscious or unconscious commitments to certain stylistic ideologies. My era will be free of all that dogma." So then I had to design a poster to announce the show. It's not possible to design with no style. You can't.

ACD asked me to write a statement for the back of the poster, and I typed out a stream-of-consciousness thing: "What is good design? Is it all these stylistic things or is it something else?" And they said, "Why don't you just print that on the front? And I said, "Oh, brilliant; a type solution. I know how to do that." But then, of course, it's what typeface? Do you use Futura, Bodoni, or Helvetica? I mean, what typeface do you put it in so that it doesn't appear to admit that it has any conscious selection of style? I sweated over that for two weeks and then finally turned to my daughter Elizabeth, who was four years old and had just learned to write. I realized that if I dictated it to her and she did it in her handwriting, that would solve my problems. She did it perfectly. It fit on the page. So it was really like God telling me what to do.

Some people say there is a Pentagram style and a Pentagram clique. How do you respond to this Pentagram-ruling-the-world concept?

You know, you don't get chosen to be a partner here completely at random. There has to be a certain affinity for the existing partners. I think just like any group that votes in its future members, it all proceeds from a certain point of view. Just like putting in a school faculty, the challenge is to try to bring in people who are compatible without being identical.

The basic premise of Pentagram, founded by five guys, has never been as kind of single-minded as, say, an office that was founded by a single person whose point of view permeates everything.

Is there an exclusive design community, a clique, a movement that you've seen developing in the last ten years?

Let me tell you about my creation myth about the graphic design field. It used to be there were just good designers and bad designers. There were so few good designers that they knew each other on sight—Saul Bass was in L.A., Chermayeff & Geismar in New York. You'd put them all in one room and they'd all hold hands and that was a wonderful world.

Now, there are so many designers, I think there's room for groups and subgroups. The fact that Pentagram, which is really just a single firm, can be considered any kind of group at all, is kind of funny. But what's really funny is the idea of dominance by one or the other. I know that if you live outside New York, you have this fantasy that there are these people in New York who are calling the shots on everything. I remember in the eighties going to AIGA meetings in the Midwest, where I'm from, and hearing questions about this idea of these trilateral commissions of Massimo, Milton, Ivan, Rudy de Harak and God knows who, who would sit around and decide everything that would happen in graphic design for the next twelve months!

But there has been a perception of a star chamber, right?

There's always this idea that other people are in control. What's interesting is, I think a lot of the contention that's developed in the last few years has to do actually with this reciprocation between groups of people feeling the other group was in control. Believe me, there's a whole group of designers who feel like *Emigre* magazine rules the world. And it's not just fans of *Emigre*. It's people who would never be published in *Emigre* whose feelings are hurt: "Why don't they ever publish anything that looks like me and my friends." Likewise, *Eye* magazine or anything else. I think there was a period in graphic design when you might have felt like you were screwed if you didn't go to Cranbrook or CalArts. It doesn't matter how much work you did or how good you are. And they would deny absolutely there's any kind of single-minded cabal happening there. On the other hand, if you're out there in Valencia, California, you imagine that there are these East Coast designers who are driving really expensive cars, who have really big, bad clients, who just for the joy of it like to grind their heels right down and squelch any kind of poor, innovative designer who is trying to design an ugly-looking-on-purpose typeface.

In 1997, is there a hot-button issue for our field? Or have we come to the point of accepting certain standards regardless of what's being done?

Ugly versus boring was the second famous argument. The first was Tibor Kalman and Joe Duffy, which was about something different. But in the same way, it was the kind of argument that was waiting to happen, and it had to do more with personal expression versus service to the client. Ugly verses boring was about what constitutes acceptable appearance standards for graphic design. I don't think that everything is settled. What people actually want is to have their point of view acknowledged and validated. They don't want to be dismissed out of hand. Designers of the older generation don't want to be dismissed out of hand as just being a bunch of schmucks who had their glory days a long time ago, and now are just blindly and pathetically defending their turf against kids who have had much less of a chance to have their moment in the sun. And the people that took offense on the other side didn't want to be cubbyholed as just a bunch of mindless nihilists who think it's fun to make things look messy because there's reason not to. Once you acknowledge that a point of view is valid, the wind comes out of some of the arguments. A mature field figures out a way to still have a discussion after that.

There seems to be a lot of discussion going on in academic circles—

As I was finishing the last sentence, I realized that if there is an argument waiting to happen, it may have to do with a theoretical approach to design versus—I don't want to say an anti-intellectual, more pragmatic, approach—a less theoretical approach to graphic design. There's this new mania now for writing about graphic design instead of doing it. I can accept all kinds of different design, but there is something about bad writing that really drives me crazy and incenses me in a way that bad design doesn't.

What constitutes bad writing in this field?

That which is impossible to understand, nonspecific, and circular. You have to really be smart to be a writer, and I think that fewer people should attempt it. If you're not smart enough to be a writer, don't simulate the process. A lot of it is written by people that aren't quite sure of what they want to say, but have learned to simulate the locutions of academic writing. It bugs me that it's become a new mandatory pastime for designers. I worry more about a talented designer who has gotten in his or her head that to really get ahead in the design world one has to learn to write this kind of "Design Criticism," that that's really the path to glory, come the twenty-first century, in our field.

It may not be a path to glory, but it's a path to tenure!

I guess in the big world out there it's progress to have graphic design stand shoulder to shoulder with a lot of other fields that are similarly opaque in their discourse. Maybe it's enough if the graphic design faculty can clink a glass at a faculty party with the head of comparative literature, and that's a great moment for graphic design.

We worked together editing *Looking Closer,* a compilation of critical writing. How do you define critical writing?

When we first worked on *Looking Closer,* it was hard to find examples of critical graphic design writing. We looked back ten years and put together a list, and there was a lot if you looked that far back. But since then, between the mainstream design magazines, *Emigre,* special issues of *Visible Language,* and all this other stuff, there's been a ton of graphic design criticism. A lot of it is fueled by people writing within academia. However, my bias is toward writing that works on a popular level, where you can tell by reading it what they're talking about. That's not to say there isn't a role for all other kinds of writing, too, but it's just not the kind that I personally am interested in.

What would be the model of effective graphic design criticism?

The best writers are able to frame an argument, have a point of view, and be rooted in things that normal people can touch and evaluate. Good writing always connects up with things that are bigger than the thing being discussed, and even connects up with things that are outside the field of graphic design.

I can't tell you how many pieces I've read where I just sense that someone has read about some French feminist, structuralist, proto something or other, and they are thinking, Boy, is there some way I could spin this in a graphic design direction? The thing can be headlined, "Graphic Design and the Feminist Dichromatic Panopticon."

Do you think there's a dumbing-down or a smartening-up of designers?

A smartening-up. All you have to do is go back to issues of *CA* in the 1970s, and graphic design feels like the dumbest fucking field on earth. Even if you were doing great work, you may as well have been customizing cars. Most of the profiles have zero, zip, nada intellectual content. Actually, it was in reviews and not profiles that Dugald Stermer and Byron Ferris always wrote very thoughtful, provocative things. In a very kind of casual way, they would let drop opinionated things that opened my eyes as a designer then. But you never got an inkling that there were things to be for or against, or things to think or worry about. Say what you will about what I would consider the most incomprehensible excesses of academic design criticism, but it all bespeaks an attempt to establish a higher rigor for things that has a trickle-down effect. The next step is for people to learn how to have fun with this stuff, to learn to disagree in a way that's erudite and smart.

Let's end with this question: What is graphic design for you?

One of my favorite movie scenes is in *Do the Right Thing* by Spike Lee. It's pointless, it doesn't advance the plot, it has nothing to do with anything, but I know exactly why it's there. It's a speech by Mr. Señor Love Daddy, the DJ who forms the Greek chorus for the whole thing. At about the midpoint in the movie, they just pan through neighborhoods, and they show him, and he's doing a rap between songs or with some music in the background, and all he does is say the names of black artists and black musicians. It's so thrilling because there's absolutely no aesthetic or ideological consistency between the names he's saying. He's saying, "Run-D.M.C., John Coltrane, Parliament-Funkadelic, Ella Fitzgerald, Prince, Sam Cooke, Steel Pulse . . ." and on and on, the names of rappers, the names of jazz artists, the names of every possible artist from the past, from the future, just naming all of them, one after another. He never says at the beginning, "These are African-American musicians who have made a contribution," never says something like "and now you realize how rich our field is." All he does is say the names. There's something about this recitation of names, and the differences between them, and the fact that a single idea embraces them, even the idea of ethnicity in this case. I just think it's absolutely thrilling.

I always thought if graphic design is an idea, what makes it powerful is the idea that you can have a litany that goes Don Trousdell, Alexey Brodovitch, David Carson, Jilly Simons, Alex Isley, Laurie Haycock, Lester Beall, Woody Pirtle. . . . You could go on and on and on. And I swear to God, I could list more graphic designers' names in any period of time than anyone else can in America. If we had to fill blackboards, I could fill more blackboards. Everyone else would have quit, everyone else would be lying dead on the floor, and I would still be writing. So what makes the field thrilling, and what always gives it a sense of possibility, is not just what I'm going to do tomorrow, but what someone else is going to do tomorrow.

Massaging the Message

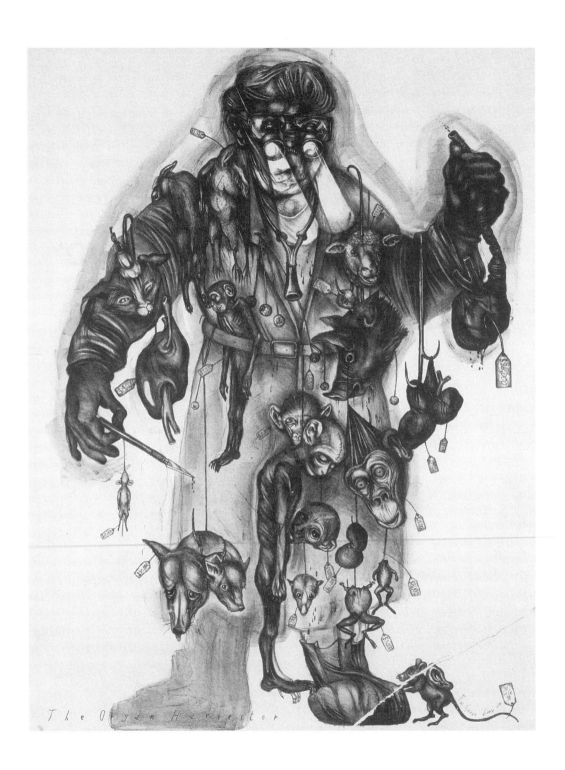

The Organ Harvester

168

 **Sue Coe** on Art and Politics

Sue Coe was born in 1951, in England, moved to New York in 1972, and has worked as an illustrator for magazines and newspapers, including the *Progressive,* the *Nation,* the *New Yorker,* and the *New York Times.* She is also a painter, printmaker, and muralist with works in the collections of the Brooklyn Museum of Art, Los Angeles County Museum of Art, Metropolitan Museum of Art, New York Public Library, Museum of Modern Art (UK), Museum of Modern Art (New York), San Francisco Museum of Modern Art, National Museum of Art, Library of Congress, National Museum of Women in the Arts, Hirshhorn Museum, and Whitney Museum of Art. She is the author of *How to Commit Suicide in South Africa* (1983), a visual essay with text on the death of Steven Biko, and *Dead Meat* (1996), an exposé of conditions in slaughterhouses and abattoirs. Her CD-ROMs include *Monkey Business* (1998) and *Dead Meat* (1998).

What caused you to marry politics and art?

Art is that vehicle that exists between the state/social world and personal life. It describes the collision that is inevitable when profit is valued more than life. I could be looking out at a vast landscape of beauty and see an empty drum of herbicides, hidden in the field, and be incapable of avoiding that reality.

In a world full of contentless images, do you believe that art can make a difference in influencing individual and/or public opinion?

There is an old story: A man was walking along the beach and saw another person doing something strange, bending down, picking something up, and throwing it into the ocean. As he got closer, he realized that in the high tide, the beach was covered with millions and millions of starfish. They were stranded and dying in the sun. As he got closer to the person, he said, "What you are doing cannot possibly matter. There are millions of them." The individual said, as he threw the starfish back. "It matters to this one."

Has illustration been a satisfying means of expression?

For many years, illustration was my only means of expression. It was through that work that I learned how to draw because I drew every day. Through illustration I learned how to communicate. It turned out to be quite useful, as a print medium, because it still contained content that the fine art world avoided. The restriction of the printed page was a challenge to be overcome.

What determines what you choose as a theme for address and redress?

If I thought about the choice of content, I would be overwhelmed with ideas. Whether it is war, prisons, the death penalty, the homeless, the slaughter of animals, the degradation of nature and human nature itself, where to begin? To take on power, one has to feel empowered. One of the classic ways to make people feel powerless is to give the illusion of hopelessness.

The camera zooms in on some very rare bird, shows all the habits of that bird, baby birds in nest, shows the ten trees in existence that the bird needs to survive, then we hear the chain saw, then see the tree fall. End of documentary. What this scenario does not reveal is all the people struggling to keep the birds alive.

The content of my work comes from friends who are activists. They are active in the struggle for change, and if we can use artwork to create change, that is all the better. I have complete admiration, and wonder, for what they have achieved. These people are on the front lines, and I am usually on the drawing board.

Many of your subjects—AIDS patients, Malcolm X, Steve Biko—require considerable dedication. How do you determine what your focus will be?

The focus comes from being in the situation. Wherever possible, I attempt to get off the drawing board and into the content—life before art. Distance from the subject creates generalizations and irony. To put oneself in that situation is to find unity with most of the world's life, and one is helpless to avoid pain and suffering. There was an occasion when I had my drawing board and pencils and was going to make a portrait of a young man who was dying of AIDS. He had other plans: he wanted me to get cigarettes, then make out a grocery list, then go and pick his dog up from the pound. Reality intrudes.

Your work is as much about research as it is about creating images. Are you looking for truth?

There are different truths; there are gender truths, race truths, class truths, and species truths. The discovery is to reveal contradiction, not to resolve it. However urgent the appeals of those identity voices, there is a universal compassion that spins a web around the fabric of life. None of us would exist at all if it were not for the compassion and love of our parents and then strangers. As a summation for the research process, I would say, the devil is in the details. You could show a visual history of the wheel and reveal social struggle.

***Dead Meat* is a ten-year-old exploration of meat and poultry abattoirs and slaughterhouses. Did this origi-nally begin as a metaphor for human violence or as a dedicated attack on inhumane conditions for animals?**

This was not a metaphor. It could have been but was not. The animals who died—and die—are like no other; they are idiosyncratic. By the time you read that sentence, thou-sands of animals would have died in slaughterhouses and laboratories. Eight billion a year. What does 8 billion mean? Those billions die and suffer unimaginable cruelties, and they do so because they are mute. Their piteous cries are not understood by the human ear. They have no rights. Their suffering is prolonged because they are property. I just saw a photograph that showed a calf with her back legs sawed off, just stumps. She dragged herself onto the auction block, and was bid on and sold to the slaughterhouse. I have witnessed the same animals with broken backs and gaping wounds left alive in the heat or bitter cold for days waiting to be dragged in chains to a rendering plant. When the animals are dragged, they are flayed, on the road surface, but still live. Food animals do not have the right to be euthanized. Activists are trying to change that.

I was interested in the mass mechanization of slaughter, why this existed, and is, for the most part, ignored and normalized. As children, my sister and I grew up next to a small pig farm, which was next to a slaughterhouse. We thought the crashing of chains and screaming of hogs at 4 A.M. was totally normal—and it is. We ate bacon and lard; it was cheap and tasty. The kids who couldn't afford to eat chips wrapped in newspaper would get, for a few pennies, the bits and "scrappings" in the congealed lard at the bottom of the fryer. If as children we questioned the sight of suffering, we were called "soft" and "sissies," "crybabies," "too emotional." The state requires the passive consumer, especially for those bottom feeders, the working class.

What did you learn from your years of research into the meat-producing industry?

The meat industry, the second-largest manufacturing industry in the United States, exists not to feed the hungry but to make profit. By deforestation, the meat industry removes natural habitat for animals and humans; it makes countries involved in raising livestock for meat dependent on the pharmaceutical industry. It takes people off their small homesteads and creates slave labor. The transnational corporations exploit public lands and parks, killing indigenous species. The industry pollutes and creates dependency and starvation. It is the most wasteful use of grains that one could imagine. Eight pounds of grain for one pound of meat. Humans need meat like a hole in the head. For most workers in packing plants, it's the only job in town. Most of them would leave in a second for another job. Unfortunately, they do often leave, with a disability. A few will put forth a frail argument about the importance of supplying the public with meat they supposedly need.

So this is the big lesson?

I learned the art of not forgetting. I learned that suffering is mute, that some animals cannot vocalize for help, make a plea or a case for themselves. They cannot compete with the chattering demands of human animals. In the history of oppression, certain humans join animals in their loss of freedom and life. It is complex to attempt to "grant" rights to those who have none. The earth and all the creatures on her do not exist to be murdered, plundered, and sold. Transnational corporations hunt down life at every turn and eventually will cannibalize themselves. It is those conditions that will create the reaction. The tragedy is that so much suffering of humans and animals is needless and unnecessary.

Upton Sinclair published *The Jungle* in 1906, bringing to light the horrible conditions in Chicago's slaughterhouses. Do you think that his work—and, by extension, your work—has made any difference in attitudes?

The situation since Upton Sinclair wrote *The Jungle* is far more sinister. He had difficulty in publishing that book then, and today it would not be published at all. Not only have the conditions worsened for both the workers and the animals, but publishing and the meat industry and the media have become hand in glove—bandits together. The small farmer has gone the way of the small publisher. Publications take money in the form of advertising from the meat industry. Now there are laws protecting the purveyors of flesh from any type of criticism.

You mean the libel trial against Oprah Winfrey in February 1998, which she won?

Although the industry lost its lawsuit against Ms. Winfrey, the message is clear. Question what goes in your mouth and be tied up in court for years. What small publisher or newspaper will take the risk? Whether it is that type of bullying or decapitating the heads of workers who struggle against cattle barons in Central America, the industry knows freedom of speech is not in its interest.

Does cloning and genetic engineering enter into this?

What Sinclair Lewis did not envision was the genetic engineering that makes it possible to splice human genes with pig genes and for that new life form to be patented, owned by a corporation. As the conditions have worsened, so has the resistance. Many more people now are concerned about the food supply and the rights of animals than in Sinclair's day. The global use of recourse is an issue, along with the internationalism of the working class.

What has been your goal in bringing this material to public attention?

I have been muckraking. I want to know why this issue is so concealed? What is the meat industry afraid of? Why shouldn't the public have access to the truth about their food supply? Why shouldn't the public see animals still alive after having their throats cut and being shot through the head? Why can't the public decide if they want to continue consuming flesh after seeing this? I think the public should get to see what is being concealed from them. Why can't the content of art be reality?

With the *Dead Meat* CD-ROM, you have created a powerful piece of propaganda for your ideas—art, history, commentary, satire all rolled into one kinetic and interactive experience. Can you describe the difference in form, content, and effect of this new medium?

That is a hard question. The CD-ROM is a massive compilation of text, poetry, live action, animation, music, and many more facts and statistics than we used in the book. It also has contributions from activists I very much admire and respect—Lorri and Gene Bauston, Peter Singer, John Carlin, et al worked on this. The process was much more of a collaboration because so many people were needed to pull all this together. I find doing computer animation to be the equivalent of swimming the Atlantic in a wheelchair; it's so much easier for me to draw and paint. So, experts like Peter Girardi and the guys at Antenna not only helped create animation from my existing static work but also improved the content. They made my paintings and drawing move without undermining the integrity of those works. The question is, Will that be more effective than looking at a simple pencil drawing of an animal about to be slaughtered? I don't know.

Is art like yours a caution, curative, or attack? Do you see any redemptive power in your work?

It's been all three. But before it is any of those, it first has to be art that is passably well drawn and painted. Technique is the test of sincerity. Redemption is hard, artistically. The crucifixion is more believable than the resurrection. It's true that people change, that people are, generally speaking, good. How to show that without falling into the pit of false humanism?

How has your art changed you as a person?

Art has changed everything, from giving me a mission to a gateway to meeting some amazing people, to a way to vent, heal, and enter painting—and get lost in it. And who knows, the work could create change for the better.

172

780465 001019

Archie Bishop '98

Stuart Ewen on Public Relations and Spin

In his role as a media critic, Hunter College professor of mass communications Stuart Ewen examines mass persuasion both with historical acuity and a jaundiced eye. In his books *All Consuming Images* and *Captains of Consciousness,* he argues that advertising and marketing have become so inextricably connected to daily life that the public has become vulnerable to many forms of propaganda. He further asserts that those who control the creation and distribution of images have tremendous power over public behavior and opinion. In his latest book, *PR!: A Social History of Spin,* Ewen analyzes one of the most pervasive forms of mass manipulation and discusses how to understand it. A uniquely American phenomenon, public relations is as old as the republic itself, and has been used to instill both progressive and regressive ideas. Its modern offshoot, spin, is the process of turning bad ideas into positive ones, of altering facts to fit a manufactured image. Many people involved in media are engaged in this activity, from journalists to graphic designers. The PR network is huge, and its impact is profound. In the following interview, Ewen examines the history and practice of PR and its remarkable impact on public perceptions.

What is PR?

There are two general definitions. In everyday life, we use the term "PR" to describe manufactured truth. In terms of the profession, the most generic description I could offer is that PR is the practice of trying to construct mental environments that will encourage people to see those environments as reality. The reason those environments are constructed is to influence the way in which people perceive the world and influence how people will behave in the world.

Has this always been the case?

At different historical moments PR has meant different things. In the early part of this century, when the primary arena of truth was the printed word—and we're really talking about muckraking journalism here—PR was used to illuminate social ills, such as corruption in business or in government. Within the context of journalism social truths began to take form.

How would you define "truth"?

By the twentieth century, people in a lot of different arenas see truth as something that is up for grabs. We're not talking about a traditional, hierocratic society; we're talking about a society in which there are real battles going on over what is reality. To some extent this is brewed in the Enlightenment. Part of what the Enlightenment does in challenging old systems of superstition is to say the truth is something that must be established through a process of verification. Truth needs to be shown to people.

Religion offers a kind of truth. How would you define secular "truth"?

By the twentieth century, truth is a secular concept and something that needs to be established. The publicists of the Progressive Era who were trying to build a movement toward social reform believed that the primary way in which you establish truth is by publishing facts. That's why journalism is such a good medium for that. In this period of time there are also certain people who are sympathetic to the interests of big business, many of whom have some experience in journalism, who understand that truth tastes, smells, and looks a certain way. They begin to discover, largely in response to the Progressive uses of journalism, that they can generate alternative journalistic truths for any purpose.

How, then, is truth manufactured?

The paradigm that's used for conveying a corporate point of view is print journalism. And the assumptions that underlie that paradigm are that people are capable of evaluating facts and rationally arriving at ways of understanding the world that will encourage them to make certain kinds of demands upon that world. So, if you look at Theodore Vail, the president of AT&T, or some of the other important early PR people, you see they're using the tool of the word to lay out factual arguments.

Did they actually call themselves PR people?

The terms "publicity" and "public relations" are used very early on. It's an old phrase, which in the eighteenth century is about public discourse within the active public sphere. By the early part of twentieth century, you have people who understand the media as ways of communicating information to a less physical public, to a public that may be, in fact, sitting in their parlors reading the newspaper. There is a sense of public relations as something that you send out. Theodore Vail was brought into AT&T to persuade the public that a privately held monopoly over all wire communications was in America's best interest, and he established a PR department to make that happen.

Is public relations an infiltration of the media, or is the media a vehicle for public relations?

There's no question that part of the way in which public relations practitioners view their work is trying to insinuate themselves into the media. But there is something about the media that makes this kind of ideological exchange of saliva particularly possible—for a number of reasons.

One is that a lot of the early PR people (and this continues to some extent today) come out of journalism, and so there are social bonds between the publicity apparatus and the news apparatus. Second is that with the daily newspapers, where there is the continual push for producing something new that will be replaced by something new the next morning, it's very easy to take material that is already digested and sounds like journalism, and put it into your newspaper. And there's a third element that plays a part, although it's a harder one to document most of the time. To a large extent, the people or the institutions who are interested in using public relations and in influencing news coverage are institutions who are also buying advertising in those papers; there is a kind of economic reciprocity.

Is there a symbiotic relationship between advertising and public relations?

When you have that rare opportunity to dip into corporate archives, and particularly when you go way back, where there is less protection of those archives, you find the footprints that you're looking for. I found, for example, in AT&T's archives from 1907 to 1913 that there was a lot of opposition to the AT&T monopoly. Part of it came from people who thought that the phone service should be a governmental apparatus. Other people were customers of local phone companies. So you had a situation, for example, when AT&T was trying to seize the monopoly over Kansas—and there was a competing local phone company in Kansas City—they couldn't get good coverage in the papers. I was able to find documents indicating that as AT&T started purchasing advertising in the papers, they started getting positive coverage, and the monopoly was transformed into the kind of Ma Bell image that was successfully proselytized.

What is the genesis of the Ma Bell image? Is it an advertising or a PR function?

Well, AT&T is a fascinating story because at a time when most businesses of that size showed contempt for the public, AT&T, because of its particular product and its long-term corporate strategy, was extraordinarily sophisticated in its vision. And I don't think you can draw a line between advertising and anything else. Theodore Vail was an industrial genius of sorts, who used advertising and public relations to achieve his goals. From a PR standpoint he instituted female operators, which meant that most people's interactions with the business were with a woman's voice.

Is PR all subterfuge? Is it all about creating a myth for some dastardly purpose?

When I first came to PR, that was my take on it because of my genetically paranoid American personality. One of the things that you discover, if you look at the history of public relations, is that while there certainly is a great deal of conscious subterfuge and propaganda being used, there are also what you might call two-way-street practitioners, people who basically feel that if you don't deliver stuff to people, you've failed. So, while most public relations is designed to persuade, some PR is benevolent. Sometimes the benevolence is an image, and other times it includes significant policies—as in the case of Vail, who created a pricing policy that meant that ordinary Americans very early on began to have access to telephone service. One could say that was certainly good for business. But it also carried ordinary Americans into the twentieth century.

In my reading of your book, the notion of "manufactured truth" fascinated and scared me. Thanks to the persuasiveness of PR, it's hard to determine what truth is, what reality is, what myth is, and which myths we should accept because they're good or should reject because they're bad.

We live in a very strange world, where people are continually surrounded by Trojan Horse messages that have some instrumental purpose behind them. It's part of the folklore of Americans—the myth of subliminal advertising. Whenever I'm teaching about advertising, one of the things that students invariably want to talk about is subliminal advertising, you know, the word "sex" written in the Ritz cracker and the penises hidden on the Camel pack. Most people who actually work in advertising say, "Look, this is nonsense; it's not there." What's interesting to me about the myth of subliminal advertising is not whether it's true, but the fact that everybody thinks it's true. In certain ways, that's an example of a myth that really speaks to the extent that people feel they're continually being manipulated by everything around them. Whether or not it says "sex" on the surface of the Ritz cracker, it says it somewhere, and every message that comes at you has a purpose behind it that may not be visible immediately.

Why is manufactured truth so prevalent?

One of the reasons the idea of manufacturing reality has become so problematic in our century is that certain kinds of dramatic shifts have taken place (1) in how the public is understood and (2) the way in which you address that public, given that understanding. In the early twentieth century, people were still holding on to an enlightened notion of a rational public. And, therefore, although people were continually trying to send out information that would help to shape how people understood reality, the assumption was that people had critical faculties and that information was something that people would deliberate upon.

Alongside this rational view of the public, there had also been emerging in the late nineteenth century a whole intellectual tradition that challenged the idea of rationality as the primary tool of human behavior. Most people are familiar with the influence of Freud and the ideas of the power of the unconscious. But in fact, much more than Freud, there was the emergence of a strain of thought that began with a French social psychologist named Gustave Le Bon, who wrote a book called *The Crowd: A Study of the Popular Mind* in 1895. It was translated into nineteen languages within a couple of years. It was, incidentally, bedside reading for people like Teddy Roosevelt and Walter Lippmann, and a lot of others who became very influential political figures.

Was this the first time the masses were seen as a unit that could be molded toward some end?

Well, I think the fear of an increasingly militant working class gave rise to the idea of the masses as dangerous, and also the masses as driven not by reason but by animal passions.

So, they were, in fact, a mob. And we all know that you can't reason with a mob.

Le Bon himself held to the idea that bourgeois people were still capable of reason; it's the mob that isn't. You have the emergence of a field known as social psychology, which alongside Freud's study of the individual mind, is beginning to look at the mass mind. And by very early on, not only is everybody talking about what Le Bon has discovered— the unconscious life of the masses—but people are beginning to assume that it's not something that is unique to the working class, it's an aspect of human behavior overall.

And what specifically is this?

The idea that Le Bon raised was that with the end of hierarchy and with the idea of democracy, now even the lowest elements of society think of themselves as citizens with rights.

Which, I assume, he believed is bound to create a kind of "mediocracy."

Worse. It was barbarism, according to him. He was not worried about a lowering of standards. He was worried about the complete fracturing of all standards, the creation of a society that is driven by mindless animal passions. And one of the things that he does repeatedly is to create associations between the popular mind and the minds of certain kinds of people who were always assumed to be irrational or prerational—women, children, savages, and so forth.

He was arguing that the political life of the present is no longer driven by rational discourse. The political life of the present is driven by these spinal influences, these primal neurological processes that are going on, and, therefore, it becomes incumbent upon those who have traditionally been the leaders of society, since they can no longer rule on the basis of respect that is paid them, to develop a better understanding of what are the mechanisms by which the mass mind works, in order to be able to mold it.

Mold or pander to?

Well, what Le Bon is talking about is the need to be able to shape this raw material into a political constituency. So he's not talking about pandering. Pandering is always the idea of somebody in a public setting lowering the culture. Le Bon is interested in using the social psychology of the mass and developing certain kinds of understandings and techniques that will allow social scientists to be able to know what the appeals are.

Did Le Bon use the tools of PR to propagate his ideas?

He never became a practitioner of what he was proposing. What's interesting about Le Bon is that he represents the emergence of a sector of the intellectual class whose primary role is one of monitoring and affecting public attitudes, and although he himself doesn't become a practitioner of that, he prefigures the emergence of what is today an incredibly large element of the American intellectual class whose everyday activities are involved in studying public attitudes and shaping them.

How were Le Bon's ideas filtered into American culture?

Walter Lippmann, the famous American journalist and pundit, is somebody who is completely entrenched in the ideas of Le Bon. He founded the Committee of Public Information during the First World War, whose job it was to propagate the war to the American public.

But Lippmann was a Progressive.

The period of the First World War marks the end of Progressivism, a shift from a middle-class intelligentsia—who are calling for social reform because of egregious violations at the top of the society but also because of fear of what's happening below—to an intelligentsia that is making its peace with the top of society and is using its intellect to assert order on what's below. If you read Walter Lippmann when he's a college student at Harvard in 1910, you know he's a participatory Democrat. But by 1914, when he is still at the *New Republic,* he writes a book called *Drift and Mastery,* in which he contends that the climate of exposé, the climate of reform, has unwittingly given rise to a society where nobody respects authority anymore and where the society is in crisis. And he begins to assert that the next job that stands ahead of Progressives is going to be one of learning how to assert mastery over a chaotic world. And at that moment, and in those words, the agenda driving Walter Lippmann begins to coincide with the agenda driving much of industrial America: How does one assert order on what is potentially a dangerous and chaotic society? By 1922 he writes a book, *Public Opinion,* which is, even today, the book through which one can understand the strategies of power of the contemporary world.

Does Lippmann provide a strategy for public relations?

Lippmann lays out the problem that confronts the modern executive in what he refers to as the "great society"—large-scale international society. By "executive," he means a political or corporate leader. The problem confronting the executive is that people believe society should be run as an outcome of their collective will. But he goes on to say, the problem with this is that people are totally incapable of understanding the society they live in. He begins to draw a picture of a society in which people are continually driven by illusions; their concept of the world is not based in the real world, but rather is driven by what he referred to as "pictures in their heads."

So, is Lippmann advocating that the purpose of public relations is to manipulate these pictures?

His feeling is that if you present people with truth, it only complicates things because then they want to discuss it. When people start discussing things, you've got trouble. He didn't completely reject the idea that people were capable of reason. He just felt that reason would only get in the way of leadership. Lippmann was perfectly willing to create the illusion of democracy. He just wasn't willing to practice it!

Would you say that this creation of an illusion of democracy is what underscores the whole practice of PR?

Absolutely. The emergence of public relations is incomprehensible apart from the rise of democracy. And to some extent, public relations has been one of the primary mechanisms by which elites have been able to maintain their position in a society that is ostensibly democratic.

Democracy creates this group of people who, as you say, feel they have rights, yet there is an elite that wants to maintain that these rights are limited.

Well, they don't necessarily want to maintain that the rights are limited, but they want to maintain limited rights. What they strategically would like to do is to maintain the idea that the rights are unlimited, but at the same time to be able to ensure that they are limited.

Which brings them back to the original framers of the Constitution. You vote if you have land. If you have power, you have power.

As long as leadership can get away with giving the vote only to property owners, you don't need public relations.

What is the fundamental difference between public relations and propaganda?

There's a part of me that wants to say there's no difference. Historically, public relations has been much more successful. That is to say, a propaganda ministry tends to be very visible. Edward Bernays in 1928 writes a book called *Propaganda,* which is all about the practice of public relations. It is read by Nazi minister of information Goebbels. So one can say that these are twins—they are born of the same parents.

So, PR exists in a democracy and propaganda exists in an authoritarian society?

PR exists in a society where state domination is anathema, and therefore, one of the most basic intrinsic faiths is that the public relations practitioner should be thoroughly invisible.

You mentioned Edward Bernays. In your book you describe him as the pioneer of public relations and social science. Can you say more?

Bernays is Sigmund Freud's nephew, and he's really the guy in the United States who takes the ideas of social psychology and normalizes them as corporate practice. He basically takes the ideas of mass and individual psychology, and applies them to public relations.

It's at that point where the journalistic paradigm begins to give way to the mesmerizing or the power-of-suggestion paradigm.

How does this mesmerizing occur?

Bernays's real innovation was, you don't send out press releases. Rather, you study what the press is likely to cover; the kinds of things that jut out from the normal and will be seen as news. Then what you do is create circumstances that are calculated to get news coverage.

Such as?

The famous campaign that Bernays did for the American Tobacco Company: George Hill, who was the president of American Tobacco, hires Bernays and says to him that there are a lot of people who smoke, but because of certain kinds of social attitudes they aren't willing to smoke in public. He was talking about women. So Bernays, rather than putting out an overt campaign trying to sell Lucky Strikes to women, hooks up with a woman who is the head of a feminist march in New York and says to her, "What might be a really good idea in this march is if you all carry cigarettes as torches of freedom." Now, from our vantage point we might say that she should have just slapped him around and said, "Hey, we don't want cancer."

But at that period of time, cigarettes were, in fact, symbols of male prerogative in the streets.

Right. So if a woman is interested in assuming that social prerogative, the cigarette was a very good symbol to use. And so they march, and it gets covered, and not only is it creating a visual image of women in public smoking, but it's also creating a kind of intrinsic association between smoking and the emancipation of women.

Isn't there a cynical side to Bernays's manipulation?

It's thoroughly cynical. It's basically viewing reality as a stage set. It's about creating mental scenery that will encourage people to see the world in certain ways, to accept certain kinds of things, to behave in certain kinds of ways. It is the mentality of the string-pullers.

You subtitle your book *A Social History of Spin*. Is this a uniquely late-twentieth-century concept?

Spin is the transformation of public discourse into public manipulation. At this point in time, spin and the tools of mass communication have become the primary vehicles with which power and truth are asserted. It therefore becomes necessary for those tools, and for a critical mentality toward those tools, to be a basic part of education. It's quite astounding that in the United States, which is the most pervasively public relations–oriented society in the world, this kind of social and cultural literacy is virtually nonexistent.

How are images used in public relations?

Generally, they're used to create impressions (and I say that because an impression is something that reaches somebody in a fairly subtle way) and to make suggestions.

So, we're not talking about the Pillsbury Doughboy or Ronald McDonald being tools of public relations.

The Pillsbury Doughboy is a piece of corporate publicity. But one of the things that's become standard practice is that people who are in executive positions are served by media trainers who basically say to them, "Here is the way you will look good in the media; here is how to deal with an interaction with the media"—individuals are being encouraged to learn how to comport themselves. This kind of proliferation of media training and speaking training that goes on is not about the word, but rather about the image.

The use of certain kinds of environmental design questions is clearly about image. The way in which products are designed, the way in which headquarters are designed, is about image. What is going on right now is that the question of image has gravitated from the locale of the corporate mascot to the entirety of corporate presentation or political presentation.

We've all heard the canard, Any publicity is good publicity. But what is bad PR?

Ineffective publicity is publicity that people have contempt for. Of course, there's also the moral issue of publicity. In our century, we have seen examples of good and bad publicity. Filmmaker Leni Riefenstahl's paean to the Nazis, *Triumph of the Will*, was bad publicity. The aestheticization and eroticization of mass murder is bad publicity. I would add similarly that the aestheticization of human dignity and the idea, for example, that America is made of all of its people (I'm talking about the imagery produced by the New Deal administration) I view as good publicity because it helped to reconfigure how people understood what is America, who are Americans, and it opened doors for a lot of people, doors that are currently in the process of being closed down again.

How do we immunize ourselves from the PR disease?

One can't protect oneself. Even if you become cynical yourself in relationship to it, you know you'll just become more and more embittered and miserable. I think that insofar as public relations is a social fact and is part of the cultural fabric of our world, if one is really interested in protecting oneself, one needs to look toward social and cultural responses to it. There are a variety of things that might be appropriate. One of them that I think is essential is making literacy about the media environment an integral piece of what's going on in education. To merely think in the nineteenth-century vision of the three Rs as the building blocks of education is to not understand what the nineteenth century was about, and certainly isn't producing an education that is empowering people in the twentieth.

How are designers used, willingly or not, as tools of public relations?

There is no question that many people participate in the world of public relations without knowing it, and that has something to do with the structure of the industries, where the discussions about what is the ultimate goal take place in different rooms from the rooms in which the product is being produced. By the time, say, a television production company receives a notice to instruct them, "Here's what McDonald's wants out of this commercial," there are assumptions and goals that have been discussed in another room but which are not necessarily apparent in the instructions, "Here's what you're supposed to do." I think that's true of designers as well.

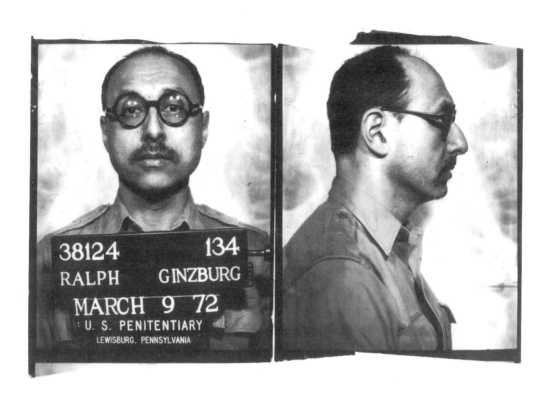

Ralph Ginzburg on the Perils of Publishing

During the 1960s and 1970s, Ralph Ginzburg published *Eros: A Quarterly on the Joys of Love and Sex, Avant Garde: Exuberantly Dedicated to the Future, Moneysworth: The Wallet Fattening Consumer Advisor,* and *Fact: An Antidote to the Timidity and Corruption of the American Press. Eros* was banned as "obscene," resulting in Ginzburg's imprisonment under a sentence of five years (owing to an outcry of protest, he was freed after serving eight months). Supreme Court Justice Potter Stewart, who voted for acquittal, termed the court's ruling in *Ginzburg v. United States* the worst in the history of American jurisprudence except for that in the Dred Scott case, which legalized slavery.

You began your career as an editor at *Esquire* magazine in the fifties (the same spawning ground for Hugh Hefner, I might add). Why did you decide to start your own magazine? And why did you decide to launch one concerned with the taboo subject of sex?

I felt there was a great need for a well-written, well-designed magazine on love and sex that would reflect psychological maturity. The government eventually suppressed *Eros,* of course. I believe a magazine like *Eros* is still needed today.

***Eros* was a beautifully designed magazine, replete with exquisite typography—which, incidentally, was cutting edge in its day—smart illustration, and awe-inspiring photography. Was this your idea? Or were you influenced in this direction by your art director, Herb Lubalin? And, finally, what role did design play in the life of the magazine?**

The decision to have the magazine well designed and expensively produced—remember, it was a hardcover "maga*book,*" if you will, not the usual softcover format publication— was mine. This was a marketing ploy to enable a hefty cover price. But beyond that, every design detail and initiative was Herb's. He gets full credit for *Eros*'s design excellence. Without his virtuosity, *Eros* would not have been the big hit among the cognoscenti that it was. Although this is little known, the publication was actually losing money because of its huge production costs, and very likely would have folded of its own accord had the government not attacked it.

How was content determined for *Eros*?

As editor in chief, I myself determined *Eros*'s editorial contents. I followed my own tastes, instincts, and interests. I know that this is shamefully egocentric, but I have always enjoyed a euphoric sex life and, thanks to four years of psychoanalysis, possess keen insight into the forces that govern human behavior. Thus, I felt completely confident in my editorial decisions. Herb and I were in perfect synch on them. He never once balked or complained about any articles or graphic features I proposed, and, believe me, he would not have been bashful about objecting. I can still hear him bellowing *"This stinks!"* when receiving design projects that he disliked—not from myself, of course, but from other clients. I must give due credit also to two other individuals who aided in editorial content: Warren Boroson, a brilliant writer, idea-man, and editorial general factotum, and my wife Shoshana, whose witty titles were the topping on our most successful editorial confections. It was also her decision to name our subsequent magazine, *Avant Garde,* and, believe it or not, it was she who made clear to Herb the overall approach he should take in designing Avant Garde Gothic, which turned out to be one of the best-selling new typefaces of the twentieth century.

How quickly, from issue one to issue four, did it take the government to intervene? And why was the magazine considered contraband?

The government did not intervene until the fourth and final issue published (a fifth issue was prepared but yanked off press at the time of my indictment; it may well have been our finest). As to why anything was considered "contraband," as you put it, or "obscene," as government lawyers put it, is a mystery to me. You must understand that the crime of "obscenity" or "pornography" is a crime without definition or victim. It is very much like the crime of "witchery" in centuries past. It is a bag of smoke used to conceal one's own dislikes with regard to aspects of sexual portrayal or behavior. It has been said that obscenity to one man is the laughter of genius to another. The very closest I can come to documentation for an answer to your question is a book written by—as I recall—either a Supreme Court justice's clerk or a member of the Justice Department and perhaps even by a U.S. attorney general whose name was something like Nicholas deKatzenbach [Nicholas deBretteville Katzenbach], in which (on about two pages of the book) he describes the meeting at which it was decided to indict me. According to that account, Bobby Kennedy (who I think preceded Katzenbach as attorney general, or maybe Katzenbach was assistant AG at the time; I'm unsure) feared that a feature in *Eros* depicting a pair of nude dancers (no genitals showing), consisting of a black man and white woman, would undermine the Kennedy administration's racial integration efforts. This has always seemed bizarre to me, but I'm giving you facts as I recall having read them in that book. My own personal belief is that Bobby (now, ironically, known to have been an energetic whoremonger—and I point this out not to put him down on moral grounds but to underscore his religious and legal hypocrisy) acted at the instigation of a New York priest, head of a local Catholic-front antipornography outfit, and a man in Cincinnati who headed a national antipornography unit of the church called something like Citizens for Decency in Literature. I believe his name was Keating [Charles H. Keating Jr.] and that he was later imprisoned for major crime during the savings-and-loan scandal. Following my indictment, both of these gents boasted publicly of their roles in convincing Bobby Kennedy to attack me. For more details, see my book *Castrated: My Eight Months in Prison* (designed, magnificently, by Lubalin), a short version of which was published in the *New York Times Magazine* during 1973, as I recall.

I remember the "interracial" portfolio very well. It ushered in a major shift in attitudes. Previously, such a

thing was called miscegenation (a term that has a biological/legal taboo-sounding ring). Were you aware when you published the photographs—indeed, when you published articles on prostitutes, aphrodisiacs, et cetera—that you were taunting the powers who could do you harm? Did you believe that you could actually go to prison for what you were doing?

> Absolutely not. I thought I was exercising my constitutionally guaranteed rights of freedom of expression.

Today it is hard to imagine that a magazine with such artful erotica was a threat to society. Indeed, your magazine paved the way for the then-unforeseeable permissiveness in today's media. What happened to you as a result of this pioneering effort?

> Clearly, my career as a publisher was all but ruined. It is tough to envision today, especially by someone like yourself in the field of art, but I became a social outcast as a result of my conviction and imprisonment—a U.S. Supreme Court–certified felon, at that—and very few established businesses would deal with me. Thus, my publishing potential after release from prison was severely circumscribed. I have always felt that I might have become a major force in American publishing had it not been for my conviction. Instead, I'm just a curious footnote.

Fact was a trailblazer in terms of content and design. It was a magazine devoted often to a single theme of social import. I remember your infamous Goldwater cover, accusing him of being psychologically unfit to be president (which got you sued for libel) after he advocated the use of nuclear weapons in Vietnam. What was the reasoning behind *Fact*?

> Well, the government itself was so astounded when the Supreme Court upheld my conviction that *ten years* elapsed between the time of my indictment and the moment when the Justice Department screwed up the courage to pack me off to prison. The strategy was to give the public plenty of time to forget about the case, and it worked. During this period, I first published a magazine called *Fact* (another design par excellence by Lubalin) and then *Avant Garde*. It was a trailblazer in inveighing against the bane of smoking as well as being *first* to attack Detroit for automobile *un*crashworthiness, and Ralphie Nader, a Harvard student, was *Fact*'s discovery; many thousands of Americans remain alive every year now as a direct result of *Fact*'s pioneering article, "American Cars Are Death Traps." Although *Fact* was hard-hitting, it was not controversial in a way that enabled the government to suppress it. It was not highly visual, like *Eros;* controversial pictures, it seems, not words, excite the ire of censors.
>
> *Fact*'s editorial purpose is best described by its subtitle: *An Antidote to the Timidity and Corruption of the American Press.* In today's journalism, where almost everyone in the field considers her- or himself a crusader and investigative reporter, it is difficult to imagine this, but back then the media really were, by and large, the mouthpieces of big business and big government. Thus, there was a need for *Fact*. The Goldwater case outcome was another free press/free speech debacle—and a catastrophe for my small company. I don't want to bore your readers with details of yet another miscarriage of justice, and so I'll pass on a lengthy answer to this question.

Fact's covers were ostensibly typographic, more like an advertisement than a traditional magazine cover. How would you characterize Lubalin's design of the magazine?

You're right. *Fact* was partially distributed by newsstand. We felt the need to try to stand out against our competition via shrieking covers.

Avant Garde was another rule buster. Published in the late sixties, it was somewhere between a New Left journal, such as *Evergreen*, and an underground newspaper. With Herb Lubalin as your art director, it was beautiful and decidedly a trendsetter in terms of type and image. What was the impetus to start this magazine?

Herb and I longed to get back to a highly graphic magazine, and, with the permission of my lawyers (remember, imminent imprisonment was hanging over my head all during this period), we launched the more highly visual *Avant Garde*. It was, by the way, my own favorite among my dozen or so periodicals.

What was the reception to the magazine, and what caused its demise?

The magazine was an instantaneous sensation among the intelligentsia—writers, toilers in the arts, academicians, et al. It was killed when, as I indicated above, I was belatedly imprisoned on the *Eros* case. I attempted to revive *Avant Garde* after my release, but its momentum had been lost and my attempt was a failure. A very costly one, I might add, which drove me to the cusp of bankruptcy. Fortunately, I was able to reverse my financial nosedive through the subsequent success of yet another periodical, the consumer advisor *Moneysworth,* which had a circulation of 2.4 million copies.

You pioneered unorthodox methods of marketing your magazines. Full-page ads in newspapers and magazines announced your products (sometimes with photographs of you as pitchman). I understand that sometimes you didn't even have the product before you began to advertise. Where did this notion come from? And was it successful?

It was hugely successful and stemmed from a great American tradition dating back to the Revolution (and probably before that to Europe). The word "subscribe," as in magazine "subscription," comes from the Latin for "underwrite." Potential subscribers who shared the vision of a particular editor would *underwrite* the cost of launching his periodical, in advance of its actual appearance, by *subscribing* to it. Thus, we were able to solicit subscriptions and collect payments for our new magazines even before they appeared. That is how, with capital of just $400, I was able to become a publisher. Ironically, it was *Fact,* perhaps more than any other magazine of its time, that promoted the consumer protection movement. But this same movement eventually got laws passed that banned the solicitation of payments for products that did not yet exist. That's why all announcements for new magazines nowadays declare, "Send no money! We'll bill you later!" It's illegal to collect money for a magazine that does not yet exist. Unfortunately, this put the kibosh on launching magazines based upon editorial content; today, new magazines are predicated mostly upon advertising potential, not editorial message. Multitudes of worthy periodicals in the nineteenth and early twentieth centuries could not have appeared except for this exciting mechanism. Its demise—and the resultant huge loss of expression for nonconformists—has never been chronicled by anyone but myself.

Why did *Fact* fold?

Because of Barry Goldwater's libel suit, alluded to previously.

After publishing, you focused on photography, becoming a stringer for wire services and New York City dailies, and then a staffer for the *New York Post*. How did this evolution take place?

Well, by the mid-1980s Herb had died, and many of my original key staffers had moved on to bigger jobs. I felt that my publications had degenerated into mere moneymaking machines. I myself had amassed more wealth than I could possibly spend pleasurably for the rest of my life, and I decided to dissolve the company. I gave my staffers two years' advance notice that the company would be folding, stopped taking new subscriptions, and methodically wound down operations. To some degree, I was weary of the struggle, I decided to try to have some pure fun. Photography had always fascinated me, and, by studying manuals and practicing on my own, I developed professional-level skills.

Has photography taken over as your passion and vocation? What are you doing now?

Yes, I'm obsessed by it, and have been for over a decade. I continue to freelance for news media across the United States and Europe. My work also appears in magazines—from *Life* to *Natural History* to the *National Enquirer*. In addition to general assignment, I shoot sports. The UPI has just retained me to shoot the Goodwill Games being staged here in New York this summer, over a two-week period. I'm something of an avian portraitist; my bird pictures have appeared on Audubon calendars and elsewhere. My biggest break in photography will be the appearance in spring 1999 of a book of 510 of my news photographs presented by Harry N. Abrams, the art book publisher. I do not wish to reveal details of the book at this time, but its approach is unprecedented. George Plimpton has written the foreword.

Tibor Kalman on Social Responsibility

Tibor Kalman was born in Budapest and raised in suburban New York. He was educated at New York University and on the streets of New York City. In 1968, he started working for the company that became Barnes & Noble. In 1979, he founded M&Co. He was art director at *Artforum,* creative director of *Interview,* and the founding editor in chief of *Colors,* for which he edited the first thirteen issues. In 1993, he suspended M&Co. and moved with his family to Rome. In 1995, he left *Colors* and reanimated M&Co. to work primarily on noncommercial projects.

For over a decade, first as the principal of M&Co. and then as editor of *Colors,* you've been on a mission to change the way people in the design field address the world. How did this missionary zeal take hold?

M&Co. started in 1979 as just another design firm. For me it was about leaving the big company I was working for, Barnes & Noble, and starting out on my own doing the only thing I knew how to do. Our first project was signage for E. J. Korvette's department stores, a chain of discount stores in New York. During the first five years of M&Co. we did a tremendous amount of garbage. By the mid-1980s we were moving to a kind of Robin Hood idea where we would do ugly work for corporations and interesting work for rock bands and cultural institutions. In 1986, we began showing our music work to corporate clients because in the mid-eighties (and suddenly!) corporate clients started becoming younger and hipper.

What made you change your focus?

Because I could see that the other way wasn't going to be enough to keep me interested in design. The mission began when I started thinking, "Does what designers do make the world look nicer or more interesting or better?"

What did you decide?

I was dissatisfied with the notion of having something look "good" or "nice." That's when I became interested in the vernacular.

How do you differentiate what you call "garbage" from vernacular?

Vernacular is the result of a lot of time, very bad tools, and no money. In New York it might be a bodega sign in Spanish Harlem or the graphics on the side of an ice delivery truck. A tremendous amount of care is taken with the work, and there's real concern about beauty and stuff like that. However, because there is no skill, it comes out kind of clunky—but beautiful, in my opinion. Garbage is bad, stupid, but professional graphics: junk mail, the Korvette's signs and Citibank brochures we designed.

Were aesthetics your only bête noire?

No. I like beautiful things, so this was not just about aesthetics. The thing that started to bother me, after we got good at producing garbage, was the extent to which we were being asked to lie and the extent to which we were asked to put pretty faces on nasty corporate behavior.

Like what?

We did annual reports for the Limited for a couple of years. Each time we were asked to do a very pretty annual report that made the company, which was having its share of problems, look like everything was hunky-dory.

So you were spin doctors.

Isn't that what most of design is about—using design to make something seem different from what it truly is? So that's the point at which I began to worry about what we designers, who are very skillful and have powerful tools at our disposal, are doing in the world, what role we are playing—making the filthy oil company look "clean," making the car brochure higher quality than the car, making the spaghetti sauce look like it's been put up by Grandma, making the junky condo look "hip." Is that all okay or just the level to which design (and many other professions) have sunk? That was the point at which the AIGA conference in San Antonio, "Dangerous Ideas," happened. Milton Glaser and I were cochairs, and we decided to raise ethical and moral issues (I'm sure it was not the first time) at a national conference of designers.

Before that, at the second AIGA conference in 1988, you mounted an offensive against Esprit, the winner of that year's AIGA corporate award. Was that the fulmination of your frustration with, say, the Limited or other companies you were dealing with?

What shocked me was that the AIGA could reward a company like Esprit just for having a semicool public relations face, just for the fact that they had hired hip designers. It didn't seem to me to be the role of design in the world. I wanted to make sure that people saw the other side of the coin and the contradiction in their positions.

You mounted an anonymous leaflet campaign calling into question Esprit's poor labor practices. It was a strong indictment, but you didn't acknowledge that you were behind it. In fact, you even denied your involvement.

Yeah, I wasn't ready to come out. I wasn't sure enough of my legs and theory.

So when did your legs get stronger?

Well, a few years later I was working for Benetton, which was the same thing as Esprit (ironically, Oliviero Toscani was creative czar for both); although my project for Benetton, the magazine called *Colors,* was totally independent editorially, I acknowledge that you can't be a designer and have nothing to do with corporations. It's almost impossible. In rare cases it's not even bad.

Do you feel like you were able to succeed at making those contradictions public?

No. I was terrible at it. I could make people laugh at it, but I couldn't solve the contradictions, and I couldn't address it in a way that would convert people. I think that the long-term series of criticisms that I made of the community have been useful. But I don't think that anything has been resolved.

A milestone of your mission to make design free from hypocrisy was the so-called Kalman/Duffy debate, where you were fairly critical of Duffy's public position about what design does for business. In retrospect, do you feel that was a useful forum for making designers conscious of their actions?

That was at a time when Duffy was owned by this big designer/entrepreneur from England named Michael Peters, who was going to turn Duffy's firm into the Gap of corporate design. They were taking full-page ads in the *Wall Street Journal* telling corporations that they could turn shit into gold. I read those ads as, "The way we'll turn shit into gold is that we'll put it in gold packaging, and we'll sell people bottles of the same old shit and just make it look fabulous, valuable, and lustrous," which is what Duffy was always very good at. To be fair, he could make good stuff look better, too. I mean, in a certain way, it's what most other designers and I are also good at. So, at the AIGA conference, there was an unsatisfying debate because I was not able to separate what I did very much from Duffy. And there were two kinds of people in the audience: those who were absolutely convinced of my position, and those who thought that it was outrageous that I, being a member of the community, would call into question the practices of the community. I think Michael Bierut said it best when he said there was no difference in what we did, it was just that I felt bad about it. In hindsight, I guess I was trying to change my role in the system and bring the contradiction to my colleagues' attention.

What was the response?

It was mostly negative. Designers are proud of what they do. No one likes to be called unethical. But to me, most design projects were about stretching the truth or embellishing it or hiding the negative aspects of the product. In this live debate, waves of responses came back saying, Where do I get off criticizing Duffy? (I used him only as an example; I was really challenging my profession, and so this was no surprise). The point was that there was a person out there yelling into the darkness, who was saying that maybe what we do, not what you do, not what Duffy does, but maybe what *we* all do is not quite right. Hadn't anyone said this before? Why was there not such a thing as criticism in our field? I'm sure there was, but everyone in that ugly hotel ballroom in that fake city in Texas seemed to be new to the idea.

Whatever success or failure you might have felt, the AIGA conference marked a moment when the design profession became self-reflective. How did you proceed from there? What changed for you in terms of your attitude?

I began to realize that I couldn't do image building for corporations anymore. And by the late eighties, much, though not all, of M&Co.'s work was shifting away from that. We began to find other ways to be busy and to survive outside the area of making brochures, annual reports, and corporate IDs. We worked on film titles, videos, our own products.

What about your philosophical direction?

I began to think about whether it would be possible to use my skills as a designer to promote good ideas instead of corporate profits. That's when I began to do a lot more lecturing and tried to move the firm from form to content.

In your missionary role, around 1990, you gave a highly publicized satiric presentation to the designers at Landor Associates in San Francisco, the nation's leading identity design company—the belly of the beast,

so to speak. Did you feel that had any kind of curative or cautionary effect, or was it ultimately for their amusement?

What I tried to do was to pick apart and expose the cynicism of corporate identity to the management at Landor. I was kind of a clown, and they probably got swelled egos thinking, Oh, we've really got this wild, revolutionary kind of guy in here, and aren't we so liberal that we allow him to speak to our staff?—probably what Luciano Benetton thought as well.

What I was after was just to throw wrenches into the works and reach some of the younger designers who hadn't quite made up their minds that Landor was going to be the way they would live their lives.

And the result?

I was beginning to formulate ideas about whether it was possible for me to use my skill at getting corporations to do self-critical stuff. That was one of my purposes at Landor, and I think to some extent there were some discussions inside Landor about what that meant. I don't know what the lasting impact of it was.

Why did you decide to close M&Co. after nearly fifteen years?

Very simply, because I became involved with a project that was better than all the stuff I had ever done at M&Co. With *Colors,* I had control over content. I was editor in chief. There was total freedom. There was even a decent budget. I had started working on *Colors* in 1991 and did it for two years and five issues in New York. At the time, there were a dozen to fifteen people working on *Colors* and a dozen to fifteen working on M&Co., and I bounced like a maniac between the two. I had two super-demanding, trying-to-reinvent the-wheel, full-time jobs! But I was having more fun on *Colors,* and it was a lot more interesting than wristwatches or album covers. I thought it would be a lot more useful to the world than the whole sum of M&Co.'s output from that period.

How did you reconcile Benetton—a clothing firm, similar to Esprit—*Colors,* fun, and usefulness for the world?

You don't become a corporation and you don't make profit in this world without exploiting people. And I knew that Benetton was a corporation, and everybody else I had ever worked for was a corporation, too. There are a couple of institutions that I've worked for, like a museum now, that is not in and of itself scummy, but it gets its money from scum. That's just how it is, and you're either going to go into a shell, go into academia, kill yourself, or figure out a way to swim among the barracuda.

At the time Oliviero Toscani, the creative director of Benetton, was doing very controversial "socially oriented" ads for Benetton that ultimately promoted knit goods. How did you feel about this?

At the time that I got involved, Toscani was doing those sweet unarguable antiracism ads where a black and white child play together or a black hand and a white hand are handcuffed together. Actually, I liked Toscani a lot as a person, and I believed that he was really concerned about those issues, and I believed that he spoke a language that was incredibly easy to understand around the world. That was the beauty of what he did.

So you were comfortable with the relationship?

I didn't have very much trouble reconciling with it at that time. I knew deep in my marrow that Benetton was probably not the nicest company in the world, but I thought that the freedom I was getting in making the magazine was worth the trade-off of having slightly filthy money in it. Remember, most ballet in the United States is funded by Philip Morris. Does that mean the dancers shouldn't dance?

You mean you're not a purist?

I'm not independently wealthy. I can't afford purity. I don't believe it's the way to be effective. I took advantage of the fact that Benetton was ready, willing, and able to fund me, making a big international magazine whose message I could believe in, especially since I played a major role in creating that message. For me, the issue was that Benetton could wear *Colors* like a medal—that they (sometimes) could get good publicity for it was fair—as long as they didn't try to influence the message. I believe I had more freedom than 95 percent of magazine editors. It wasn't a magazine for everyone, but it was a magazine that I believed could reach young people in lots of different places around the world. I felt that the concerns and interests of the audience—young people, whether they were in Manila or Philadelphia—reflected similar frames of reference because of the global village, MTV, Coke and Pepsi, Adidas and Nike, technology and a shrinking planet, and that we could actually address issues that were relevant to both.

You did issues that were extremely powerful. One of the most striking was an issue on racism, which to me is still an exemplary piece of publishing activism from this decade.

I want to mention that we also did issues on sports and travel. Because what I wanted to do was take the serious issues, like racism and AIDS, and treat them with humor and sexiness, and take the issues like sports and travel and treat them more as issues of social relevance and politics.

Where did you, coming back to the United States, want to resume your career?

The one thing I didn't want to do was to begin where I had left off. I didn't want M&Co. to work "commercially" any longer—that is, I didn't want it to sell stuff. What I really wanted to do was to find—or better yet, invent—a magazine to edit. There have been a couple of projects in my life that I would have been happy to continue to work on for the rest of my life. One of them was *Colors*. The other one was the Talking Heads video.

The video, which introduced moving type as a visual element on the screen, was a wonderful piece of form, but how could you do that for the next century?

I think there is a thoroughly exploited but equally unexplored relationship between image and type, especially moving image and type. While we see a tremendous amount of type on television now and on commercials because it's such an effective way of communicating two messages in the space/time of one, I sincerely believe that the extent to which it's being done is still only scratching the surface. What we were doing in the Talking Heads stuff back in 1989 was really ahead of its time. It was a way of creating narrative with design, using words as pictures and, maybe, using pictures as words. That was the relationship in *Colors* too. I'm fascinated with telling stories using images as opposed to words. And a lot of my work right now is about the ways in which images can be arranged as messages.

Since returning to the United States, are you happy or are you disappointed in where design as a community has gone?

I'm disappointed. A couple of things bother me: one is the extent to which technology has evolved. The evolution of technology has been tremendous. I'm not computer-literate at all. And at the risk of being thought an old fogey, I mistrust what computers do to ideas. But given the impact of computers within the design world, the impact of computers on photography, the impact of the Web, I think that there has been a really fundamental sea change, a kind of shift of the critical mass.

For better? For worse?

For both. It's made it much easier for designers to become more responsible about the things that go through their studios. That's an opportunity that right now is wasted.

Wasted in what sense?

It's wasted on obfuscation. It's wasted on a trashy kind of commercialism instead of even cool commercialism. It's wasted on corporate Web sites that are pointless. I think a thing like the Levi's Web site, which everybody talks about as being really cool, is useless because they haven't figured out what it should do. If they could figure out what it could do, it would be revolutionary, but designers are failing to do that. Again, they're failing to consider that content begets form, not vice versa—you can't get around that. If something is useless, it does not mean that it won't sell. Look at the stuff on the shelves at Kmart; watch the home shopping channel.

Has the word "cool" replaced "meaningful"?

Well, I think the word "cool" has replaced the word "content." If you have enough attitude in your work, if it's cool enough, then it doesn't matter that there's no content. The best example of this is David Carson. It's cool, and so it doesn't need to say anything. And I think this is a fundamental misunderstanding of what design is. Because it's just a language. It's just a means of communicating. It's a medium. It's not a message. It doesn't have any message in it unless somebody comes along and puts a message in it. Just because you make something cool doesn't mean that it is something. If nothing is cool, then it's nothing. And that's why this sort of work is disappointing for me.

And yet you feel that given this new technology, designers have more power and therefore should have more responsibility?

Because of the technology, we have the opportunity to become really important. We don't need publishers anymore to do this. Just look at the Web designers, they can single-handedly reach the world—eventually with full-motion video and stereo sound. We can do this for free; we can all do it at home, not only designers, but also everybody else in the world. So, I am excited by it because I am hoping that people are going to be serious enough to not be constantly in search of something that's just cool, but to be in search of ideas that can eventually begin to fill these huge empty vessels of technology.

Are you gearing up to preach to the design community again?

No. Yes. No. I'm just trying to do good work. I'm trying to make it really hard on myself, and I'm trying to make it really hard on my audience, and I'm trying to do work that just leaps forward. That's what I want.

RICHARD SAUL WURMAN

INFORMATION
ARCHITECTS

In·for·ma·tion Ar·chi·tect [L *info-*
RALPH APPELBAUM
tectus] n. 1) the individual who
PETER BRADFORD
organizes the patterns inherent
CARBONE SMOLAN   MURIEL COOPER/DAVID SMALL
in data, *making the complex*
RICHARD CURTIS
clear. 2) a person who creates
DONOVAN AND GREEN
the structure or map of infor-
NIGEL HOLMES   JOHN GRIMWADE
mation which allows others to
MARIA GIUDICE/LYNNE STILES
find their personal path to
JOEL KATZ   KRZYSZTOF LENK/PAUL KAHN
knowledge. 3) the emerging 21st
DAVID MACAULAY
century professional occupation
DAVE MERRILL
addressing the needs of the age
CLEMENT MOK   DON MOYER
focused upon clarity, human un-
BRUCE ROBERTSON   NATHAN SHEDROFF
derstanding and the science of
ERIK SPIEKERMANN
the organization of information.
ALEXANDER TSIARAS   RICHARD SAUL WURMAN
-In·for·ma·tion Ar·chi·tec·ture
PETER BRADFORD *EDITOR*

Richard Saul Wurman on Information Architecture

In his best-selling book, *Information Anxiety* (1990), Richard Saul Wurman developed an overview of the motivating principles that stem from his desire to know rather than to already know, from his ignorance rather than his intelligence, from his inability rather than his ability. He received both masters and bachelor's degrees in architecture from the University of Pennsylvania, where he was awarded the Arthur Spayd Brookes Gold Medal and where he established a deep personal and professional relationship with the architect Louis I. Kahn. He founded Access Press Ltd. in 1981 and The Understanding Business (TUB) in 1987, and created an annual design competition for the AIGA in 1995. A major project of TUB was the restructuring and design of the 30 million Smart Yellow Pages directories distributed in California by Pacific Bell annually. In 1984, he created the TED conferences—Technology Entertainment Design—of which he has been and remains the chairman and creative director.

"Information architecture" is a term that you coined over two decades ago to define the real schism in visual communication. What does this mean to you today?

I coined the term formally in 1976 when I was national chairman of the AIA [American Institute of Architects] conference, and I called it the "architecture of information." The whole conference was about information architecture.

How were you defining "information architecture" at that time?

The ability to make the complex clear, and an emphasis on understanding as opposed to styling. Now, twenty-two years later, there actually are some people who focus their attention just on doing this. There are several people who now use the term "information architect" on their cards as opposed to "graphic designer." But the schism remains fundamental. The people that are held near and dear by most of the members of the AIGA, the gold-medal heroes of our profession, are still the stylists.

Is that the key difference?

It is the fork in the road: Make something look good or be good.

And the twain cannot meet?

Oh, sure, they can meet. You can make something be good that will also be handsome. But you can't just go to make something look good, look different, look stylish, and then hope to find your way back to making something understandable. My fundamental emphasis is on the celebration of understanding. I think that's really our duty as communicators, to make things understandable, and if you truly, in an artful way, make them understandable, they are also handsome, without a doubt!

So, it's the old "form follows function" issue?

Well, it's the form follows performance. Function is taking a shit. Performance is the art of the working theater of digestion.

A vivid description, to be sure. How do you see the role of the graphic designer having changed over the past decade?

Well, this small group has changed from mascara to meaning. Because they've recognized what I predicted twenty-two years ago, that this is where all the business is going to be, where more and more work is going to be for the profession, and this is a much more noble and artistic thing to do. The rest is really fashion. David Carson is fashion. He is Mr. Armani. He's not even Mr. Armani. He's Mr. Versace. I mean, that's bullshit. You know, here today, gone tomorrow. I can't tell you how boring fashion magazines are and fashion shows are. I find them utterly boring. It is so shallow and thin that I can't get it up to even watch them.

Historically, who would you say prefigures the information architecture movement?

Beck's London Underground map. This is the ubiquitous piece of graphic design that embodied in it the desire to communicate and make things understandable to masses of people. And it is certainly handsome.

What about the Swiss school? Was that style or was that information?

It's a formality and an arrangement. It's just not a deep way of *understanding*. It's not as fundamental. I mean, there are people in that movement who have made wonderful pictograms. Is that information? *Yes*, they help understanding. But it's like serving tea, it's not a whole dinner. I think they're good. I'm not trying to throw the baby out with the bathwater. It's not a way of life; it's manners.

You have a problem with pictographs?

I don't think pictographs are bad. I'm not trying to be picky. They are nice things for an information architect to do and to use, but they're not information architecture in the broadest sense. There are wonderful pictograms, such as those that are done for the Olympics and all. They clarify things. They help you make choices. They are a kind of a vocabulary of understanding. I find it strange that they redo them every time there's an Olympics, though.

I guess that's the nature of graphic design—difference and newness are virtues, even if the existing thing is already functional.

Hopefully, information architecture is not just graphic design. The TED conference is information architecture because I design how people communicate in real time, and I change the structure of my conference so that what I design gets rid of the anxiety of understanding in real time, in physical space and time. It's all information architecture. A good phone call is information architecture. Good words, the appropriate relationship between words and visual things, is information architecture.

What is the cure for the anxiety of understanding?

The disease is when "information" doesn't tell you what you want or need to know. Most things we call information are not information. There's not been an information explosion; there's been an explosion of noninformation. When it's not in a state that informs—

and most of the word "information" is the word "inform"—it's just meaningless stuff. The cure is good information architecture.

Is noninformation really misinformation?

They are different things. You might have a whole bunch of numbers that could be absolutely accurate, but you can't understand them. That's not misinformation. That's data. And we get huge amounts of data, and much of this we think we're supposed to understand because people call it information. We get accordion printouts on our desk, and if you are an executive in a large company and you think that the person down the hall understands them, you give more money in your budget to the department that produces things that nobody uses or understands.

Who should be an information architect?

People who have a passion about understanding, which in my opinion should be any healthy human being. I get several e-mails every day from individuals from someplace in the world who find my name, who want me to suggest a school or books and courses that they can take and other people to write to because they want to follow the career of information architecture.

You said it earlier, graphic design is at the fork in the road. And unless graphic designers can understand exactly how they can play a role in the world that you're talking about, they opt for the easier world, or they opt for the easier road to take, which of course is stylization. It's fashion because fashion is hipper.

They've got to realize, fashion is easy, really easy. Yet our society glorifies the people who are the best at doing fashion.

The last decade has seen an increase in information in more media than I suspect even you anticipated. What is the role of the info architect in this new media world? And I'm presuming that not even you foresaw the extent to which the Web and other electronic media would be taking over. Or did you?

I certainly didn't know about the Web. I saw the explosion and the power of communication. But did I see it in the numbers of what's happening now? Probably not. But I certainly said in speeches fifteen years ago that "this is where all the work is going to be in the future; don't you guys get it?" I went around school by school to say, "You should get a degree in information architecture; this should be a real focus of attention. It's not a matter of doing a real beautiful map; it's about doing a map that works." I did that at Art Center, and I did it in Philadelphia College of Art (as it was called then) and at RISD, and nobody cared.

Is information management the designer's final frontier, or is there something else on the horizon? In other words, are we going to bypass graphic design?

I think the art of understanding will always be the final frontier, and the art of understanding hasn't changed since the invention of words. Why should it change? The goal of civilization is to make information understandable, and that's been in words, songs, pictures, and numbers.

But is it going to be, should it be, will it always be the goal of the graphic designer?

I don't think there will be graphic designers. I think there will be information architects! There will be people who understand words, pictures, numbers, and the technology to communicate them. Nobody is being trained to do that now.

Who or what in your opinion is leading the way and why?

Failure always leads the way. The fact that most graphics don't work dances with the need for understandable communication, understandable information about things, understandable instructions. Web pages don't work, and TV news programs don't work, and there are more and more of them, and therefore it's clearer, the failure. Actual catastrophe, or the perception of catastrophe, promotes creative change.

Are we talking about stripping things down to the barest essentials?

No, just deciding how you find something. How do you take a journey? How do you empower people to take their own journey? If I wanted to get in my car and drive to California right now, I could go a lot of different ways. I could go the fastest way. I could go the scenic way. I could go the way—because I have a convertible—where it's just most fun to drive. I could go a way that hits all the best museums, or all the best anything. Or I could go because I want to stop and camp along the way, God forbid. I could go because of the weather; I might have to take a certain route. I could go on a gastronomical tour. I could go many different ways. Correct? In every way, the journeys would be different, but I would be empowered to do it because I know how to drive my car and read a map, and I could decide how I want to find these things, and I'd have to research how to get there.

Is information architecture in part providing the ability to decide whether you want to make that trip a fast one or an enriching one?

No. It's empowering you to make those decisions on how you want to go through it.

But you could go through it any way.

If we're talking about a really good Web page, you could find your own journey through the stuff that's behind the Web page. That's the point.

What do you think the influence of your TED conference has had on this electronic manifestation of the Web or CD?

I'd rather you ask people who come to TED.

Well, what would you like to have had come out of it, given all the input that you put into it?

Much more comes out of it than I ever tried to have come out of it or anticipated. I did not plan the success or the power of the meetings. I still don't fully understand it. You know I'm arrogant about almost everything, but I don't have arrogance about this because I'm constantly surprised. It's just much more of an event than I ever meant it to be. And people create new ideas, new projects, new magazines, new companies, new conversations, new friendships, new epiphanies, new things that come out of it that I never anticipated. And it continues to be that way. I mean, I have big ideas for this TED-X February 2000 conference. If it follows the pattern, it will have much more power, many more and longer legs.

Is this why you created a TED MED conference?

The need in the medical profession is also for information architecture. The importance and power of understanding healthcare information effects the delivery of lower-cost, better-value healthcare, *and creates* better patients and better doctors. Nobody has looked at that slice. That slice is the information architecture slice of an industry that's 10 percent of the GNP. Few graphic designers care about it or focus on it!

Technology Entertainment Design, how do these forces interact?

The choice of the word "entertainment" rather than "education" is important. A lot of people think "education" seems to be a more responsible word. I find it the least responsible word because we have boards of education that have given us really terrible learning experiences. It's "entertainment" because it's information in an entertaining form that allows us to learn. And "entertainment" is not a bad word. And I'm not talking about stand-up comedian entertainment. Although I must say, some of the clearest notions of politics have come to me from comedians saying something. That's why at my conference I always have musicians and jugglers and magicians. Simply, it is the design of information in an entertaining form using appropriate technology.

So take out the *E*, and you can't have *T* or *D*?

In order to do technology that relates to communications today, you need entertainment and design, and you can go through the three of them each way. Is design becoming a science? No. Just more systemic. Just more thoughtful. But then, I wouldn't call psychology a science either.

Where do you feel you must go next with the TED idea and ideal?

I will take this celebration of understanding public in February 2000. I don't know what I'm going to do after that.

Is this what we, the people, want?

I don't care. That's what I want. The minute you start judging your work based on forces and intellects and minds outside of yourself, you don't know how to make judgments. I make judgments based on what I want to know, based on my ability to understand. And my innocence and my ability come from being a dumb shit.

Michael Ray Charles on Racial Stereotypes

Michael Ray Charles is a representational painter whose work in the early 1990s addressed political and social issues with homage to such nineteenth-century commentators as Goya and Daumier. In 1993, he began painting racial stereotypes (mammies, Sambos, and coons) derived from vintage commercial art that incorporate wit and irony to attack both the racism of the past and present. His paintings are rendered in a primitive style, and he quotes old circus banners, vernacular signs, and folk paintings—a pastiche that underscores the fact that these disturbing images were once America's most popular art. Charles was born in Lafayette, Louisiana, and teaches painting at the University of Texas at Austin. He has had solo exhibitions at the Art Museum of the University of Houston; Tony Shafrazi Gallery, New York; Moody Gallery, Houston; and Galerie Hans Mayer, Düsseldorf, Germany. His works are in the permanent collections of the Museum of Fine Arts, Houston; San Antonio Museum of Art; and the Albright-Knox Art Gallery, Buffalo.

In your recent catalogue, *Michael Ray Charles: An American Artist's Work,* you ask, "What if the Jews never talked about the Holocaust?" Do you feel that nineteenth- and early-twentieth-century caricatures of African-American representations—the Sambo, mammy, minstrel, and coon—are ignored by blacks and whites?

A lot of blacks don't want to see images like mine; perhaps they bring up too much pain. A lot of whites are embarrassed and feel ashamed by them. But "out of sight, out of mind" doesn't mean that it doesn't exist. It happened, and I feel it has not been dealt with.

Do you feel that these images are still being used?

Let's talk basketball. When I look at some images of black basketball players in today's advertisements, I see references to the talented man-child or the ungrateful and unruly servant who should be happy to be receiving millions of dollars to entertain. It is unfortunate that the image of the Negro athlete, by my standards, has become the most visible definition of black masculinity.

How did you become aware of these stereotypical historical images? Were they introduced to you as a child or later?

As a child I may have seen a lot of such things around Louisiana, but I did not think much of them. When I was in graduate school, a colleague of mine had given me a little Sambo figurine. At the time I was doing paintings about the American flag, and so I didn't use these stereotypes initially—I didn't think it was what I was searching for. However, ever since I began to use such images, I haven't viewed life in the same way. They have taken me on a ride. And a wonderful ride, I might add.

How do Sambo, mammy, minstrels, Amos and Andy, and other images of this kind have relevance today?

I think the importance of these images to the development of American culture has been, in many cases, overlooked or misunderstood. Images of this nature are so significant to our definition of who we are, how we are, and what we shall be.

I've heard the argument that bringing this stereotypical imagery back to the surface merely rekindles old antagonisms. For a period of time, this was endemic to American mass media—one couldn't get away from ethnic and racial stereotypes. But after a certain amount of time, those specific images were eliminated, and there is at least a generation, if not more, that has never been exposed to this.

That's right. Such imagery was supposedly killed off. But I think that the images were repackaged and reintroduced to us in the images of J. J. from *Good Times,* Raj and Dee's mom from *What's Happening!!,* George Jefferson from *The Jeffersons,* and the woman who played Clifton Davis's mom from *That's My Mama.*

That leads me to Ellen Degeneres coming out of the closet on *Ellen*. Some people say this is a great thing. I recently asked the writer and performer Quentin Crisp his thoughts about this. When he was living in England (for the better part of his life) openly as a homosexual, and was being persecuted, arrested, and tried in court for his sexual orientation, could he ever have imagined something like this—a person's decision to admit homosexuality is broadcast over national media—and how did he feel about it? His response was, "It's still a caricature." Forty years ago, *Beulah* starring Ethel Waters (and later Louise Beavers) was the only American television show to feature a black woman as a leading character—and she was a maid. Later there was *Amos and Andy.* Today there are many television shows starring black men, women, and children. Do you feel that these spawn a new breed of stereotypes?

Yes and no. I can't blame the actors, producers, directors, or writers because we've all been affected by these images. They're drawing upon what they've consumed. One of the biggest problems I have with stereotypical imagery about blacks is that so many of the people that these images were made to mimic or to define have accepted such variations as their equal. I think a lot of the stereotypes have been internalized and made human by blacks as well as whites.

Are you reprising the minstrel character, the Sambo character, the mammy character, and the Sapphire character (from *Amos and Andy*) as a kind of object lesson? Are you saying that the stereotypes we see now really have their roots in this, and we need to understand the essence of what a stereotype is?

I'd say yes. It's self-exploration. I want to know about these images—how they were used, why they were used, and when they are being used. There's more to my work than just blackface imagery or the clown caricature. On one level, it's me trying to say that what we're seeing now, in different variations, was originally rooted in these caricatures. On another level, my work goes beyond that. I am deeply motivated by various forms of communication. I like finding out how things have evolved to mean what they mean. I see images of the black basketball player everywhere. I know it's a hot fad, but I remember watching the Olympics when the first Dream Team was assembled. Oh boy, did America jump on the backs of those athletes! It's like, "These are Americans; we can kick everybody's butt." Everybody seemed to be blown away that the team was as awesome as it was, how they just walked over these other countries' teams. It was like the flag blowing in the wind, all shining and shit. The beautiful red-white-and-blue flag at its best, with the right amount of wind passing through it so that you get the full flap—confidence, cockiness, whatever you want to call it. But the reality is that the flag is more torn, *worn,* and tarnished, and that's the flag I think I find more attractive, more intriguing, because that's not a false face for me. You know, it's funny, I'm a very optimistic person. But in terms of the representations of the black in this country, I don't think much has changed.

But doesn't that ultimately present a positive and powerful image of black men and women?

It depends on who you're asking. I think that in some cases, however, an inaccurate abstraction of blacks remain.

The stereotype has changed from the poor, shiftless black field hand to the mighty supermen who are getting million-dollar contracts. But one of the things that I have found as I study historical stereotypes is the desexualization of black people. The mammy is certainly not a sexual character, and when placed in a couple situation, she's always the harpy, the one who won't let her husband get away with anything. How and why were these characters desexualized?

The black male and female images were desexualized so that they could not appear to be a threat to whites, in any capacity. I think they had to remain childlike, overweight, lazy, and unintelligent for whites to remind themselves of who they were. In some of today's advertising I now see the Negro athlete as this superbeing who is able to be all things within the confines of the arena. The image of the athlete is juxtaposed with the image of the criminal and the image of the rapper. When combined, you have the same old shit—a dangerously, uncontrollable, powerful physical specimen. In the nineties, this is beautiful. When something is thought of as beautiful, it is considered sexy. In this case, the sexually charged black male remains.

How does the minstrel show—that once popular form of entertainment where whites, stealing an essence of black people, put on blackface and cavort onstage—fit into the idea of deracination of black culture?

Minstrelsy was whites' attempt to mimic and make fun of blacks, but the "essence" of black people was not stolen. It cannot be stolen. Minstrelsy was a desire to become something or someone that was as great as the human longing to be. The essence of blackness, for me, is defined as being able to withstand, to evolve, to grow in spite of, to show one's wounds, to wear one's scars, and to get right back up because there is nothing else left to do.

But didn't the bombardment of these stereotypes in mass media influence how black people saw themselves?

Not only do I think those images influenced some blacks' interpretations of themselves, they continue to influence white, Asian, European, African, and many other cultures' perceptions of American blacks as well as how they see themselves. These images are forever part of the vocabulary of what one should want and what one should not want.

How do black people respond to your imagery?

I receive mixed responses. One black woman once asked me, "How does it feel to be the Clarence Thomas of the art world?"

I don't see the logic of her metaphor.

It seemed to me that she believed that Clarence Thomas was a sellout, and, by association, she was giving me the same label. She had a very limited perspective. I am an individual who happens to be black. The fact that I am black does not mean that I represent or support every black cause. Her comment initially bothered me. Ultimately, I found it more humorous than anything. Maybe she saw a part of herself in one of my paintings.

I wonder whether people have trouble distinguishing between these as insulting pictures or charged symbols?

I had a journalist walk up to me and say, "So tell me about the black woman in this painting." I responded by saying, "It's not a black woman; it's an image that I use to refer to a black woman." She then replied by asking about another painting in the same manner. I don't think she was able to separate the caricature image of a black person from the reality of what a black person actually is.

What about the aesthetic force of the image? Despite the grotesque caricatures, the drawings and paintings are often masterfully done.

Thank you. I think that there's good and bad in everything, and there's a beauty about these that I'm attracted to. I'm not going to tell you a lie. I'm very attracted to those images.

Whenever I lecture about black and Jewish stereotypes, I preface by saying that these are not the racist bile produced by hate groups. They are mainstream concoctions. Often the characters are very appealing. In the advertising trade literature of the early twentieth century, Aunt Jemima was called the most "friendly" American trade character. Do you see the images that you're drawing from here as essentially racist?

I have to say yes because of the time in which images like these flourished and the social conditions blacks were subjected to. I don't quite see today's evolved variations in the same way. It is obvious that we are living in a country that has grown and continues to evolve. How we are evolving is the issue: Have we reached a limit on what's new? Or is everything recycled, repackaged, and reprised until someone grabs the bait?

When I look at the original source material, I can't help but be repulsed by the fact that this is about promoting infantilism and reducing people to objects. I call it a cancer. For me, as a child, it must have had a subliminal impact on how I perceived black people. The first time I could think of a black woman as truly beautiful was when Diahann Carroll starred on television as a nurse in a show called *Julia*. When do you think perceptions among whites toward blacks began to change?

I am sure that was one of the times when it occurred. Perceptions about blacks didn't change overnight. It's evident that some white people's perceptions about blacks have never changed. This process of change has been a gradual thing that is consistently gaining and losing ground. I think that when Africans came to this country as slaves, the lust for the other began. Opposites have always attracted. The perceptions of blacks always change when whites find ways to utilize blacks for profit. However, the lust for blacks remains.

Speaking of beauty, once I gave a talk before a Jewish group of women and men between sixty and seventy years old. I showed them illustrations from *Little Black Sambo,* among other things, and talked about the negative connotations of that book. A woman came up to me afterward and said, "I loved that book. That was my introduction to black people."

I had the same thing happen to me recently. An elderly white woman came up to me and said, "Please don't make the Sambo ugly; I love little Sambo. I grew up with the Sambo; it's so dear to me." She started crying. I said, "You're speaking of this image as though it were a person." She went on to say that she's not racist, her children grew up around black people, they had black people over all the time, and she worked in a school in which she taught black students. This woman began making a cradling gesture as if she were holding a little baby. She didn't get it. She did not see that image as anything but a black person. That's one of the things that really motivates me to continue my exploration into these images and how they affect us.

How difficult has it been for you as an artist to use this taboo imagery?

At times it has been slightly discomforting. But I always seem to find inspiration to follow my heart.

In your catalogue, you talk about also being interested in the subculture heroine, pinup, bondage mistress Betty Page. How does that get integrated with your interest in black imagery?

I want to do a pinup series. I would like to explore some other ideas about beauty that I have been having for some time now. Besides, if you are going to do a pinup painting, you have to go to the source.

Among your paintings are images of mammies on the covers of the *Saturday Evening Post*. What is the motivation for those? Was it because the *Saturday Evening Post* never, or rarely, had a black person on the cover? The only Norman Rockwell painting I remember in the magazine with black people was the now-famous painting of the young girls being integrated into a Little Rock public school.

There were mammy images that surfaced on the cover of the *Saturday Evening Post*. I don't think that Rockwell did any of them, but there were some of those images there. My doing a parody on the *Saturday Evening Post* had nothing to do with whether or not an image of a black person was included in the magazine. I've been a big fan of the *Post* covers, more specifically the work of Rockwell. I think during this time he managed to capture an America in his art like no other I have seen. I gravitated toward his work the first time I saw it. Parody was my vehicle of expression, but after completing one painting I quickly became interested in how I could use the feelings I got from those covers to my advantage. This is what gave the Forever Free [a series of paintings using slave stereotypes] products their biggest push very early on.

We talked about how black people react to the paintings. How do white people react to them?

Mixed, you know. A lot of women cry. Some people feel apologetic. Some people just don't get the irony; they walk in and say something like, "I really enjoyed your show; it's very funny," then move on. I say, "Thank you for coming out." I don't worry about it anymore. You've just got to do what you've got to do. And when it's all said and done, then people do what they have to do.

Does the response of the viewer enter into your artistic decisions?

It used to bother me because I think deep down inside of me I wanted every black person to really understand my work and appreciate my work. I think my work challenges ideas about who black people are and who white people are—in terms of interpretation representation. Whatever responses I get about my work now, I evaluate them according to what I can or cannot learn from them. Otherwise, into the trash they go.

After years of involvement with these stereotypical images, how do you personally feel about them?

They deserve a certain respect. But you know, I think about so many people whose lives these images have affected. A lot of black people have died, and many are dying under the weight of variations of these images. That's motivation enough for me to explore and deal with these things.

Der Distriktschef von Krakau

ANORDNUNG

Kennzeichnung der Juden im Distrikt Krakau

Ich ordne an, dass alle Juden im Alter von über 12 Jahren im Distrikt Krakau mit Wirkung vom 1. 12. 1939 ausserhalb ihrer eigenen Wohnung ein sichtbares Kennzeichen zu tragen haben. Dieser Anordnung unterliegen auch nur vorübergehend im Distriktsbereich anwesende Juden für die Dauer ihres Aufenthaltes.

Als Jude im Sinne dieser Anordnung gilt:

1. wer der mosaischen Glaubensgemeinschaft angehört oder angehört hat,

2. jeder, dessen Vater oder Mutter der mosaischen Glaubensgemeinschaft angehört oder angehört hat.

Als Kennzeichen ist am rechten Oberarm der Kleidung und der Überkleidung eine Armbinde zu tragen, die auf weissem Grunde an der Aussenseite einen blauen Zionstern zeigt. Der weisse Grund muss eine Breite von mindestens 10 cm. haben, der Zionstern muss so gross sein, dass dessen gegenüberliegende Spitzen mindestens 8 cm. entfernt sind. Der Balken muss 1 cm. breit sein.

Juden, die dieser Verpflichtung nicht nachkommen, haben strenge Bestrafung zu gewärtigen.

Für die Ausführung dieser Anordnung, insbesondere die Versorgung der Juden mit Kennzeichen, sind die Ältestenräte verantwortlich.

Krakau, den 18. 11. 1939.

Wächter
Gouverneur

Morris Wyszogrod on a Designer in Captivity

Morris Wyszogrod was a graphic design student in Warsaw, Poland, at the time of the Nazi occupation in 1940. As a Jew, he was prohibited from plying his trade and instead forced by the Germans into a succession of labor and concentration camps. Using his skills as a calligrapher, typographer, and illustrator in the service of camp officials, he managed to survive the unspeakable horrors of the Holocaust. After being liberated in 1945, he immigrated to the United States where he went to art school and was ultimately hired by Paul Rand as a layout person and designer in the art department of the William H. Weintraub Agency, where Rand was chief art director. Wyszogrod continued to work in the advertising field. His memoirs, *My Brush with Death,* illustrated with drawings done after his release, is published by the State University of New York (SUNY) Press.

How did you come to be incarcerated in Nazi concentration camps?

The Germans occupied Poland, and they set up so-called Jewish Councils, Judenrat, whose assignment was to execute the orders given by the Germans. They gave out all sorts of decrees, but the main decree was to deliver groups of Jews to do slave labor, starting with cleaning the ruins that had been caused by bombing. Jews had to submit to the worst type of labor. The concentration camps came later on, when they decided to plan a mass extermination.

How old were you?

I was nineteen years old when the war broke out in 1939.

This was prior to the establishment of the Warsaw Ghetto?

Oh yes. The Warsaw Ghetto was established in 1940 on November 15, on a Monday morning. But the persecution started immediately. My first encounter with the Germans was in '39, a few weeks after they conquered Warsaw, when I was caught one morning walking toward the school of graphic design from which I graduated but did not receive my diploma because of the outbreak of the war. I was stopped by a soldier on the street, and he said, "Jude?" I said, "Jah" in German. He ordered me to climb into a truck, where forty Jews were assembled already. I dared to ask one of the soldiers where we are being taken, and he said, "You are going to work." We were driven to the central institute of physical training, north of Warsaw. The Germans asked every one of the Jews, "What type of work do you do, what's your profession?" I told them I was a graphic designer.

What was the response to saying you were a graphic designer?

The guy who was interviewing us said sarcastically to another soldier, "Look, we got an artist, a Jew. Can you imagine?" Then he said to us, "Today you'll be doing artwork." I was very happy because I saw big signs written in German Gothic, and I knew I could do that. He gave an order to follow him, and as we approached a building that was half in ruins, he said, "Line up against the wall, and take off your clothing and underwear." We thought that this was the end. Instead of shooting us he said, "With the underwear you clean the shithouse. This is going to be your artistic work today."

Were you ultimately sent to the ghetto?

No. First we were recruited to submit to forced labor by the Judenrat. They would march out thousands of Jews from the Jewish district to different points in Warsaw, mostly military barracks or military headquarters, to clean and do all kinds of dirty work like washing underwear, cleaning rooms, toilets, and so on. The hunger was horrible. So a neighbor of ours, whom I will never forget because his guidance led eventually to my survival, said to me, "Why don't you volunteer?" By volunteering, instead of being rounded up on the street, you had a chance to get maybe a better job or work indoors; most of us were forced to do work outdoors, with the exception of some professionals. To work outside meant rolling barrels of gasoline, cleaning up pavements, and working in the fields under constant beating and scary screams. The Germans liked to give orders screaming and beating at the same time. So I volunteered.

What did you volunteer for?

I didn't know. But they took us to the Warsaw airfield, where we had to start cleaning and repaving the runways, which the Poles destroyed, expecting the Occupation. The man who led this particular group was a teacher, a Jew from northern Poland by the name of Alan Eisenberg, and he asked me what type of work I did. Finding out what a Jew could do meant something for him and for the Jew because if he could contribute, he would calm the German Beast. So I told him I was a graphic designer. And I was brought into one of the old mansions at the airfield, and I was introduced to a young second lieutenant, who told me that he would investigate to see if I was telling the truth. If I was telling the truth, I would have a chance. If I didn't tell the truth, there wouldn't be any chance. So he introduced me to a higher-ranking officer, telling him that I was a Jew who claimed to be an artist. The officer laughed, and said, "We'll find out what kind of an artist you are." So I said, "I have no tools with me." He said, "We'll give you paper and ink." I said, "I have no brushes, I have no pen to calligraph." He couldn't find a pen, and so he gave me a simple pen point.

What did they want you to do?

Some calligraphy. He brought in a big sheet of paper, a target, and said that I should pick it up and hold it in front of me. I thought he was going to kill me, that he was going to aim into the target. He started laughing and said, "This is not meant to harm you. You will cut up the paper and you will work on the back. You will do calligraphy." In the meantime, I thought that I'd lost my heart.

Still, you didn't have a pen?

I said, "I am going to go strike something in the form of a pen. But I need a knife." We were warned that no Jew can have any tool, not even a spoon, or anything sharp—it

212

meant instant death. But I said, "If you give me a pocket knife, I am going to strike the pen." And I went outside into the garden, and I broke away a branch from a tree, and I made a flat pen for calligraphy. The officer watched me like a hawk. He was afraid that I would do something with the knife. So I put it back gently, took my tool in hand, and said, "Will you please give me your initials?" He said, "W. P., Wilhelm (or Willy) Pomeranten." I drew the *W* and the *P* in a nice, calligraphic way. He showed it to the lieutenant, who asked me, "Where did you study that?" I said, "In the city of Warsaw at the school of graphic design of the Marshall Joseph Pilsudski School." He asked, "Who were your teachers?" I said, "Both Poles and Germans," and he liked this and gave me an assignment to make three main signs for each soldier—for the closet, the bed, and his valise. And they loved it. I proved to them that I was not a liar, that I knew as much German Gothic calligraphy as the next German. And I proved it to them because I'd studied it, and I knew it well. This was my first job with this particular Luftwaffe unit.

Was this a regular position with them?

No. This was not a continuous career; I had to go through all sorts of efforts and assignments and scares and horrors for six years.

In the camps, how did practicing graphic design save your life?

I was rounded up and delivered to the flames of the Warsaw Ghetto. From there on, the destination was death. I was brought to the infamous Camp Majdanek, but I was lucky, with a group of other Jews, to be selected and be taken away to a subcamp that was a so-called labor camp, which was attached to the Heinkel Flugzeugwerk (airplane factories), set up in the area that was used before the war for Polish armament factories. This was the central district of industry in Poland. And they had all the machinery and all the equipment that they captured and their own equipment. This camp was supposed to do repair on planes. Later they brought in trucks and tanks. It seems that the Jew was able to adjust under severe conditions, and the so-called merchant became a good mechanic, a mechanic became a good electrician. And I was assigned by a miracle, chosen from being killed even in this camp, to do wall painting.

Regular housepainting?

Regular painting, inside and outside, painting walls in the newly erected barracks, factories, or big hangars, where they would bring in the damaged planes and parts. And from here on, again, I proved that I can paint not only the wall, but also nice letters. This was observed by somebody, who said, "Okay, can you make a sign?" The first sign I made was "For Jews and Dogs Entry Is Forbidden." I did similar signs and also very funny signs for their orgies that took place outside the perimeter of the death camps.

Was doing this artwork and this lettering considered an essential job? Did you believe that it was going to save you?

It saved me. I was getting assignments to make beautiful drawings for the Germans' loved ones back home in the "beautiful West" from the Schweineland, from Poland, from this piggy land where there is filth, vermin—the Jew and the Pole. I received my assignments from a man who was a murderer, while he described his love for art, and he made me draw in calligraphy a beautiful poem to his wife, with beautiful phrases to his beautiful family from a land that was devastating his soul. Because after all, he did not like to do what he was given to do, but "we have to do it." It was for the sake of the longevity of the German Reich and Hitler and the world. He did not like to dirty up his hands in filth and shit and blood. But this was something that he was lovingly assigned to do because there was a good reason for it. While this was going on between me and the murderer, I felt secure. My mother, the angel, was standing behind me and delaying my execution, delaying my death. But I was not always lucky to encounter these so-called clients of mine.

It is difficult to think of them as your "clients." Once you told me about another client, an SS commandant who made you copy master paintings for his personal collection.

He was an art lover. He had rolls of canvases. I don't know where the canvases came from. And he made me copy one because he borrowed it from a friend, and he wanted to have a copy. I did not expect him to give this explanation.

Do you remember what the painting was?

A landscape by Delacroix. He was very nice to me. He would come in to visit me and would take out a cigarette, and I would apologetically tell him, "Unfortunately, I cannot smoke this cigarette because I don't even have a match; I'm not supposed to have a match." He said, "Well, with me you don't have to play. Here is a match; light the cigarette while you work."

Did you have the proper materials for this kind of work?

It was a big problem to get tools and paint. I told him I had no canvas and I had no brushes, and the only tools I painted with outside the perimeter of the camp in the factory were big brushes for wall painting. He said I should not worry; he'd get a car, he'd change my striped clothing into a German suit, one of these linen-type combination trousers and blouse that were buttoned up—they didn't have any zippers. And he told me to wear a cap because I had a special haircut in the camp, what they called "the avenue for lice." Of course, they had these storerooms with tons of clothing taken away from the living before they were dying or after they were killed.

So, he allowed you to leave the camp?

Yes. They drove me to Lublin, and it was nice and quiet, and I got access to paint stores, where I got turpentine and linseed oil and some brushes and some canvas. The SS man with the gun who took me there signed a voucher. The Poles were unhappy. They assumed who I was because the relationship between me and the guard was somehow strange, very formal, and I didn't want to talk too much. Of course, I spoke Polish to them.

Did you do other kinds of assignments as your career progressed?

I did a horrible poster, a skull on a black background, a skull and into the eye of the skull a crawling louse, and it said, "Jew Pestilence. Be Careful." I did all kinds of slogans on the wall. There were slogans that were taken from the SS lexicon. For instance, "My Life Is Devoted to the Führer, to the Dream"; "Love, Smoke, and Gorge Yourself to Death"; "Drink Yourself to Death." Filthy slogans, pornographic slogans, which they used for parties. Pornography they liked.

Were you segregated from the other members of the Jewish population? Were you in some cleaner studio or barracks or something?

For a short time I was isolated from the barracks because they claimed that if I came in touch with them, I might bring lice and pestilence. Therefore, they put me in a barrack with two more Jews, a father and a son. He worked in the administration, and because of his position he managed to sneak in his son, who was not feeling so well. So we slept for a short time in a little cubicle next to the barracks. This was a special privilege because they were afraid that I would bring lice. They were scared to death of typhus.

Was there any time during this career when it seemed as if your usefulness was over to them as a designer?

Yes. They sent us to different camps to do different types of work, like digging up graves and burning the bodies. This was no artwork. This was death work. One of the camps was Plaszów, where Steven Spielberg set his movie. I was not privileged there.

Did you end your time in the camps as a graphic artist?

No. As a plain mortal. I was liberated in Theresienstadt.

Wasn't Theresienstadt the so-called model camp, where the Germans allowed a modicum of freedom to prove to the Red Cross that concentration camps were more or less humane?

Yes. But it wasn't so. This was a transfer camp to the death camps. Most of the inmates were German Jews, Austrian Jews, mixed marriages, half-Jews, three-quarter Jews, all kinds of people—devastated people. They had an orchestra there, but not in my days. I was there the last days of its existence. We were 36,000 prisoners destined to go up in the air with dynamite. The whole camp was set to be dynamited. And the camp was saved thanks to the SS commander (whose English-German dictionary I brought with me to the United States)—he decided to give himself up to the Russians and disclose the situation that the place was about to be dynamited.

Did you ever draw when you were there—pictures of what you saw?

No. I have a good memory. I recorded it, just like you are recording now. I recorded it in my mind.

Because of the threat of death, you didn't do it on the spot.

Absolutely. By having a pencil without permission, you were dead. A piece of paper meant carrying a message. So it was forbidden to have any sort of tools. However, since I was the so-called *Kunstmahler,* the artist, I was permitted to carry a pencil or a brush, and I always carried it openly.

Do you feel that having been a designer and an artist really saved you?

The graphic stuff saved my life, yes. And even in the SS you could find a human approach, a certain understanding, but it was also done mostly for the sake of their selfishness—because they could use me. It's just like they used a shoemaker. I was not any different, maybe a little more because I delivered something that was beautiful, which pleased them. I could see a smile on their face. There was a certain satisfaction. The fact that an SS man took out a cigarette and threw it at me over the shoulder like to a dog meant, "Good, fine," under these circumstances. I felt that all of us who gave them something were kept alive for a time.

A Swell of Interactivity

Jules Feiffer on Children's Books

Jules Feiffer is a Pulitzer Prize–winning cartoonist whose weekly comic strip of political and social commentaries has, since 1956, addressed, attacked, and changed the mores and attitudes of the American public. His satiric jabs at sexual and interpersonal relations, in books such as *Jules Feiffer's America,* plays such as *Grown-Ups, Knock Knock,* and *Little Murders,* and screenplays including *Carnal Knowledge,* have been key in breaking the strictures imposed on the post–World War II generation. In recent years, he has somewhat turned his attention from the baby-boomer adult world that he greatly influenced, to the post–cold war children's world, with novels and picture books that deal with the travails of growing up. Now in his late sixties, while continuing to make political commentary, he has turned from his theater and film audiences to their children and their children's children.

How did this new interest in authoring children's books come about?

The first satire I wrote back in the fifties was *Munro,* about a four-year-old who gets drafted by mistake. It was written as a children's book for adults. But the notion of writing about children *for* children didn't occur to me until after I left the theater in 1990. I stopped writing plays, and being a creature of obsession, needed a new one. If I am not obsessed about work in at least one of the forms I play with, I tend to be very unhappy, pissed off, and bored with myself.

Why did you leave the theater?

I left the theater, or maybe the theater left me, after *Elliot Loves,* which took six years to write and was produced in 1990. It was directed by Mike Nichols. During rehearsal I said to him, "This is my best play. If they don't like this one, I'm out of the business." He said, "So am I." As it turned out, he lied and I didn't.

It was as simple as that to walk away?

I felt that at an advanced age, with a sizable family and lots of expenses, I could no longer afford to be a pro bono playwright. The theater scene in New York had changed to a point where outside of the production itself, I didn't enjoy it all that much. In the years of *Little Murders,* I was writing for a specific audience that was identifiable, that I felt needed what I had to say and could get value out of it. In subsequent years, I think that audience stopped going to the theater, and the audience I was dealing with more recently treated works like *Grown-Ups* not as illuminating pieces of stage craft that told them something about their lives they wanted and needed to hear, but as assaults on their very being.

So the audience that you were writing for—and I consider myself part of that audience—started having kids?

And I started—late in life—having more kids, too. (I have a three-year-old and a thirteen-year-old, in addition to my older daughter, now pregnant, thank you very much.) So, I was having these young kids, looking for new areas to work in, and also looking for a form in which I could show the more positive side of myself—less critical, less combative. But the particular incident that drove me into children's books was purely accidental. What happened was, a close friend of mine, a brilliant illustrator, had a terrific idea for a kids' book. He wanted to illustrate it, but he didn't have a real story to go with the idea. He asked if I would come up with the story. Since the story had to do with our common background in the Bronx as kids back in the thirties and with movie stars, I thought it was terrific. A summer went by, then finally I started to click on it. I called him up and said, "I've been working on it for two weeks now; it's going great." A long pause, and he said, "Uh . . . I guess I should have told you; I decided to write it myself." "When did you decide to do that?" I asked. "Two weeks ago," he said. "That's when you should have told me," I said, and hung up in a fury. He called back immediately and said, "I'm a schmuck. It's your book; *you* do the book." I said, "No, I'll do my *own* book, and my book will be better than your book." So, what got me into writing for children was spite. If you've been around kids long enough, you know it's a feeling that's not inappropriate.

I can appreciate that.

Then I thought, what other subject going back to my childhood was I nuts about? Since my friend's idea was movies, I thought about old-time radio, but that certainly had nothing to say to today's kids. So I thought of comic books. Then as I started fooling with the idea, it went from the passive idea of a kid who read comic books to a kid who drew them, and suddenly I was in autobiographical territory, which I really hadn't planned at all. I didn't want to set it in the past. Like all the fictional things I do based on my life, *Grown-Ups, Little Murders,* even *Carnal Knowledge,* I get bored when I'm dealing with facts out of my past; so I make up a story that is true to my sense of the past, only the facts are changed. That is what happened in *The Man in the Ceiling.* Nothing in the book ever happened, and everything in it is true.

Why do you get bored with your own experiences?

Lots of people whom I find enjoyable, love telling entertaining anecdotes about their experiences—"And then this happened, and then I went, and then I did, and then I won. . . ." But if it happened to me, I know the ending, and I'm not interested in relating it except, perhaps, with a drink or two. And to work on a story that simply tells what happened to me, it's predictable, I already know the story, having lived the story—I don't know how to make that art. But if I take my feelings, sensibilities, attitudes, and maybe incidents that did occur, and reshape them, reangle them, reposition them, throw them in with other things, and mix them all up—that's an aspect of writing I can bite into, that godlike aspect. It's the only time in your life where you really control events.

Right. You're the creator.

And even here, in the controlling of events, losing control can be very exciting—when the characters take off and do things that you didn't expect them to do. That game, that playfulness, that fun (and fun is a very important part) takes on a joy that borders on and sometimes crosses into pure euphoria.

What are the parameters for you? You said everything is fictional, but is everything, really?

The form is chosen by the idea. Once I had the idea for *The Man in the Ceiling*, it had to be naturalistic. There's no other way of doing it. Once I had the idea for *A Barrel of Laughs, A Vale of Tears,* it had to be an absurdist fairy tale, written deadpan, without tongue-in-cheek. So the idea dictates to me the style of the writing, and it even dictates to me the style and number of drawings.

Did you have to alter your writing style and your sensibility to write for a child audience?

Only in the beginning. *The Man in the Ceiling* was the first time I'd tried this, and I didn't have an author's voice; the first voice I fell into was coy and condescending. Rereading my first day's work made me blush in embarrassment.

And you knew immediately that it was the wrong direction?

Yes. And I said, "This is no good, but what would be good?" I didn't have a clue. So I thought, "To hell with it; I'll go to the best," and I picked up copies of *Tom Sawyer* and *Huckleberry Finn*, read Mark Twain, and saw clearly that this was a man who took no prisoners, condescended to nobody, just spoke in a language that was very much his own—in vernacular, but serious vernacular, without any attempt to kowtow to a young reader. I had to find my own vernacular for Jimmy, my hero—one that wouldn't kowtow. And I did. Once I had guidance from Mr. Clemens, I knew how to proceed, and then it just took a few hours to find the voice and to start working on it.

Was Mr. Clemens your only mentor in this regard, or did you have an editor?

I'm sure I couldn't have done this without having read the children's books of E. B. White, *Charlotte's Web* and *Stuart Little*. Thurber did not help, because Thurber, if you read *The Thirteen Clocks*, is very arch. A lot of writers taught me, through negatives, what not to do.

Thurber's *Last Flower* was similar. It seemed like it was for you and me, and not for children at all.

Also, Thurber had a lot of contempt, which you don't find in White at all. With my books for grown-ups *and* kids, I've always believed that this work must be approached out of innocence—wide-eyed with a sense of discovery. And not *mock* wide-eyed, not with a cynic pulling the strings.

How do you do that after being a grown-up for so long?

You know, I think it helps to be a broken leftist, with virtually every dream that came true either turning into a nightmare or reversing itself entirely. When I was a kid and when you were a kid, we didn't think that social Darwinism and racism would be legitimate and respectable concepts.

Stop, you're depressing me.

Well, you have two ways to go with this information. There's the kind of cynicism that allows you to throw up your hands in disgust. I had seen what that cynicism had done to people whom I admired as a young man, people like Fred Allen and Henry Morgan and others who, not having things work out as they wanted, just went sour. I clearly knew from the beginning that if I ended up as a success at the difficult work I was determined to do, I was bound to get kicked in the teeth now and again; I made an early promise to myself that I wasn't going to let it get me, that I wasn't going to give my critics the power to decide who I was or what I became.

How much mentoring for your first two books came from your own children?

The child I was working most with in *The Man in the Ceiling* was me. But in Jimmy's youngest sister, Susu, there is a lot of my daughter Halley. And the stories Jimmy tells Susu are stories that I told Halley. She was also my unofficial editor on the book. I'd read it to her, and she would not understand certain passages (she was about seven at the time); the questions she raised would guide me to rewrite—and that was an enormous help. But where she *really* mentored was on my next picture book for children.

Is that *I Lost My Bear*?

Yes. *I Lost My Bear* is about a little girl who loses her pet stuffed animal in this huge, rambling West Side apartment and searches for it everywhere. But what the book really takes a look at is the nonlinear logic of children. Time and logic as understood by grown-ups is unknown and unusable to children. So the book follows this girl's winding, circular, in-and-out trail, looking, pretending to look, forgetting to look, looking for other things, as she's going after this stuffed bear. I studied Halley as an older father—I didn't have my second generation of daughters until I was in my fifties—at an age when I've slowed down enough to spend more time with her, watch her, and see how, if you insist on keeping to your own concept of time, you'll go out of your mind with a small child. You have to not be impatient, not rush them along, kind of Zen yourself into a time-freezing stupor and let whatever happens happen, in order to be with them. You have to, in order to enjoy them, enter their minds or enter their world as much as you can. It's impossible, but there's really so much there.

How hard was that for you?

It was very hard, then it got easier. Now it's getting hard again.

Getting hard again because you have a much younger child or because of your interests?

When my career was not a problem and everything was more or less in place, I could do these books and sort of wander in time with them like the heroine of *I Lost My Bear*. But because of things that happened last spring, career suddenly became a major factor in my consciousness again [after forty years, the *Village Voice* ceased publishing Feiffer's weekly comic strip], and I had to scramble to figure out how, two years short of seventy, I was going to make a living. So, career forced itself into the forefront of my mind again, and until I'm reasonably rich, it will stay there.

What's the difference for you in terms of the first two books, which are novels, and the last two, which are picture books? Is there a shift in approach that you have to consciously explore?

There is. The picture books go so much faster, at least the writing does. A day, a day and a half. So there's an element of condescension—that this isn't men's work—that I don't have toward the longer novels. But when I look at the finished work, it's every bit as serious, every bit as involved in the kids' world. It's just that if I haven't spent a year on a book, I feel as if my mother wouldn't approve.

Your editor, Michael di Capua at Farrar, Straus and Giroux, is a highly respected children's book editor. Did he take a hands-on role with your book?

From the time he accepted *The Man in the Ceiling*, he and I went over virtually every line. He took something that began as an act of unconsciousness and made me aware of what I had done and should do—not from his point of view but my own. So that when I did a second draft, and later went on to future books, I had much more control over the writing process than I had before. He helped put everything into focus.

And what was that?

I can't even quite tell you. But it was a kind of attention to detail and structure and language—the casual repeating of certain words or restating certain locutions. I felt that not since working with Mike Nichols on *Carnal Knowledge* had I learned so much or been helped so much by an editor.

Is your newfound obsession for children's books a way of postponing the inevitability of your own children getting older?

I hadn't thought about that, but it may well be so. I also couldn't help noticing, once I started this, how many cartoonists we know in middle or late middle age who started for the first time doing books for children. And what is that all about? Jim Stevenson. Bill Steig. A lot of it is about the need to make money and other markets drying up. Certainly there's that in me, but why this form seemed like the right one as opposed to something else, I don't know.

Leo Lionni is another one. He didn't start until he had grandchildren. Does it have to do with having accumulated a lot of experience already?

Well, as you say, it may have had a lot to do with having so much experience that a certain calm settles or semisettles on your life. You're no longer in anguish about the present or the future, you look on things—just as kids do—with a greater simplicity. I've done cartoons and talked endlessly over the years about how we never actually leave adolescence. It keeps coming back. It has different names when it comes back. When you're a kid, it's adolescence; when you're older, it's neurosis or midlife crisis, "male menopause." But it feels the same: confusion, self-hate, lack of worth, insecurity about what you're doing, what you want to do with yourself, are you wasting your time? nobody likes me.

Is turning to the children's world a rejection of the adult political world?

Absolutely. I had the illusion, coming of political age in the fifties and sixties, that me and mine could change things, affect things. My cartoons were not done from the start simply as attacks on the empire. They were meant to overthrow the government. And looking back, I realize that we did overthrow the government. And what replaced it was a mess! The education system that we worked to undermine was undermined. Getting people to distrust their government has worked so well that the Far Right distrusts the government more than the Left ever did. So many of our initial aims became part of the body politic and the body psyche that you look at it and say, "Well, wait a minute; did I really mean for this to happen?"

In shifting much of your creative and psychic energy to the children's book arena, do you see this as a way of educating kids?

Well, remember it's not only the kids' books I do. Each week I still do the cartoons in syndication. Each month I have a cartoon on the *Times* Op-Ed page. I contribute to

Vanity Fair. And I'm still saying what I think, trying to make it as fresh as I know how. But with all of that, the kids' books are as important to me as anything I've ever done. There's so much money going into kids, so much lip service; still, it's clear that outside of selling them products or buying these kids off, we don't really give a damn. Our kids, yours and mine, are likely to have a harder time growing up than we did. What I hope to do with these kids' books is what kids' books and comic books did for me when I was growing up. When I couldn't find a conversation going on at home or in school, I found it in the literature I read, which made me feel that I wasn't a freak, that I had a friend out there, which made me feel less isolated and less alone.

That sounds like your early strips. It is what you were doing for those of us who were alienated and needed a voice. You were creating characters, like Bernard, that could be looked upon not as Everyman, but as Every-Nerd. In short, me.

I go back to that point in *Catcher in the Rye* where Holden reads a book and wants to call up the author. You want to be that writer, where the book is your friend. Certain books and plays were my friends. And the desire is to return the favor. The books that change your life seldom change your life after thirty. It's the books you read from eleven or twelve on that give you clues about where to go and who you are.

Are you implying that you have a moral agenda?

I can't stand a book with an agenda or a book that teaches us that people of all colors should get along or that Billy is no different from you and me just because he comes from a funny place and looks funny or talks funny. Books that teach lessons, that have morals, make me want to throw up. They did that to me as a kid, they do that to me as a grown-up. I think if there is a lesson to be taught, it should be organic in the story you're telling, and the kid picks that up out of the incidents, the story, the characters and relationships. If I have a message in a book, it has to be so wound up in the character, in the storytelling, that no labels appear.

Now that you've found this obsession, are you constantly thinking of new stories, the way you once used to think of ideas for plays?

In fact, more so. Because with plays, a year would go by. You write a play and then there's the period of time it takes to get the play into production, find a producer, find a theater in or out of New York, et cetera. It was impossible to start work on a new play while the last play was in the process of production.

With the children's books, I found that before *The Man in the Ceiling* came out, I was able to start work on *A Barrel of Laughs*—and so on. I've been able, to my relief and great pleasure, to be in the middle of something or actually finish a new book before the previous one is published. At this moment, before *I Lost My Bear* is published in the spring, and just after *Meanwhile* was published a few months ago, I have two books in the works—one where the dummy has been completed, very little work to be done; and another where I don't have a dummy but I pretty much have the book under control. And then there is a long cartoon narrative for grown-ups, a kind of backstage Twentieth Century Fox musical about tap dancing. That's a year away.

What other projects are you working on?

I've written the text of a new book for older kids, another picture book but with complicated ideas, about running away and abandonment. And there's a book I've started but haven't gotten back to, also for older kids about a family of Lefties back in the 1950s.

So children's books really have many of the Feiffer obsessions that came out in other media.

What the children's books seem to have done, as they move more and more into the area of picture books, is move me closer to my roots as a cartoonist, so that I do this cartoon narrative for grown-ups that goes back to the days of *Sick, Sick, Sick* and *Passionella*. I haven't worked in that mode seriously in many years, and suddenly here I am again, doing this stuff. I've been finding all sorts of ways and means that hadn't occurred to me before. I seem to be using everything I learned in my years of playwriting and screenwriting, and turning it all back into my first form, my first love, the comic strip. It really is a ball.

©Rodney Alan Greenblat / Interlink

Rodney Alan Greenblat on the Candy-Colored Cartooniverse

Rodney Alan Greenblat is a creator of intriguing and whimsical art. His paintings and sculpture have been exhibited in galleries and museums around the world. He is the author and illustrator of children's books, and director of the Center for Advanced Whimsy, an independent creative company that makes artwork, design, and music for children and adults. His four children's books, *Uncle Wizzmo's New Used Car, Aunt Ippy's Museum of Junk, Slombo the Gross,* and *Thunder Bunny* have been published by HarperCollins. The Center for Advanced Whimsy has created four commercially available software products. *Rodney's Funscreen* (1991) is an entertaining learning game for children published by Activision. *Rodney's Wonder Window* (1992) is a collection of interactive animation, and *Dazzeloids* (1994) is a comic storybook; both are published by the Voyager Company. *Parappa the Rapper* (1997) is a musical action game for Sony PlayStation, and was a collaborative project created by Sony Computer Entertainment.

You are known as a painter and sculptor, but your repertoire also includes children's books, computer games, CD-ROMs, and, most recently, video games. Before we examine each individually, please tell me how all these diverse media fits together.

I have to create a cozy candy-colored "cartooniverse" that spreads joy like peanut butter over the burnt toast of so-called reality. I don't know why I must do this, but I use whatever means seems to fit. To me, all media are like art supplies: computers, paint-brushes, lumps of clay, television production teams, musical instruments—they are all the same. Children's books, video games, TV commercials, Soho gallery shows, comic books, illustrations, I really don't care what the medium is, as long as it's something I am inter-ested in exploring—and of course it must extend the cozy candy-colored cartooniverse as far as it can possibly go.

So, can you describe what is important about your various media? Let's start with children's books.

Children's picture books seemed like a completely natural way to augment the cozy candy-colored cartooniverse. Unfortunately, it was a lot more difficult than I thought (as many things are). It takes a lot of love and sensitivity and marketing to have a success with this medium, and it takes a long time. I have four books out now and am planning to con-tinue.

And CD-ROMs?

CD-ROMs seemed perfect for the cozy candy-colored cartooniverse quest, and if you look at *Wonder Window* or *Dazzeloids,* you will see I was right! I love those two projects, but I had no idea the computer entertainment audience would be such a limited and closed-minded bunch. As Microsoft Windows proliferates, I have less and less interest in creating fun products for this medium.

And video games?

Video games are a different story. Unlike PCs, game machines like Nintendo and PlayStation work perfectly. The problem with this medium is, it is extremely expensive to develop the software on your own. In this case I took the collaborative corporate-studio-contract approach. Working with a big company is like another very difficult box of art materials—you can't work with it alone. In the case of *Parappa the Rapper*, I was actually hired by Sony to extend my cozy candy-colored cartooniverse in their direction. It was a brilliant idea for everyone involved.

Has your standing in the "art world" been compromised in any way owing to your immersion in these various popular arts?

I don't think I have much of a "standing" in the art world at this time, but I am still represented by Gracie Mansion Fine Arts here in New York. The simple fact is, I haven't had time to make any paintings or sculpture, and I do miss it. Fortunately, the structure of the art world never really changes; someday when I start making big heroic paintings (I'm planning on it), I'll attempt the art world again. It will be another challenge.

You are truly a pioneer of digital/computer art as entertainment. *Rodney's Funscreen* and *Wonder Window* took the then-nascent medium to a new plateau of wit, humor, and artistry. How did you get involved in this area? Indeed, what did you learn as a pioneer that is second-nature today?

When I first saw the Macintosh in 1986, I believed that it was a magic art-supply kit designed with creative people in mind—and it still is. This is the only reason I became interested in digital art. It was the possibility of creating the cozy candy-colored cartooniverse on a musical light-up screen without cumbersome video equipment and without teams of specialists. I could handle it. It was made for me.

When I started working on *Wonder Window,* I didn't know I was a pioneer. I just wanted to make some funny art on the computer. CD-ROMs were exotic at the time, and so I was surprised when I met people from Voyager who actually wanted to publish my stuff on that medium. This experience made me think of CD-ROM as a viable fine art medium. It was exciting then, but now I think of the computer as my most important production tool, not the delivery platform.

Obviously, your work, your imagery, is rooted in the vocabulary of children—even your loft is designed like a playland. But why the realm of children?

I never think about working "in the realm of children." I think only about the cozy candy-colored cartooniverse. For some reason, people assume I do this for kids. Kids are naturally creative and open-minded. They don't even need a cozy candy-colored cartooniverse. I divide the world into three kinds of people: children, adults, and parents. Anyone can behave like child, adult, or parent at any time in his or her life. Young people are usually called "children," but sometimes this is not true. Many young people are more mature and honest in their thinking than so-called adults. They just lack experience. Adults act childish quite often, but they are the ones who create things like governments, religions, and fashion. Parents are the most difficult—always judging things. I make my art for adults of all ages.

Your drawing and painting style is virtually primitive, and your children's books are prime examples of that. Tell me why you work in this manner rather than a more finished form?

I love the directness and spontaneity of cartoons. My work seems primitive in that way. It is actually the most natural way for me to draw.

Do the fantasy worlds you've created in sculpture, and presumably intended for adult audiences, influence your children's work? Or are they two separate worlds?

I think the only time I separate my work into age categories is when working on children's picture books. Picture book publishers and buyers are very conscious of these age restrictions. If the work doesn't fit into their age categories correctly, it can be a disaster.

***Parappa the Rapper* is truly weird, from a graphic and conceptual point of view. I've never seen a video game like it, which just goes to show that most video games fall into a few clichéd categories. How did you conceive of this?**

Parappa was conceived of by Masaya Matsuura, a Japanese musician and digital artist. He had been working on a PC- and Mac-based music-sequencing toy that became the basis for the game. His original concept also included using me as the graphic designer. He and his wife were big fans of my illustration work. The great part of this deal was the fact that he was already working for a division of Sony called Sony Creative Products in Tokyo. We have designed a line of licensed characters for sale as products like stationery, toys, and T-shirts. These characters became the supporting cast for the game. The name Parappa came from Matsuura, but it was my job to design the character and fill out his personality.

Can you explain the point of *Parappa*?

Parappa is a young and hopeful boy dog who wants to impress his cute daisylike girlfriend Sunny Funny. He thinks learning to rap from various masters will help him do this. These masters include Chop Chop Master Onion (a martial arts teacher), Prince Master Fleaswallow (a salesman at a flea market), Cheap Cheap the Cooking Chicken (a cooking-show host), and a few others. The game works like an extended version of Simon Says. The "call and response" song lyrics get the player into the game, but the trick is to improvise along with the beat. That is the only way to "rap cool."

Executives at Sony Computer Entertainment knew that this was a unique game idea. At the same time, they weren't sure if it would work—but they had a lot of confidence in me and Matsuura and his team. They left us alone to create the game we wanted, and they are very happy about it now.

I understand that you did all the artwork for *Parappa* via fax. Describe the process of making this come alive.

Because of the short time allowed for my work, and the limitations of working in New York on a Tokyo-based production, the fax machine turned out to be the fastest and most reliable way to get my designs to the animators. All the character and set designs were hand-drawn by me on paper and sent by fax with Pantone color specifications.

Your children's books are linear; even your computer-based toys are more or less linear. What about working in such a multileveled, nonlinear environment as this is the most difficult?

I don't like "nonlinear" storytelling except in some very special cases. I think James Joyce's *Ulysses* works well, but computer-based point-of-view games like *Myst* or *Final Fantasy* seem overly complicated to me. I think paintings or novels are a great place to create these nonlinear narratives, but on the computer I find it boring. I'm not sure why anyone would create a story where parts of it might never be seen by the viewer. I love a well-crafted story with a beginning, middle, and end. I would much prefer to get one of these right before attempting anything more complicated.

Do you think that art and design are moving more toward interactive realms, or are you an anomaly?

I would love to be an anomaly, but I think there are a growing number of artists like me. The technology of entertainment is trickling down to the level where almost anyone who really wants to can afford the tools. Digital video is the best example. Fifteen years ago it took two or three technicians and hundreds of thousands of dollars in equipment to do what can easily be done on any appropriately equipped computer for under ten thousand. There is an emerging group of artists who can work with video and audio in their own studios the way more traditional artists use paint.

Even so, I don't think art and design are moving toward "interactivity" any more than they were before the personal computer fad. Games, by their nature, are interactive, and some sculpture, installation art, and conceptual art all demand interactivity from the viewer. These forms have existed and continue to flourish. The computer is only another tool in creating these forms.

And the future of the computer in art?

I am actually anticipating an antitechnology backlash by artists and designers. Oil paintings and handset type may again be the ultimate form of expression. I also hope the artists who cling to the digital mediums will find ways to destroy the current entertainment-distribution system. If full-screen video can be successfully broadcast on an Internet-like system, there could be a fantastic new opportunity for free-form television, which is practically impossible now.

David Vogler has been designing and producing kids' content for the past ten years. He was the creative force behind Nickelodeon consumer products including the gooey substance known as Gak. In 1995, as the vice president of kids' content, Vogler joined Disney Online, where he helped launch the acclaimed Disney's Blast Web site. Vogler is currently vice president, creative, of Nickelodeon Online. Prior to this he was a creative consultant with studios in Manhattan and Los Angeles. His clients included MTV, Nickelodeon Online, TV Land, the Cartoon Network, and Towers Perrin. In his spare time, he enjoys juvenile humor and cocreated the TV series *Monkey's Uncle* for Saban Entertainment. His work can be sampled at *www.davidvogler.com*.

Before entering the digital realm you were a magazine art director, specifically working on parodies of mainstream magazines. How did you end up on the Web?

I started my career in traditional media and evolved into working on the Web. The transformation has been mostly by accident and good fortune. I was quietly into "online" long before it became the fashionable craze we see today. I still really enjoy doing print, packaging, and logo work in addition to my Internet projects.

And then you moved on to Nickelodeon.

I was a creative director by day and an online computer geek by night. I was working at Nickelodeon overseeing Nick's off-air products: toys, games, home video, CD-ROMs, and the gooey substance known as Gak—basically, all the things a kid could blow his or her allowance on. In 1994, Nickelodeon's parent company, Viacom, wanted to put its strongest brands online. By that time I'd gained a reputation within the company for being an online evangelist. Upper management acknowledged this and asked me to devote my time to launching Nick Online. They gave me the creative and financial support to turn my personal hobby into a full-time job.

What is the difference between print and Web work?

There's a huge difference in regard to execution and deployment. The fundamentals of printing ink on paper have remained virtually unchanged for the past century. In the world of the Web, the medium changes with every quarter. The tools, content strategies, and business models are constantly evolving. It's an incredibly volatile medium. Depending on your outlook, the Web is either incredibly exciting or terribly frustrating.

Print and Web work have a lot in common creatively. The Web still follows a "page" metaphor that's based on magazine mechanics. The fundamentals of clear communication and smart graphic design transcend any medium, whether it be print or pixel.

From Nickelodeon you moved to Disney Online. What is the fundamental difference between the two companies and their products?

It's like night and day, and really quite simple. Nick is for kids, Disney is for families. Nick takes risks, Disney plays it safe. Nick is urban, Disney is suburban. Since the companies have two very different philosophies and target audiences, their products are informed by very different agendas.

On the surface, one might think they're competitors, but that's really not the case. Nickelodeon is the most powerful and creative brand for kids. Everything about Nick is driven by kids, their humor and their point of view. Nick believes that it's tough to be a kid in an adult world. Disney is driven by fantasy, nostalgia, and family values, and believes childhood is "happy" and "magical." It's often mistakenly considered to be just for kids. Disney aims to capture children in the context of the family. This sounds subtle, but there's a big difference.

Another difference is that Nickelodeon successfully appeals to kids of all ages, especially the elusive eight- to twelve-year-olds. Disney, however, is strong with pre-schoolers but struggles to retain the older kids. As the audience grows up and enters that rebellious 'tween age, they consider Disney to be uncool. At a certain point in every kid's life it becomes a right of passage to shun Disney and all things Mickey. In the past few years there have been some Disney initiatives that tried to expand the Disney image and make the brand more modern. At Disney Online I'm proud to have been part of that effort.

Disney is a major brand with tamperproof characters. Are you able to expand the boundaries—experiment and play—or are you shackled to the Disney cast?

The "shackling" that Disney enforces is to maintain the integrity of their characters and brand. You can't fault them for it. It's just good business. When you sign up to work for the Mouse, this goes with the territory. It's naive to think you can fight Disney City Hall. Unfortunately, many creatives quickly burn out and slip into the quagmire of mindlessly cutting and pasting Disney assets.

In the proper dosages, working with the Disney characters can be rewarding. They're a rich palette with deep emotional equity. Even the most hard-core anti-Disney folks have a soft spot. With a little prodding they'll eventually fess up to a favorite Disney character. (In my case, it's King Louie from 1968's *The Jungle Book*!) Disney is an American institution, and its legacy is an indelible part of people's lives.

Disney digital toys, D-Toys, are not the stereotypical Disney fare. How did they come about?

When I first proposed the D-Toy notion it was met with nervous resistance. The concept of making content that wasn't based on the current Disney animated feature conflicted with the preprogrammed inner workings of the Disney synergy machine. Originality was alien, let alone kid content that was a little smart-ass. I started to make them on weekends and evenings as a means of maintaining my sanity.

So, the mother of invention was pure survival?

I don't think one can thrive on a diet of pure Disney material. It just isn't a balanced creative diet. I soon realized this applied to the audience as well. It's refreshing to explode preconceptions about the Disney brand and the online medium. Whenever the Web site was reviewed, the press went out of their way to celebrate these humble nuggets of creativity. Once the positive fan mail started rolling in, Disney stopped scoffing at me and acknowledged that I had struck gold.

What are D-Toys exactly?

D-Toys are small Shockwave applications: a kid can play with them in the Web page and has the opportunity to download a corresponding projector to play with them locally offline. D-Toys are meant to be like prizes in a Cracker Jack box—fun, easy, and fast. This is a notion I pioneered while I was at Nickelodeon Online. Back there I called them Clickamajigs. I'm personally fascinated with interstitials, the short subject and tiny entertainment that is byte-sized!

My creative mission behind them was to produce a small nugget of play that was open-ended. Kind of like a Slinky, Lego, or Gak. There's no right or wrong way to play. They're gender-neutral and work for any age group. They require no prior knowledge or back story. Best of all, no D-Toy looks or operates like the one that preceded it. Each one loosely tells a story and features unexpected surprises. They're all based on original characters and stories that I've written, designed, and art-directed from scratch. By design, they have nothing to do with preexisting Disney characters and films. For Disney, that's considered a bit progressive.

"D-Toy" stands for either Disney Toy, Digital Toy, or David Toy, depending on how you look at it. The D-Toy franchise is a home for unconventional art styles and UI (user-interface) executions. The interfaces range across the extremes of pencil sketches, photography, collage, and even crude Claymation. It's encouraging to see this kind of liberal and adventurous art direction coming from a Disney unit. I'm still amazed and grateful to upper management for letting me create them. As a footnote, for every one D-Toy accepted, there are two or three that are banned. More often than not, my ideas are deemed too radical for the Disney brand, and I can't particularly blame them.

Do you have any problems reconciling the digital toys with the Disney Web site, which is a heavy dose of convention?

Not really. The Disney's Blast site contains content for children ranging from as young as four to as old as eleven or twelve. I'd like to think of the site as a content buffet. There's something tasty for kids of all ages. The D-Toys give the site more texture and credibility.

How do you feel about designing for children? Are there times when you would like to address a more sophisticated audience?

Actually, I don't think there's a more sophisticated audience than kids. They see right through everything and know when you're full of shit. Kids are the toughest to entertain and the most challenging. They have little or no baggage to color their perceptions. It's the adults who are easy to entertain. Just look at mainstream television sitcoms, CD-ROMs, or movies. Snooze. It's all pretty much paint-by-number entertainment. You really can't get away with such formulas with kids.

Is humor aimed at kids, regardless of media, fundamentally different from that aimed at adults?

If humor works well for kids, then it'll work universally. It's better to take kid-based humor and "grow it up" than to take adult humor and "dumb it down."

Do you think that the Web is going to be a wellspring of innovation in the visual realm, or have we fallen into a new litany of conventions?

As bandwidth increases and authoring tools become more sophisticated, the Web will become the ultimate visual and creative melting pot. Even in its current primitive condition, the Web is a rather delightful visual experience. It'll only improve over time. History has shown that all new emerging mediums adopt the conventions of a medium that proceeded them. Luckily, the Web is changing so rapidly that most conventions we force upon it don't have the opportunity to stick.

Edwin Schlossberg on Interactive Environments

Dr. Edwin Schlossberg, a student of and assistant to Buckminster Fuller, is a designer, author, and artist with a Ph.D. in Science and Literature from Columbia University. He founded Edwin Schlossberg Incorporated (ESI) in 1976, a multidisciplinary design firm with more than fifty people on staff, to create dynamic interactive experiences in a variety of contexts, such as museums, public attractions, retail stores, TV programs, and computer information systems. His environments include ECHO at Chicago Symphony Orchestra; Sony Wonder Technology Lab and Sony Plaza; Innovation Station at the Henry Ford Museum, Dearborn; Macomber Farm; and the Brooklyn Children's Museum.

I would call you a kind of social engineer. You move people from here to there on an educational pathway, with the purpose of inspiring individuals to interact among themselves for the purpose of learning. How did you come to this discipline?

I am not a social engineer, but perhaps a new category called a "social designer," someone who considers how people respond and interact and are affected and effected by how an event or environment is designed. The challenge I have always felt is to make things that would enable people to learn more about (1) a subject, (2) themselves, and (3) other people—both living and recorded. The process that led to my having the good fortune to design things has been very erratic and fortuitous. I think that getting a doctorate in science and literature was a big help, since it propelled me to solve problems of explanation and description. I also think that working with Buckminster Fuller and seeing him strive to solve problems by redescribing them helped to focus my effort.

In the course of your career, you've adopted psychological models as touchstones for your work, but your work is also very much about the design of plans and spaces. How important is design in the interactive process?

Design is always central to the expression of an idea. But I do not try to visualize how a new communication tool will look until I have really explored what I want to communicate and how I want a particular conversation between people in an environment to unfold. Design for me is the process of animating and bringing life and drama and excitement to that conversation. Usually, the physical, spatial, and graphic design occur as ways to enable the scripts of the conversation.

In _Brave New World Revisited,_ Aldous Huxley warned against the invasive power of mass media. Essentially, are you taming or controlling mass media in what you do?

I think what Huxley was imagining was a mechanistic model of communications and control that is more about predictable delivery of materials than it is about dynamic interdependent conversation. I don't think about controlling mass media because most of what I do is to activate smaller physical spontaneous communities in public places. I am very interested and concerned about creating tools that enable one hundred or five hundred people to have an interesting, exciting time communicating with each other and being engaged in trying to find more ways to do that. I love the thought of someone taming the mass media as if it were a rude beast. No one has that big a chair.

Taking a chapter from your latest book, *Interactive Excellence,* how do you educate a mass audience—what are your tools and strategies—as opposed to control them?

The key ingredient in engaging and educating a mass audience is to provide many points of access to a conversation, and enabling all the people to participate in the conversation in a meaningful way. The more our society fragments, the more important it is to offer public contexts in which people can come together and share experiences that engage them on a deep level. In these public contexts, it is possible to model a successful conversation, which is the respectful give-and-take of ideas. Especially now, with the proliferation of the electronic media, more people have more access to more information; all kinds of audiences need to be educated about how to engage in successful conversations, and how to be critical and how to look at information from different perspectives. People with different educational levels and cultural backgrounds all can participate in the conversations, and I try to provide points of access that change with each person's level of experience or knowledge so that, for example, parents will not be burdened by their ignorance in front of their children. Doing this is making a developmental interface, which is a very useful tool and possible to implement with the electronic media such as the Internet. By providing such points of access and tools, we can equip audiences to become more critical, to appreciate different perspectives, to have more meaningful interactions and build better communities, and be better able to participate in the give-and-take of ideas.

You do projects for adults and children. Is there a fundamentally different approach to each group?

Children see their job as learning to control their world. They try anything to make something work. Adults think that there is a right way, and if it doesn't work, then they have failed. Children don't measure failure by their inability to get the right result. They measure it by the feel and consensus that occurs around the experience. Knowing this makes me design experiences for children and adults in very different ways.

How do you design an environment for children? What is your frame of reference?

Of course I use my experiences with children in general and my children in specific—imagining how they would want to explore an idea or how they would enjoy a kind of experience. Also, I try to imagine what experiences between the children would engage and enliven what happens, not only focusing on the communication between the design and an individual child. I also try to develop the metaphor about the experience and the links to other experiences so that it is a design that has a context.

I remember you telling me about a multileveled interactive environment (goal- and task-oriented) that

you had devised as a high-tech entertainment center. How does this differ from, say, Disney World or LaZer Park?

The design I developed for a multiperson interactive entertainment center is based on the idea that the games serve as means to enhance the conversation between the players. They are real games that enable the outcome of each move to affect the outcome of all subsequent moves. They are collaborative and conversational and competitive. They are meant to serve as a new paradigm for people to enjoy being with strangers and learning from them and having a productive time. Disneyland experiences are based on a linear narrative, and Lazer Tag promotes the logic of "I win, you lose"—the willing suspension of disbelief is the primary engine of entertainment. I designed my experiences to lift out into the world the rich diversity and quality of the people who play them—leaving the game as the means by which to overcome resistance to enter into a conversation, not itself becoming the main focus.

What has been the response to this kind of interactivity? Is it what you expected?

The response has been enthusiastic among those people for whom growth and discovery and other people are attractive, and it has been resistant among those who feel otherwise. In my naive enthusiasm for making the world better, I expected everyone to embrace the idea, and, of course, they did not.

In your work, interfaces are not simply graphical devices on computer screens. What is involved in creating a successful interface?

A successful interface is invisible as a means to connect people. Just as a good match-maker retreats into invisibility once the match is started, a good interface explains and explores all the parts of a system and enables the users to grab hold of them like a comfortable tool that lets them work effectively. I think that creating a successful interface is truly a modern skill that means bringing to the design knowledge of physical design, behavioral issues, graphics and image, story and script, and being able to orchestrate them in a very new and attractive way. It is what I hope that design schools are training their students to do, since it is and will be one of the biggest design tasks of the next decades.

What are the new standards of excellence needed to make interactivity a valuable exercise?

(1) To be excellent, interaction must enable its participants to learn more about the subject, themselves, and others within the experience. (2) To be excellent, an interaction must provide access to the subjects within it from a variety of points of view, levels of education, and ages. (3) To be excellent, interaction must develop from the use by its participants—it must learn and change depending on its users' action.

This is a first take at rules that I am sure will grow and change.

Decades ago, Marshall McLuhan spoke of a global village. It seems with the Internet we have come close to that prediction. However much interactivity brings people together, it separates them as well. Do you feel that we are more or less communal today?

I think we are less communal in our ideas about ourselves and are becoming more communal in our actions. The Internet provides a context for large and small communities, as do CB radio, ham radio, et cetera. We need more awareness of our communities of interest and more efforts to connect into physical communities and reengage our neighborhoods. All of this takes experiences that shape and celebrate the reality that we have things to give and get from one another.

The moderns, and Bucky Fuller was one of them, believed that good design could enhance the quality of life. Do you subscribe to that notion? And how in the electronic world can this work?

Yes, I do, and I spend every day living that belief. Design in the complex and very challenging electronic world will create context and reweave the cultural fabric if we all uncynically give it a whirl.

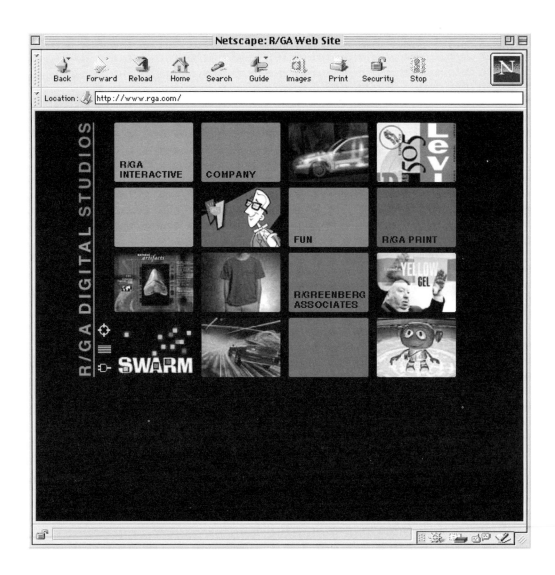

Robert Greenberg on Technology and Design

Robert M. Greenberg is chairman and CEO of R/GA Digital Studios, a design and production company known for pioneering new media and the creative integration of film, video, and computer-imaging techniques. Greenberg founded R/GA in 1977, forging a unique interdisciplinary approach to media, and along the way has won many industry awards for creativity, including the Academy Award, Clios, and Cannes Lions.

From humble surroundings to a major technology and design company, you are in the forefront of just about everything that concerns visual communications. Tell me, what are the biggest challenges facing designers in new media today?

Working in multimedia is very interesting because you are constantly learning. Nowadays, everyone is being bombarded with information that needs to be sorted through and prioritized. Information architecture and navigation design are critical to making sense of that information. Intelligent agents, collaborative filtering, and distributed systems are examples. New ideas are based on design, making complicated things understandable and developing vehicles for getting information. We are way into the information age, and the next stage will be based around collaboration. Collaboration requires things like groupware and shareware; it's experimental, but the whole point is in learning more about how people might do that. R/Greenberg Associates (R/GA) is not a pyramid structure but a horizontal structure whose modular components can be reconfigured efficiently to solve problems, then pulled apart and put back together. It's definitely the way it's going, not just here but at General Motors.

You have gone beyond the simple definition of graphic or motion design into areas of social structure and planning. How is your new, collaborative world realized through your projects?

Things fall into either education, information, or entertainment. Currently, we are building an informational space for a large pharmaceutical company geared toward doctors who never have enough time to address patients' needs. We are also doing a total design for Ticketmaster. If you're interested in the Cleveland Indians, for example, through a computer interface you can go into a stadium and pick your seat as well as preview the view from your seat. We are experimenting with parts that will reside on your computer as a knowledgeable device and will let you know when a certain opera is at the Met or when Bruce Springsteen is in a ninety-mile radius. We are also developing Stream-line, a very sophisticated grocery-shopping system that remembers your shopping preferences and allows you to order things very quickly and have them delivered right to your garage. It is currently being prototyped in Boston.

That's not Boston, it's heaven!

It's not happening in New York, yet; it's really the furthering of another system in Chicago called Pea Pod. There are more and more people transacting online.

Does this relate to your earlier film and TV motion design in any way?

What it's going to look like is not that much different from what we were doing in the late seventies, but more important is that it is all coming together at the turn of the century. It's very interesting because I've been tracking technology for a long time, and the year 2000 is very meaningful in terms of convergence. Whether it's the technology installed in the base of computers to advances in satellites and telecommunications to broadband networks to developments in software, it is all coming together in a meaningful way in that time frame. Interactive production is utilizing the same kind of digital production tools that we're using on the studio side.

Do you still work in any of the, well, old-fashioned, preelectronic ways?

People are getting fed up with the feeling of insecurity, that they have no control. What is ironic is that all this technology stuff is supposed to give you more control. Nevertheless, I always try to find the time to do something to remind me that technology is not all that is important—what one does with one's hands is also important.

You can't beat pencil and paper.

No, you can't. I love the juxtaposition of technology and the primitive, the handmade. I collect outsider art, which is the antithesis of our work at R/GA, where what we produce often involves the collaboration of hundreds of people and is viewed by millions. Outsider art is a world apart from the mass-media vocabulary, often created for the artist's eyes only, without a thought given to communicating to others.

I always like the metaphor of the relationship between painting and sculpture. In sculpture, you have to deal with technical issues—material, gravity, making things that go together—whereas painting is much more intuitive; it's direct, it's you and the brush and the canvas. It seems like you start off with sculpture and you are working toward painting. You're working toward your transparent tool, where you can be intuitive. The way people are taught now, abstraction comes first.

Is this a better method?

No, a lot of the kids that apply to R/Greenberg Associates are smart about new media because all of their attention is focused in that area, and they do some wonderful things, but sometimes they lack exposure to other forms of communication. They are going to have to focus on traditional graphic design, film, lighting, photography, art direction, and so much more.

These new methods of design seem so fundamental. Can they really go back? Isn't it hard for them?

It is hard. There are very few people I meet who have the perspective that I had when I started out. Somewhere along the way, they all fell off the train. Now, kids come right out of computing without having done anything by hand. There is not a structure in interactive multimedia that people can use as a touchstone. If the vocabulary is set, then it's a lot easier. They know about a lot of things, but they just don't know anything about traditional design and typography. Then on the other side are very sophisticated designers who aren't going to make this transition because they aren't interested in this new technology.

If you mean "sophisticated" in terms of those designers who come from the traditional school of design, I suspect one gets used to tried-and-true methods.

Yes, but nobody is too old to learn new tools, and there are a lot of people who are open to it, like Paul Rand, for instance. Toward the end of his life, he loved all this stuff. He came here once and I'll never forget it. After he went through the place and saw what we do, he said to me, "Bob, now I understand what you do." And I said, "What's that?" And he said, "A camouflage for bad concepts."

How will the designer who understands history and masters current technology be able to make a fundamental difference in our society or culture?

My girlfriend, Corvova Choy Lee, has a vast education in art and architecture, and I have a great understanding of computers and the art and science of communications. Corvova has taught me about Titian and Piero della Francesca, and I have taught her about Stephen Hawking, Intel, and virtual learning. At R/GA, we encourage artists to be more technically astute and technicians to be more artful.

WIRED

May 1995

BRIAN ENO
GOSSIPISPHILOSOPHY

The Wired Interview
with Kevin Kelly

Duckman: What the hell you starin' at?

Jon Katz on Thomas Paine, father of the Internet

Gateway: Beats skinning hogs

$4.95 / Canada 5.95

248

John Plunkett on the Wired World

John Plunkett is a partner with Barbara Kuhr in the Park City, Utah, design firm Plunkett + Kuhr (P+K). They are also the creative directors of *Wired* magazine and Wired Digital, which they helped found in 1992 and 1994, respectively. As *Wired*'s creative directors, they are responsible for the look and feel of *Wired* magazine and Wired Books, as well as HotWired, the world's first commercial Web site. Plunkett is a 1976 graduate of the California Institute of the Arts. In 1979, he joined with Dan Friedman and Colin Forbes in a corner of George Nelson's office to help bring Pentagram, New York to life. Plunkett remained with Pentagram three years and went on to direct projects for Saul Bass, Deborah Sussman, and James Sebastian before opening Plunkett + Kuhr in 1990. P+K's past projects include signage for the Musée du Louvre (with Carbone Smolan Associates and I. M. Pei), exhibitions for Carnegie Hall, and the graphics for the Sundance Film Festival.

Where did the idea to start *Wired* come from?

I met Louis Rossetto in 1984 in Paris, where he was the editor and I was the designer of an investment newsletter. We became good friends after discovering we were both closet media junkies—we'd go out and buy an armload of American mags, and end up in some café, critiquing them. Louis kept saying we should start a magazine, and I kept laughing at the likelihood of that. Four years later, though, Louis was working for a technology magazine in Amsterdam, where he first began to encounter the people and subcultures that *Wired* would later report on. Barbara Kuhr and I were back in New York when we got a call from Louis in the fall of 1988. The conversation went like this:

> "I've got it; I know what our magazine should be about!"
> "What?"
> "Computers!"
> "Oh."
> "You don't understand—computers are going to be the rock 'n' roll of the nineties!"
> "You're right; I really don't understand that at all."

As it turned out, Louis was able to persuade me and a lot of other people that he really was onto something. Technology would become a dominant cultural force in a very short time.

What is your design background? Were you already "wired"?

When I was a student at CalArts in the early seventies, my mentor Louis Danziger used to tell his design students that "one day we'll all be working on computers." We thought he was nuts.

What changed your mind?

At Pentagram in the late seventies/early eighties, I spent a good deal of time devising proportional systems for American Express and other clients so that they could "proof" text for their annual report on their word processors, cutting their typesetting bills in half. We'd design the reports and then build silly-looking, oversized templates—but with accurate character and line counts—that could be output directly from their machines. But I still didn't view the computer as a tool I wanted on my desk.

In 1984, when I worked on the newsletter in Paris, that changed. They had one of the first Macs, and I became very excited to have Apple's handful of typefaces to work with directly. This was before any page-layout programs, and so we output the type and made traditional mechanical pasteups.

In 1986–87, Barbara and I were hired to create the visitor information system for the Musée du Louvre, working with Carbone Smolan and the office of I. M. Pei. Somehow we survived a year of speaking French, arguing with Parisian government bureaucrats, and learning PageMaker, which we used to lay out the whole (giant) signage program on a fourteen-inch screen. It was like scanning a football field through a microscope. Perhaps more importantly, though, we began working remotely and in real time on a giant "facsimile machine" with the office in New York. This technology stuff was beginning to get interesting.

In the late eighties, I began working on projects with Jim Sebastian at DesignFrame in New York. I introduced the Macintosh to his office, and Barbara and I bought our first home computer when the Mac II was released (like a lot of designers, I doubt that I would ever have touched a computer if the Macintosh interface hadn't been invented). At DesignFrame, we created the ColorCurve Color System (which itself was based on computer calibration of colors) entirely on the Mac, and devised a desktop-publishing system for the Hillier Group, an architectural firm in Princeton, New Jersey. We also began using modems to transfer files, combining the networking of fax machines with the increasingly sophisticated design tools of the Mac.

Between FedEx, modems and faxes, and the computer's ever-increasing power, Barbara and I began to think it might be possible for a small design office to do national work from a remote location. We began looking for a small town near a good airport in the West, which brought us to Park City, Utah, in 1991, with no clients and a lot of fear. In the next two years, though, we designed exhibits for Carnegie Hall (remotely) and graphics for the Sundance Film Festival (down the street).

When did *Wired* get wired?

Ironically, the first prototype of *Wired* was made (in the spring of 1991) by hand-collaging color prints to look like it was done with the high-powered computers and programs we knew we needed but could not afford. Once *Wired* received funding in late 1992, we began what has now become five years of near-weekly commuting to the San Francisco office, accompanied by high-speed telecommuting from our home office in Utah. For better or worse (or both), we are committed to living the life *Wired* reports on.

Couldn't you do the entire magazine electronically from a distance?

Ironically, considering the editorial mission of *Wired,* this is the most highly collaborative effort I've ever been involved in, requiring huge amounts of face-to-face interaction. We've experimented with videoconferencing, which works well enough for deciding logistical problems, but is terrible for blue-sky creative sessions. Maybe one day there will be high-res, real-time video that somehow captures a sense of "being there" for all the participants, but in the meantime, there's no substitute for our weekly editorial/design meetings.

In designing a magazine that chronicles the present and heralds the future, what were your primary concerns regarding form and style?

The science-fiction writer William Gibson once said, "The future has already arrived. It just isn't equally distributed." We used this formulation to guide the design of *Wired.* Our job as both journalists and designers was to track down the future, and then make it visible to our readers. But in 1992, the future of communications was invisible to most people.

The chief formal issue to resolve then, it seemed to us, was the inherent contradiction of using ink on paper in a fixed, old medium to report on this emerging, fluid, nonlinear, asynchronous, electronic world. Since we couldn't *be* the new medium that we were reporting on, what could we do to signify it? What does that invisible future look like? Perhaps more importantly, what does it feel like? Is the future good or bad? scary or friendly? a threat or a promise? et cetera. Then there was the technical question of how "electronic" could ink on paper look? I'm no lover of fluorescent ink—it just seemed appropriate to this particular problem.

There were also the more pragmatic issues of packaging the product. How do you differentiate yourself from the competition on the newsstand? How do you gain attention? Louis wanted *Wired* to be a premium-priced magazine—$5 instead of the average $2 or $3. That led us toward a look and feel that might be closer to a book you wanted to collect, as opposed to a magazine you throw away.

We also deliberately tried to avoid as many contemporary magazine design techniques and clichés as possible. It remains nonobvious to me why most magazines look alike. And, in particular, we wanted to ignore the unspoken design taboo: good design = subtle, tasteful, elegant, restrained. My feeling about that is, maybe so, depends on the context. We felt it was more important that *Wired* be *alive* than subtle.

Now that Wired is online, too, what are the hierarchies and characteristics of the parts of the media-mix that Wired Inc. has become?

Our goal is a Wired "brand" that signifies useful and entertaining information about the future, delivered via any media that make sense. To date we've developed the magazine, books, and various Web media and tools, all primarily text based. We've also begun to experiment with television, which seems better suited to delivering the emotional subtext rather than anything approaching deep content. We're also interested in TV in a more pragmatic sense, in that we'd like to be present on the day the Web and television collide.

Do you see the wired world as having already developed design clichés and stereotypes?

We put ourselves in the business of developing some of those very clichés six years ago.

This is, of course, a double-edged sword. We try to develop visual metaphors that are meaningful in relation to the content they are meant to serve. It's sometimes painful then to see the surface appearance of our work picked up and used as decoration, detached from its original purpose. This is not a new problem for designers—we are just more aware of it now from our experiences with the creation of *Wired*.

What are some examples of these stereotypes, and their appropriate context and use?

Fluorescence = electronic future is the obvious one. To some degree, it's become part of the Wired brand, although when investment banks begin using it for capabilities brochures, one wonders. We've sometimes used a layered technique that, while not novel in the design community, was unusual to find in the context of newsstand magazines.

Along the lines of stereotypes, how did *Mind Grenades* develop? And is it a visual code for the future?

Mind Grenades was Wired's first book. It's a compilation of the first thirty intro quotes we created for the magazine in collaboration with a lot of extremely talented designers and illustrators—Giles Dunn, Erik Adigard, Max Kisman, James Porto, Jeff Brice, Nick Phillip, among them. We conceived the intro quotes as advertisements for ideas. They were meant to compete with the actual advertising in the front of the magazine and win. Ironically—or is it inevitably?—the ad world seems to have responded to our attempts to fuse word and image. The intro quotes are also an homage to our patron saint, Marshall McLuhan, and Quentin Fiore's amazing 1967 design of *The Medium is the Massage*. But is it a "visual code" for the future? I'd prefer to think not, that the visualization of the future is by definition a moving target, one that we at Wired hope to keep up with.

What about the wired or digital world do you find most challenging for designers?

Lots of things. First, we need to move on from seeing the computer as a box on our desk that isolates us like TV, and embrace computers as big magic that increases our connection to each other, transcending time and space.

Which brings up collaboration. The nature of networked computers is to break down the distinctions between disciplines, between clients and consultants, boss and junior. Designers who embrace this notion will prosper.

Equally important, if we don't quickly move from a print-based paradigm, a good chunk of the design profession is likely to be replaced by film-school graduates in the next few years. Think real-time filmmaking, not print or graphics. The means of storytelling are changing. Previously separate and distinct technologies and disciplines are all migrating to desktop, one-stop shopping. Combine this with quickly expanding bandwidth, allowing the Web and television to merge, and you enter a new world of telling stories with sound and motion from your computer to other computers/TVs. Print isn't about to disappear, but the center of the design profession is likely to gravitate toward this emerging media form. Witness the work of graphic designers who have gotten their hands on a Media 100 machine, like Laurie and Scott Makela at Cranbrook. Amazing!

And lastly, not all, but most designers are still far too in love with their shiny new machines. There is the temptation to use every new bell and whistle that comes along, sometimes simultaneously. The loss of typographic craft has begun to be corrected, but now we very much have the same problem with prepress and printing, which accounts for a lot of murky imagery and crazily contrasted colors (gee, they looked nice onscreen). I say this having committed each of these sins and more in public a number of times over the last five years. I only hope one sees a trend over time in *Wired* to solve these problems rather than repeat them. Color and contrast that look beautiful via the transmitted color of one's monitor can look *terrible* when transmuted into the reflective color of ink on paper.

As a creative director/publisher of a magazine and books, how do you see the print environment changing vis-à-vis the digital?

My own sense is that ordinary information delivered in ordinary ways will tend to gravitate quickly now to electronic media. My hope is that extraordinary information presented in extraordinary ways will become the future of print. This is much like the futurist John Naisbitt's "high-tech/high-touch" notion. I think there is a possibility for certain books to tell their stories entirely visually. We did a book last year on the Burning Man Festival in Nevada that attempts to tell the story of the event through 160 pages of photos. It's a story with a beginning, a middle, and an end—and a few diversions on the way. But, hopefully, readers come away with a greater understanding of the event than if they read the accompanying essays. In a different sense, *Mind Grenades* tries to operate on a purely visual level, separate from the text track.

Is there a typeface that says "future"?

I think there are typefaces that can say anything, but it depends almost entirely on the context, and then on the designer's knowledge of the world around us and especially our collective history.

Should we, as designers, be concerned with how the future looks?

I don't think we have a choice. Design, or any other creative endeavor for that matter, is inherently concerned with giving form to the future.

Is design a vehicle for spreading notions of what the future "should" look like?

Spreading notions of how things *should* be? No. Creating notions of how things could be, yes.

Do you still consider yourself a graphic designer? Do you think graphic design can contribute essentially to online design?

I've never been any more comfortable with the term "graphic designer" than with the previous misnomer, "commercial artist." The term "graphic design" connotes only that which you can see: the end product, the tip of the iceberg of a long and primarily invisible problem-solving process. But it's the problem-solving process that matters, much much more than the end result it provokes.

I'm really from the classical modernist school of design on this subject. I believe that designers design, and whether it's a book, a chair, or a business strategy is immaterial. One brings the same problem-solving approach to bear regardless, and through a combination of luck, experience, and timing, one is sometimes able to solve a problem well and truly. So yes, designers can certainly contribute to online design if they choose to. It's just that, from my point of view, the designer concerned with matters of content is more likely to make a meaningful contribution than the designer who is primarily concerned with form.

Index

Page numbers in italics refer to illustrations.

Books from Allworth Press

Education of a Graphic Designer
edited by Steven Heller (softcover, 6¾ × 10, 256 pages, $18.95)

Design Literacy: Understanding Graphic Design
edited by Steven Heller and Marie Finamore (softcover, 6¾ × 10, 320 pages, $19.95)

AIGA Professional Practices in Graphic Design *by the American Institute of Graphic Arts, edited by Tad Crawford* (softcover, 6¾ × 10, 320 pages, $24.95)

Design Culture: An Anthology of Writing from the AIGA Journal of Graphic Design *by Steven Heller and Karen Pomeroy* (softcover, 6¾ × 10, 288 pages, $19.95)

Looking Closer: Critical Writings on Graphic Design *edited by Michael Bierut, William Drenttel, Steven Heller, and DK Holland* (softcover, 6¾ × 10, 256 pages, $18.95)

Looking Closer 2: Critical Writings on Graphic Design *edited by Michael Bierut, William Drenttel, Steven Heller, and DK Holland* (softcover, 6¾ × 10, 288 pages, $18.95)

Careers by Design: A Headhunter's Secrets for Success and Survival in Graphic Design, Revised Edition *by Roz Goldfarb* (softcover, 6¾ × 10, 224 pages, $18.95)

The New Business of Design
by the International Design Conference in Aspen (softcover, 6¾ × 10, 256 pages, $19.95)

Licensing Art & Design, Revised Edition
by Caryn R. Leland (softcover, 6 × 9, 128 pages, $16.95)

Business and Legal Forms for Graphic Designers, Revised Edition
by Tad Crawford (softcover, 8½ × 11, 208 pages, $22.95)

Legal Guide for the Visual Artist, Third Edition
by Tad Crawford (softcover, 8½ × 11, 256 pages, $19.95)

Electronic Design and Publishing: Business Practices, Second Edition
by Liane Sebastian (softcover, 6¾ × 10, 216 pages, $19.95)

Selling Graphic Design
by Don Sparkman, foreword by Ed Gold (softcover, 6 × 9, 256 pages, $18.95)

Uncontrollable Beauty: Toward a New Aesthetics
edited by Bill Beckley with David Shapiro (hardcover, 6 × 9, 448 pages, $24.95)

Please write to request our free catalog. To order by credit card, call 800-491-2808 or send a check or money order to Allworth Press, 10 East 23rd Street, Suite 210, New York, NY 10010. Include $5 for shipping and handling for the first book ordered and $1 for each additional book. Ten dollars plus $1 for each additional book if ordering from Canada. New York State residents must add sales tax.

If you would like to see our complete catalog on the World Wide Web, you can find us at *www.allworth.com*